Pastoral Theology: An Inquiry

Centre for
Faith and Spirituality
Loughborough University

Pastoral Theology:
An Inquiry

——•——

David Deeks

EPWORTH PRESS

British Library Cataloguing in Publication Data

Deeks, David
Pastoral theology: an inquiry.
1. Pastoral theology—Methodist Church
(Great Britain)
I. Title
253   BV4011

ISBN 0–7162–0437–1

First published 1987
by Epworth Press,
Room 195, 1 Central Buildings,
Westminster, London SW1H 9NR

Typeset by The Spartan Press Ltd
Lymington, Hants
and printed in Great Britain by
Richard Clay Ltd, Bungay, Suffolk

Contents

Acknowledgments

T. S. Eliot: Lines from 'Little Gidding' from *Collected Poems 1909–1962* reproduced by permission of Faber & Faber Ltd.

I. Murdoch: Extract from *Nuns & Soldiers* reproduced by permission of Chatto & Windus.

F. Sagan: Extract from *The Unmade Bed* reproduced by permission of Aidan Ellis.

The extract from the Litany in *The Alternative Service Book* 1980 is copyright © the Central Board of Finance of the Church of England and is reproduced with permission.

The extracts from the *Methodist Service Book* and the Conference Report 'The Ministry of the People of God' are copyright © the Methodist Conference and are reproduced with permission.

George Mackay Brown: 'The Poet' from 'The Year of the Whale' from *Selected Poems* reproduced by permission of Chatto & Windus: The Hogarth Press.

R. S. Thomas: Lines from 'Guernica' from *Ingrowing Thoughts* reproduced by permission of Poetry Wales Press.

H. J. M. Nouwen: Extract from *Reaching Out* reproduced by permission of Collins.

W. H. Vanstone: Lines from 'A Hymn to the Creator' in *Loves's Endeavour, Love's Expense* reproduced by permission of Darton, Longman & Todd Ltd, London.

Introduction

The primary longing of the Christian is to live the faith of Christ. This book focuses on two important elements in the Christian life – prayer and pastoral care. It is infinitely more important and much more demanding to pray and to care than it is to read (or write) books on these themes.

I am confining my use of the word 'prayer' to private prayer. This limitation is not meant to suggest that private prayer is more important than the worship of the church. It is not. Private prayer is my concern because it is an inescapable partner of pastoral care as practised by individual pastors. Prayer is the 'heart' exploring and critically examining things; it is the means by which we attend and respond to God as he continues to love all that he has made. It is the interior task without which the exterior activity of pastoral care cannot function well.

Pastoral care is one facet of pastoral work. Pastoral care is itself a broad category including many sorts of actions: healing, sustaining and guiding individuals; reconciling people to one another; enabling people to co-operate for the well-being of human communities and in the struggle for justice, freedom and peace in society. Even so, pastoral care is but a sub-heading of the larger notion of pastoral work. I illustrate this from my own experience as an ordained minister, though I do not wish to suggest by this that pastoral work is done primarily by ordained people. In addition to pastoral care, my job includes studying and expounding the scriptures, preaching, leading worship and presiding at holy communion, baptism and a large number of other ritual actions performed by the church. All these tasks, and much else besides, are part and parcel of my pastoral work. So we say that ordained ministers are authorized to take responsibility for the ministries of the word and sacraments as well as pastoral care.

Prayer and pastoral care together form our subject. All Christians participate in them in one way or another. They are integral components of the calling which all Christians receive to a life of love and service. None of us can become involved in the adventure of loving to which God calls us without praying and caring. The sole justification of this book will be found if it encourages some to pray better and to care more effectively.

Better praying and caring should not be confused with more praying and caring. God calls each of us to discern, develop and use the particular gifts he bestows upon us. In some situations or at certain phases of our life, God gives us capacities for prayer and care we never dreamed we would be capable of; in other contexts or at other times, very little prayer or caring will be required of us, if we are to be faithful to some other, overriding vocation. Young parents, for example, burdened by the demands of several small children in confined accommodation, may have little opportunity for prayer but will exercise pastoral care with an extraordinary and exhausting intensity. In contrast, a middle-aged woman badly hurt in a car accident and forced to spend many weeks in hospital may discover a longing to pray a lot precisely when opportunities for practical compassion are restricted.

Most of the time our prayer and care happen informally, spontaneously and unreflectively. They are none the worse for that. It is the experience of some that detaching themselves from doing what comes naturally and trying to understand how in fact they do these things kills the joy and uninhibited giftedness of their love. Some natural cricketers, it has been argued, have been spoiled by coaching! A book such as this is not for them. Others, however, discover that practice and reflection upon experience can enrich each other. Reflection can enable us to dig deeper into experience and disclose hidden levels of meaning. Reflection can help us to do more effectively what we intend by enabling us to define goals and tasks more clearly; to know ourselves better and thus to capitalize upon our strengths and compensate gently for our weaknesses; to analyze situations where we are confused or insecure so that confidence and skill can be developed. Reflection forges links between what we do and what we believe, both about ourselves and about God.

A distinction worth making is between sharing informally in the Christian ministries of prayer and pastoral care (which we all do to some degree or other) and exercising formal leadership in these ministries in the name of the church. The degree of responsibility carried by a prison visitor, a lay hospital chaplain, an ordained minister or (in Methodist terms) a class leader or pastoral visitor is so great that, in my judgment, *some* context needs to be found for critical reflection upon the task.

I am not suggesting a book like this is the normal or preferred way of opening up a conversation between prayer and pastoral care on the one hand and reflection on the other. A more natural context is a small group assisted by wise leadership. It is, however, as a further contribution to this dialogue between experience and understanding that these chapters are written.

My conclusion is, therefore, that many Christians may be helped in their prayer and pastoral care if they stand back a little from what they do and try to make sense of it. Some should feel an obligation laid on them to participate in this reflective work. A few are required to do so as part of their public accountability to the church for the responsibilities they carry. The formal names we give to this task are spiritual theology and pastoral theology. The aim of this book is to clarify what is meant by these phrases and to encourage people to share in the tasks these phrases represent – always in such a way as to nurture the practice of prayer and pastoral care.

A few preliminary points may be useful straight away to clear the ground for what follows. In essence all theology – talk of God – seems simple. Christians say, 'God is love' (I John 4.9). Prayer and pastoral care are the means we use to express the basic Christian obligation to love God, to love ourselves and to love our neighbours as ourselves (Mark 12.28–34). Such notions, however, are not as easy as they look. Here are three prominent themes which make the production of any theology of prayer and pastoral care a daunting task:

(*i*) 'Love' is a word which in English carries a huge range of meanings in different contexts. It can refer to a mother cuddling her toddler who has become distressed after a fall down a step; to a schoolteacher feeling relaxed and fulfilled in the performance of his daily work; to a wife loyally supporting her husband when he has been deeply hurt by a sense of failure or inadequacy; to a social worker dispassionately evaluating the best course of action for a family under threat of eviction from their home; to two adolescents daringly holding each other's hands on the back row of a church; to a volunteer at the hospice holding the hand of a patient as she dies; to two people discovering each other's bodies and the exhilarating and explosive experience of sexual intercourse; to a self-employed craftsman falsifying his income tax form in the quest for more wealth; and much else besides. So what is the meaning of 'love' in our understanding of God and in our practice of prayer and pastoral care?

(*ii*) We cannot easily love what we do not know. The pursuit of knowledge, however, is a frustrating experience. On the one hand, there is the sense of being overwhelmed by the 'explosion of knowledge' in the modern world. Psychology, sociology, anthropology, economics and biology all make significant contributions to our understanding and practice of pastoral work; all have become major areas of research and specialized knowledge. The information which needs to be taken account of in our understanding of ourselves and of what it is to be human is enormous. So what hope is there for any but the most prestigious intellects to know enough to be able to love well?

On the other hand, knowing more and more about less and less (which is the fate of so many specialists) provokes an awareness of the *limits* of our knowledge. Our understandings are bound to be partial, distorted and provisional. Is our capacity for love also to be thought of as partial, distorted and provisional?

(*iii*) Western society in the twentieth century has been marked by a rapid growth of professionalism. The caring or helping professions have become a normal part of our culture: doctors, nurses, social and community workers, counsellors – each group sub-divided into specialists concentrating on particular human concerns, individual or social. What are the values and ideologies upon which these professions are based, and how do they relate to the Christian ideal of love? How do Christians who are encouraged to participate in the ministry of pastoral care relate to or differ from the caring professionals? Should those who carry formal responsibilities for leadership in Christian pastoral care – whether as ordained ministers or as authorized lay persons – see themselves as fellow-professionals alongside the secular professionals? What are the particular questions for those in the helping professions who are also Christians endeavouring to practise Christian love?

My intention is not to attempt an exhaustive commentary on the three themes I have just referred to. I shall have them in mind, but my aim is more modest. It is to reflect from my experience on how such difficult issues give shape to pastoral care and pastoral theology in our contemporary setting. I shall draw on the work of countless others. If you like, I am wanting to venture over bridges others have built or are in the process of constructing, and to encourage you, the reader, to join me on the journey. That sounds fairly safe; in fact it can be deeply disturbing.

From time to time I suffer from vertigo. One of my most frightening experiences happened when I was having a bad spell with dizziness and insecurity about keeping upright. I had to walk across the Thames on the footbridge from Waterloo Station. It was a blustery day. Partway across I was paralysed. I clung to the railing for dear life, convinced that the next step would plunge me into the swirling river. I had to crouch down to regain some semblance of stability and renewed confidence. I deeply envied other pedestrians who passed by without a care in the world, and who probably were looking at me out of the corner of their eye as if I were a drunk.

Theology of the kind I am hoping to clarify in the following chapters is markedly different from what traditionally passes as 'theology' in the Western churches. Leaving behind the conventional and moving towards the new involve dislocation and reorientation. We can be left feeling quite giddy at times. I have the suspicion, however, that Christian living (or at least, praying and caring) could flourish more easily if the churches re-ordered their programmes for theological education and personal development. If this book could encourage more to move in the new direction and could suggest the new agendas and methods which will be necessary, it will have surpassed my wildest hopes.

I   In Search of Meaning

1 Basic Resources: Words

Pastoral care is the practice of love, in words and deeds. The most loving thing anyone can do for us is to encourage us to search for the meaning of our lives. I take it for granted that I cannot help someone else to make sense of life unless I am involved in seeking life's meaning for myself. Therefore everyone who practises pastoral care needs also to receive pastoral care.

Each of us is deeply affected by the dominant culture in which we have been brought up. In Western society the prevailing culture has pushed religion to the margins. We are 'secular' men and women, living in a world which has no obvious relation to God or any memory of his impact on our history. If meaning is to be found, it will be discovered in the course of our day-to-day living. The desire to make sense of life in a secular context is a deeply serious business. How do we go about it? We begin by exploring how story-telling and conversation can help us. In the following chapter we shall reflect on how we act in the world. Finally there will be a glance at what art, science and history contribute to our search for meaning.

Telling my own story

The effort of remembering and recounting the story of our lives is one of the most vital experiences in which we can engage. My young son is at the stage where his bedtime demand is for me to tell each evening a different 'true story' from my own childhood. Memories have to be dredged from the deep well of the past. Yet the memories come. How much we can recall from our past amazes us. The story our memories stimulate has a life and moving quality second to none.

A narrative carries our experience simultaneously at several levels – intellectual and emotional, and maybe at other levels too. (We shall examine that phenomenon more fully in Chapter 7.) There is a sense in which our telling of our own story is a re-living of our experience. Everything is placed in its own time and context and reveals its 'reality' and authenticity. A story simply will not let us reduce our experiences to dogmas, abstract ideas or laws.

Any story of our lives is bound to be selective. The task is not to recapitulate every moment of our previous experience. If that were the objective, we should live only half a life – and spend the other half repeating the first half. In fact we select from our total life experience certain key categories of remembered moments. Things we feel deeply about form one important category, for example: falling in love; the death of someone close to us, perhaps in tragic circumstances, provoking in us grief and anguish; occasions in life when we have felt cheated or badly let down, so that their memory is always discoloured with anger and rage.

A second category consists of experiences which, on reflection, seem to have been significant for the course our life has taken: they matter to us. In this category come: a chance meeting, a book or a casual conversation which changed the direction of our life; a decision which was taken which blocked off for ever all sorts of possibilities for our life; or a task laid upon us which released gifts, capacities and devotion of which, up to that point, we had never dreamed we were capable.

Thirdly our story must include particularly puzzling experiences. I mean not simply those that appear to us as confusing or as apparently insoluble problems. I mean those very rare moments that make us stop and ponder deeply. They point beyond themselves to something essentially mysterious. They claim our attention, require us to look and look again; and, in a way we find it difficult to express in words, draw us into themselves. They request urgently some form of participation, and hold out before us the promise of untold richness. Yet every step forward leaves us with the feeling of insecurity, of being in danger of being swallowed up. I have touched on such moments elsewhere[1] and here simply highlight the main categories:

> The experience of encountering another individual as a unique centre of mysterious personal 'otherness' – like me, beckoning me in love, yet revealing an unbridgable chasm between us.

> The experience of awe before that which is holy.

> The experience of uncompromising moral demand of such intensity that a 'No!' would inevitably smash me to pieces.

> The experience of discovering vitality, purpose and significance for myself and my tasks in life even when all around speaks of meaninglessness and despair.

> The experience of anger mingled with compassion in response to life's obscenities and human barbarism.

Although the story of our life selectively concentrates on challenging and deeply textured experiences, the task is not simply to dwell on them as isolated highlights. The story we tell connects them together in a continuous thread, incorporates them into a personal history. That is the means by which meaning may be glimpsed. When we see the meaning of an event in our story, it becomes real for us. We enter into its reality in the past, and at the same time it clarifies the reality of our present. In her novel, *The Unicorn*, Iris Murdoch makes one of her characters say:

> I lived in your gaze like a false God. But it is the punishment of a false God to become unreal. I have become unreal. You have made me unreal by thinking about me so much. You made me into an object of contemplation. Just like this landscape. I have made it unreal by endlessly looking at it instead of entering it.

The story I tell of my life at the present moment is inevitably shaped by my vantage-point. Where I am here and now creates a perspective on my past, a perspective which is necessarily limited. However, my present situation is not *simply* a viewing point. It is a part of the thread of my life, and potentially highly significant in its own right. One of the things that happens when I remember and recount my own story is that it enables me to see the value and significance of the present moment more clearly. My history gives a perspective on my contemporary situation.

> And the end of all our exploring
> Will be to arrive where we started
> And know the place for the first time.[2]

But the present situation will change. The future will create new vantage points. My story therefore has constantly to be re-told. What seemed a while back to be highly significant now fades into insignificance. Then I was looking back from the bottom of a valley; now I find myself on a hillock, and the view of the same journey is vastly different. Or, of course, the change of perspective may be the other way round – from peak to pothole.

How I tell my story, how I select its highlights and depressions, is coloured by many other factors besides my present vantage point. Some of these other factors have their effect without our being conscious of them. The earliest months and years of our lives fall into this category; in Chapter 10 we shall explore further their contribution to our self-understanding. Another example of largely unconscious influence on our life-story is the cultural context or contexts in which we have lived. It is hard to overestimate the degree to which culture shapes our experience and the form our story about ourselves takes. There is an essential Englishness about the way that all English people in England experience the world and discover themselves; just as there is an inescapable and distinctive Frenchness about the experience and self-awareness of the French. Sometimes it takes the perplexity and disorientation of a 'culture shock', resulting from a move into a strange context, to bring home to us the powerful formative influence of our indigenous culture.

Culture is a large concept, and we experience it as constituted of many distinct groups and institutions: family, local community, school, college, the firm for which we work and the associations in which we find recreation. When we focus attention upon these smaller units, we quickly notice how much of our identity is bound up with their structures, values and histories. In our society so much, perhaps too much, of the identity of men is related to their daily work. That is why the early questions in establishing relationships follow a predictable pattern: your name? what do you *do*? your family? For the same reason, men being made redundant or passing through a major transition in the work they do experience a major psychological crisis. It is nothing less than a loss of identity.

One important way in which we sift out what is more authentically our own identity, as opposed to the identity pressed upon us by significant institutions to which we belong, is to listen to the stories told within these institutions. Groups and institutions communicate their stories in all sorts of ways: memorable anecdotes, formal and critical histories, the way things are done, the patterns of relationship and rituals which are taken for granted, and the rhythms and structures of the corporate life. By these means the identity and common purpose of the group or institution are disclosed with lesser or greater clarity. As we listen to this story-telling we are all the time making a judgment about the degree to which our personal stories resonate with or jar with the stories of the institutions and groups with which we are involved. We are assessing how much we feel 'at home' in any particular group. That way of putting it reminds us that there are some basic groups, especially our families, whose influence upon us is so profound that they shape our personal identity to an extent that we can neither measure nor leave behind. Even so, my understanding of myself is never totally absorbed into the story of any particular institution, even a close-knit family. My freedom remains in however restricted a form, and my story explores the meaning I can find in my unique journey through life. (Chapter 10 explores this theme further.)

No story I tell about myself can be complete. The story of my own life cannot be taken forward to its conclusion. The future is unknown, except that it must include my death. So the full meaning of my life remains an open question.

The story so far, however, is not without its points. If nothing else it suggests some basic attitudes to the future which is still to come: fear and foreboding, or cautious optimism; expecting more of the same, or eager hope. Especially in the latter half of life, my story so far may suggest overarching patterns for life's journey which can be projected with reasonable confidence into the future – though nothing is certain. The sorts of patterns into which our narratives may fit include the following:

A journey whose destination and route are freely chosen at a very early stage; the scenery *en route* is of only marginal interest; the stoppages and diversions on the journey are frustrations to be coped with as courageously as possible.

A headlong and terrifying rush into oblivion.

An unplanned ramble or tour, but one which is marked by unexpected discoveries or compelling landscapes which leave rich impressions on the memory and make the travelling worthwhile; it may be that the constant movement will end up somewhere meaningful – or it may just stop.

A hike on which we keep losing our way; from time to time the goal becomes visible, but more often than not it disappears from view and it is no longer clear that what we are doing now is getting us any nearer the journey's end.

A pilgrimage, leisurely and worth savouring for its own sake; there is time for stoppages and explorations along digressions from the main route; there are amiable companions to converse with on the way, to support and be supported by; many have gone this way before and that knowledge, together with our picture of the holy shrine at the approaching end of the pilgrimage, excites us.

Patterns of these kinds need to be handled with some caution in the telling of our incomplete life-stories. They contribute positively to our search for meaning when they are disclosed to us, when they leap out at us and offer themselves to us as a gift. It is rather like those posters which are made up of nothing but black dots of various sizes: when we are too close we see nothing but confusing arrays of dots; at a distance the same dots may reveal themselves to us as a design or picture. The danger arises, however, when the pattern takes on a greater prominence than the narrative itself, so that experience is forced into a mould. Life will not be so restricted. Patterns fluctuate and change as life proceeds. When I started writing this book I had a rough outline of its chapters and themes. As I get down to the business of constructing sentences and paragraphs, the material takes on a life of its own. It will not fit into my preliminary outline. The pattern has to be reformulated as the book is being written.

The art of conversation

John was an up and coming young manager in a large commercial enterprise. As a sign of his upward social mobility he and his wife bought a house on a small private housing estate being developed on the edge of a town, within a few metres of unspoilt countryside. Next door lived Bill and his family. Five years before, Bill had struck it rich on the pools and had decided to invest a proportion of his winnings in a new house. Bill worked on building sites as a labourer; his employment was casual.

John and Bill inhabited different worlds. Both, however, had to tackle the gardens at the back of their houses. Bill was a keen and skilful gardener. John was reluctant and pedestrian; he was overawed by the overgrown mess bequeathed him by the previous occupant of the house. A low brick wall with a wooden fence on top separated one garden from the other. At first John and Bill each tackled his plot without reference to the other. Then one hot Sunday afternoon, in a pause for breath, John and Bill noticed each other; they broke the silence between them by introducing themselves to each other across the garden fence. As the months went by, John and Bill found themselves from time to time working simultaneously in their gardens. They would occasionally stop to pass the time of day, or to chat about common experiences in the arduous task of creating gardens.

The day came when Bill and John found themselves in conversation. It had not been planned; it began spontaneously. An announcement in the local press of hundreds of redundancies in a nearby engineering firm triggered the conversation. Over the preceding months enough basic knowledge about each other had been built up for them to speak to each other with a measure of openness and confidence. It was not easy. The garden fence felt like the thick barriers separating their different upbringing, culture and life-style. The conversation, however, created the possibility of transcending the boundaries whch hitherto had isolated John from Bill. They knew instinctively that this involvement in a 'conversation' was different from the talking they had engaged in on previous encounters. The conversation had a life of its own. John and Bill were drawn together into this experience; they forgot about the passage of time, as if they were caught up in something like a trance. But it was not a trance. Rather, John and Bill found themselves alert and attentive. Each wanted to listen to the other while the other was speaking; and the speaking was done with care and sensitivity. Neither was particularly skilled with words, though John was a deal more articulate than Bill. In the alternating rhythms of listening and speaking each was searching to say what he meant and to hear what the other was trying to communicate. They felt free to question one another, to seek greater clarity, to check that what was heard was what was meant. Into John's mind there flashed at one point a slogan he had heard about from a New York sub-way:

I know you believe you understand what you think I said, but I am not sure you realize that what you heard is not what I meant.

The conversation carried its own momentum. Without either Bill or John organizing anything, the conversation opened up all sorts of subjects which neither had anticipated at the beginning. Yet they did not feel as if the experience was disjointed, or the subjects were disconnected. One theme seemed to flow into another effortlessly. When at last the conversation came to an end, John and Bill knew something important had taken place between them. They had become neighbours in a deep sense: they had struggled towards, and to an extent achieved, understanding of each other; they had discovered some things they agreed on; they had discovered some measure of shared meaning, or common sense, about life and therefore they felt bound to each other in a suggestive form of obligation, respect and dependence.

Weighing our words

We can now leave the story of John and Bill. In doing so, we will be conscious of the fact that not all conversations are as fruitful as this was. Some conversations simply come to a stop: 'I understand what you say but I disagree profoundly'; or, 'I understand what you've said, but I can't see what it adds up to.' On other occasions conversations drift into arguments; a shared enterprise becomes a war situation, each looking for victory over the other. I suggest, however, that our broader experience of all sorts of conversation leads us to a generally accepted conclusion. Conversations are like our attempts to tell our own stories: they are treasured and precious ways of using words, set deep in our experience of what it is to be human, not in the least trivial, superficial or wasteful of time. That justifies us reflecting critically on story-telling and conversing, to understand how they 'work' and to unearth their limits and weaknesses as well as their strengths in our struggle for meaning.

The most obvious insight we gain from reflecting on story-telling and conversation is that our personal quest for meaning, value and purpose in life does not take place in a vacuum. We explore the meaning of our lives in openness to others. In story-telling we are open to our culture, and the network of groups and institutions whose values shape our lives. Culture and upbringing act as a lens or filter for what we can hear or experience in life. Conversation points to our openness to other individuals. Usually these two forms of openness overlap and interconnect. The simplest way in which the influence of my parents and their culture is transfused into me is through the conversation that takes place between me and them. Sometimes, however, conversation takes us beyond the boundaries of our native culture and context. We meet a stranger, as it were from another world. In our conversation cultures meet and interact. I begin to see that being human transcends the confines of race, class, sex and occupation.

There is, however, a subtle but important difference between openness to culture and openness to other individuals. Culture influences us and orders our experience almost automatically. We do not choose it; it is given to us, even determined for us. It is an accident of birth that I was born in England in the twentieth century into the particular family and social network in which I was reared. Conversations, by contrast, are much more under my control. I can choose to enter a conversation, or refuse to converse, or withdraw from a conversation. Openness to other individuals is thus a problematic thing – an indicator of my confidence or fear, my naïvety or my anxiety. The intertwining of trust and mistrust has very deep roots (Chapter 9). The art of conversation is, however, built on trust, a confidence that outside, beyond and beneath us, are life-enhancing realities which can nurture our identity and influence creatively the direction of our lives. 'Faith is always an opening to a meaning which comes to me, which is given to me from somewhere else' (C. Geffre). Part of the struggle that goes on as we tell the story of our lives is to sift out those persons, places, institutions and artefacts to which we return time and again because they have proved themselves trustworthy and especially illuminative of the meaning of our lives.

The second obvious theme we draw out of our experience of story-telling and conversation is the role of language. Without language of some kind, experience remains unfocused and we cannot fully appreciate it. Language, of course, is more than words. There is such a thing as 'body language', and it is prominent in our conversations: the grimace on the face, the restlessness of the legs and feet, the look in the eye, the nervous fiddling with a button, the seductive posture. But language is largely words. Words are fundamental to our humanness; without them we could not think or conceptualize. Words have meanings. In fact words transmit to us the common experience and the meaning of experience which has accumulated in a culture; or they inform us of what is going on in the public worlds of nature and society, and how events may be understood. Words also have the capacity to invite us to participate in our culture's common experience and shared meanings, and to respond to what is going on in the world. That happens when we use words to form our own sentences.

Some words have a single meaning, like technical words and step-by-step instructions in a car maintenance manual. Other words – metaphors and images embedded in a poem – carry many levels of meaning. A poem bears reading time and again, and constantly unveils new insights.

So how does language work in a conversation? Not in an abstract way, as it does when we consult a dictionary. A conversation is an encounter with something concrete and particular, with the experience and meaning of a culture focused in another individual and transmuted by that individual's unique personality. A fresh perspective on common sense, a nuance on the familiar, comes to my view. This presents me with a challenge, but a challenge which it is not easy to grasp, because words are slippery in their meaning. So conversation takes time – time for speaking and listening, for questioning and affirming. Even with time its success cannot be guaranteed. Conversation is an art to be practised, a process to be engaged in as long as we have life.

Thirdly, story-telling and conversation make us more aware of ourselves. As we notice how things have gone for us during our life and how others react to us in conversation, we see more of ourselves. It is as if story-telling and conversation enable us to step out of ourselves and look at ourselves with some detachment. We become self-critical, we reflect on who we are, what our lives add up to, and how coherent we are as persons. The importance of this in our search for the meaning of our lives can hardly be over-estimated. There is, however, a dark side to the development of self-knowledge: it can become all-absorbing. Is self-awareness the only goal of story-telling and conversation? Are the past, the culture we have imbibed and other people merely mirrors in which we see ourselves reflected? Do they not have a reality of their own which is different from ourselves? Could one of the possibilities in a conversation be to *enter* the meaning and reality of another person? When John and Bill finished their conversation they felt not only that they now lived with each other as neighbours and had drawn enrichment from each other in their meeting; they also felt an obligation to each other. John and Bill would now live for each other. The bond between them represented mutuality, giving and receiving. In which case, the meaning of either of their lives now involved the other, and the relationship between them.

The conversation between John and Bill is not representative of all conversations. Others end in confusion or acrimony. In general our experience of conversations is that the tension is never fully resolved between our concern to know ourselves better and our willingness to reach out to the other in neighbourly love.

*   *   *

Our conclusion so far is that in story-telling and conversation there are signs of hope in our quest for the meaning of our lives. These activities underline the truth that meaning arises only out of the deepest possible concern, commitment and attention to ourselves. The more aware we become of ourselves the better. But meaning for a person is inextricably bound up with the meaning of the past and of our culture, of other people and of what is going on in the world. It is elusive. It constantly needs to be rediscovered and reinterpreted. The desire to make sense of life needs repeatedly to be rekindled with a new openness to the world. It calls for resources of courage, trust and singlemindedness.

2 Basic Resources: Deeds

The flowers! Thanks from all of us for the seven marvellous roses. They opened up into countless petals, then died yesterday. But they lived long enough to bring us a ray of light. It doesn't matter that they didn't last long. The important thing is that they had the courage not to stay closed up in their buds, that they were wise enough to come out of themselves and rise toward the sun in delicate red petals. They left the mark of your presence here.[1]

These words were written on May 10, 1970, from a prison in Sao Paulo, Brazil. Their author, Carlos Christo, a Dominican student, had been arrested by the military authorities on charges of subversive activity. His letter was addressed to his sister's friend, Silvia. Silvia had sent the flowers to the prison – an action we now see which had opened up many levels of meaning for its recipient. The primary significance of the gift was Silvia's friendship. A letter had accompanied the flowers and had expressed that friendship in words. The paragraph of Christo's reply which precedes the one cited above talks of friendship as uniting people into a single family. 'The only thing that bothers me is that I can't talk with [my friends].' However, the gift of the flowers did more than signify friendship. The flowers 'left the mark of your presence here'.

From a different point of view the roses represented the world of nature, another world invisible to the inmates of Tiradentes Prison. Once more, however, disclosure of many levels of meaning took place. The opening and eventually the dying of the petals spoke of light in the darkness, hope in despair, and of openness to the world and to the future.

The meaning of actions

An action is a concrete event, which can be dated, measured and categorized. An action leaves a mark in history and in the memory of anyone who appropriates the action. An action is a means to an end. It endeavours to express an 'objective' intention, that is it directs an inner intention towards someone or something other than the person acting. The consequences of an action, however, always have some element of uncertainty about them. An action can be interpreted in all sorts of ways. Will a kiss on the cheek be interpreted by the recipient as a conventional greeting, an offensive sexual advance, or an invitation to a warmth and intimacy that needs to be explored in future – preferably private – encounters?

Why do our actions produce uncertain consequences, when we intend them to achieve a particular goal?

(*i*) An action is the means we choose to achieve our intention. But we may choose an inappropriate means. The goal will not then be achieved. For example, I am at a party with a friend, who falls asleep during the after-dinner conversation. I find this embarrassing, and I know she will be embarrassed if she sleeps for a long period. I decide to wake her up. Gently but firmly I kick her left shin. She wakes up startled. Unfortunately the action is badly misunderstood. She assumes I feel free to kick her around at my pleasure. After the party I am bitterly criticized for my overbearing male chauvinism.

Every action needs careful consideration, so that it matches as well as possible the intention and achieves the intended goal. It is a bit like building a complicated toy with Lego. The foundations of the construction are straightforward. Near the conclusion, however, great delicacy is required in fixing tiny features. Too much pressure, or the insertion of the wrong piece, can make the elaborate device collapse.

Society assumes that normally we can choose actions which are more or less appropriate to the goal we intend. This is the basis on which society holds us responsible for our actions and their effects. In a court of law, for example, a person guilty of an illegal action pays a penalty. In the case of a serious crime, action and intention have to be clearly distinguished; but even when an action produces a far more heinous effect than was intended, it can never be overlooked.

(*ii*) Our actions often betray hidden motives and needs, or irrational behaviour of which we ourselves are largely unaware. (Chapter 7 will explore further the unconscious world of values, feelings and instincts each of us carries inside us.) Conscious and unconscious purposes may become intertwined and present confusing signals.

(*iii*) An action reveals something of the culture and context in which the author of an action is set. Actions are shaped by tradition. For example, custom and etiquette in a particular society largely control the actions by which we greet one another. But conventional actions are far more powerful than 'mere conventions'. They act like symbols, suggesting and making present many levels of meaning which have become deeply ingrained in the experience of a community. In the college where I work we like to share the Peace in the holy communion in a relaxed way: a warm hand-shake with everyone present, and sometimes a more expansive embrace or a kiss. These actions carry the community's world of meaning. They are additional to the personal intention and hidden motives of each participant in the Peace. What, however, if the cultural meaning of an action does not coincide with my personal intention? Conflict and intense anguish arise if I do not intend to make peace with a particular individual in the community, or do not feel he or she seriously purposes to make peace with me. Is my personal intention to be lost in the community's expectations, so that I feel a loss of integrity? Yet if I refuse to shake an individual's hand, how will my non-action (which is really a freely chosen action contradicting social expectations) be interpreted?

In this question is focused a crisis which has arisen in Western society since 1945. At the end of the second world war, many felt that the European cultural tradition had failed abysmally to nourish truly human values. Particularly in the USA, men and women deliberately cut themselves free from the constraints of the tradition, and by their personal actions created new identities for themselves. This movement was pioneered by avant-garde artists[2] and blossomed generally in the late 1960s. Today we take it for granted that we should be free to wear what we feel like, marry (or cohabit with) a person of our choice, take up new (non-sexist and non-racist) roles, and choose our own work and causes. We feel responsible only to ourselves for the identity we create. In reality, however, the free 'self-made' individual is locked into all sorts of networks and sub-cultures, so that the attempt in principle to jettison tradition in favour of uninhibited, freely-chosen actions was a failure. Making sense of life remained a struggle. Hence the malaise and restlessness in so much of contemporary life.

At least the point has been scored: tradition does not convey unambiguously good values and meanings. It does indeed seem impossible totally to liberate our actions from the influence of tradition; but culture and custom can cripple and destroy as well as liberate. In one of his poems, Alan Bold describes tradition as

> That insidious coalescence
> Of anachronism, obsolescence, and expediency.[3]

Even so, some in Western society believe that the culture we inherited from the latter part of the nineteenth century is as wholesome as we shall get. Anything created by post-war modernism is much worse, and should be abandoned in favour of Victorian values. Others are left pondering how the tradition can be transformed freshly to illuminate the meaning of our lives and to respect the new, extended limits of our personal freedom.

An action, then, is orientated towards a goal, but its intention is not always crystal clear to those who receive it, and maybe to its author. What can help to signify the intended purpose of actions? First, we may consider that *words accompanying an action* may provide a fairly precise clue to the purpose of an action. Often this is the case (like Silvia's letter sent with the flowers). However, words-with-actions do not always succeed. Sometimes this is because words themselves are difficult to understand, or are symbolic in character, suggesting several levels of meaning. When I baptize a baby, I pour water over the child's head and say, 'I baptize you in the Name of the Father, and of the Son, and of the Holy Spirit.' That sentence, however, is so dense with tradition and layers of interpretation that in itself it does not necessarily clarify the purpose of the action – especially if the child's parents rarely attend church.

Another situation where words do not help us to comprehend the purpose of an action is where conscious and unconscious purposes have become intermingled. Ironically, words may then aggravate the difficulties. The words, for example, may express much of the conscious intention of the action's author, while the action itself may be confused or indicative of contradictory unconscious longings. The person performing the action then reminds us of an actor in a play, living as it were in two worlds simultaneously – the 'real' world and the world created by the plot and characters in the play.

Second, the intention of an action may be simplified if it is *not considered in isolation*. We judge a particular action in the context of a relationship or a series of actions from the same author. The broader perspective may suggest a clearer and more consistent set of purposes than one action taken by itself.

Third, *critical reflection* upon actions may clarify motive and intention. Through reflection I am endeavouring to notice in what I do the hidden assumptions, values and intentions in my inner being, and to compare them with my conscious intentions. Actions reveal more of my inner self than anything else. But even actions can deceive.

Not always actions show the man: we find
Who does a kindness is not therefore kind.[4]

Also in reflection I am pondering the degree to which what I do and say coincide. In every culture human wisdom has been distilled in a proverb such as 'Actions speak louder than words'. In a number of ways, therefore, reflection illuminates self-understanding, and is a crucial element in the struggle to create a consistent life.

Self-awareness can also develop in those who appropriate an action. 'Appropriate' is deliberately a strong word which includes not only my being a recipient of an action but also my *re*-action. When I react, and how, and for what purposes: these questions disclose to reflection a great deal about myself. I can, for example, choose to react in a way that enhances or develops the initial action. That is, I can contribute to a shared action, representing shared meanings and intentions. Or, of course, I can do the opposite.

In the mutuality of action and reaction, as in a conversation, we clarify our identity. If someone reacts to my initiative in a way that coheres with earlier actions and reactions on their part; and if their response is within the bounds of expectation set by the customs and culture of our society, their identity and mine are confirmed. 'A common tradition, a common way of life, is not sustained by discussion alone. It requires the structuring of common experience, and the pursuit of agreed goals and purposes in common action.'[5]

Conversely, if someone reacts 'out of character', or 'out of proportion' (over-reacts or under-reacts), her identity becomes problematic to me. I am puzzled. I may not know what to do next. I break the flow of action and reaction. Or I act in a completely fresh and disconnected way – as if I were starting a sentence on a new theme before the previous paragraph was completed. Either way, my reaction may disclose something to her about herself. She may say to herself, for instance: 'I see now that the way I first reacted reveals something inside me: a deep confusion or anxiety, or some unresolved conflict or pain.'

Action and Activity

An activity is different from an action. An action is a means to a goal. An activity is something we do which is an end in itself – like thinking and seeing. An activity is not without purpose. An activity has a 'subjective' purpose, that is it is directed to the subject generating the activity. Hence running to keep fit, or listening to music as a form of recreation, are activities.

Sometimes we are absorbed in an activity. We lose all sense of the passage of time. We are immersed in pleasurable sensations. In an absorbing activity we are at one with ourselves. Our identity is confirmed. Hobbies focus our experience of activity. Hobbies are for adults what playing with toys is for a child. A child enraptured by a toy has grasped in his or her hands the whole universe. Nothing else exists or matters but that toy.

When we reflect on an absorbing activity, we see ourselves clearly. We say: 'When I get involved in that activity, I really let go; I feel free; I can be myself!'

On occasion actions can glide into activity. Learning to read, for example, requires the co-ordinated application of many skills – sight, hearing, speech, memory and so forth. When eventually reading comes easily, we often read for a purpose – to glean information, or to gather ideas for an essay. But reading has a happy knack of becoming enjoyable for its own sake. Action has merged into activity.

Many activities take places most naturally in silence.

Each order of experience has its own atmosphere. The atmosphere of presence, of giving, of wholeness, is silence. We know that serious things have to be done in silence, because we do not have words to measure the immeasurable. In silence men love, pray, listen, paint, write, think, suffer. These experiences are all occasions of giving and receiving, of some encounter with forces that are inexhaustible and independent of us. These are easily distinguishable from our routines and possessiveness as silence is distinct from noise.[6]

If we were to find the meaning of our life, living itself would become an activity, a silent bliss transcending time.

Behaviour, activity and action

In everyday speech and in imaginative literature, 'behaviour' covers the whole range of things we do. In scientifically-coloured contexts, however, behaviour is taken to mean a response made to an external stimulus. As far as animals are concerned (this was the important discovery of Pavlov), what they do can be understood completely in behavioural terms, that is they make instinctive or conditioned responses of a predictable kind to stimuli. According to Konrad Lorenz, animal instincts are automatic and involuntary responses to a specific selection of stimuli from the animal's environment which concern the animal's survival or the survival of its species. These constitute the animal's behaviour.

In human beings, also, quite a lot of what we do can properly be called behaviour in this technical sense. We blink when a bright light is flashed in our eyes. We withdraw at lightning speed from the pain of an unexpected pin prick in our finger. This example, however, points us beyond behavioural explanations of what we do. If in the presence of an experienced nurse or doctor we are asked not to flinch when a hypodermic syringe pierces our skin, we discover we can control instinct. Indeed it seems to be characteristic of human beings, within limits, to be able to supress or sublimate instinctive behaviour in favour of actions which pursue freely-chosen goals or values. The consistent demotion of behaviour in favour of action is a long and tortuous process, though one which is infinitely worthwhile. Mahatma Ghandi represents a massive achievement of this kind. He drew on the ascetic disciplines available in Indian culture. For him it was necessary to fast and to forego sexual activity in order to fulfil his life's work, which included non-violence.[7]

Ghandi's is a particularly instructive example, because it focuses upon what Lorenz, with many others, has shown to be the hardest instinct to control in favour of rationally intended actions: aggression.[8] Lorenz argued that aggression is often a destructive instinct in human beings because it is no longer needed to ensure our survival as a species. That does not deny the truth that there may be occasions when as individuals we find ourselves under threat (e.g. someone attacking us with a knife), and the instinct of aggression ensures our personal survival: we hit out at our attacker. Even in this situation there are some difficult moral issues to be considered – is it morally defensible to defend oneself with aggression, or should one always turn the other cheek? – but this is not the place to explore these questions. On the whole, however, human life flourishes when aggression is controlled by moral actions.

At the social level, too, human beings in the modern world can ensure their survival by rational actions and activities, without having to resort to aggression. We create social and political structures which make available education and health-care, and which ensure a wide distribution of basic resources for human life. We encourage scientific and techno-logical research to overcome disease. We negotiate with those who are very different from ourselves, or whose interests clash with our own, to create common understandings about how to inhabit the same space without resorting to mutual destruction or bloody conquest. In short, we create a culture. Even so, violence is never far away. It is as if no rationally constructed culture can adequately absorb or control the aggressive instinct within us. That may be due in part to our never being able to construct a perfect culture. No culture, for example, is perfectly just. Power and access to resources are always imperfectly distributed through every human society. If the injustice and oppression reach significant levels, within a community or between communities, violence flares up. The violence expresses the frustration and the sense of being less than human which are felt by the victims of unjust structures. If there were no other reason for political struggle towards social justice, the reduction of violence would be a sufficient cause.

Wisdom as well as justice plays its part in our attempts to handle aggression in society. Wisdom suggests, for example, that violent action (i.e. a rationally conceived use of force to achieve a defined goal, as in a 'just war') is likely to be

overwhelmed by violent behaviour (i.e. the irrational outburst of the aggressive instinct). I myself would conclude
from this that it is a horrendous mistake to base a military
defence policy upon the idea that nuclear weapons can be
used in a limited or controlled exchange.

Another perspective on the problem of violence is the wise
use of ritual combat. Polarization takes place in every society
and large community. Destructive violence is not the only
means of expressing and working through the conflicts.
Controlled and non-destructive rituals which enact the competition and conflict also have their part to play. Football
matches illustrate this function in English society, as do the
baying and shouting during debates in the House of Com-
mons. Sartre went so far as to write: 'When a lot of men get
together, they have to be separated by rituals or else they
slaughter each other.'[9]

Ritual is a form of play, or drama. In a play, individuals or
groups take up roles. They represent attitudes, feelings,
ideas and relationships which are not strictly their own. The
play or drama represents worlds of meaning which are not
identical with the meanings the actors have discovered or
embraced for themselves. But there is some point of connection between the 'real' and the 'imagined' worlds. That is
why actors can often externalize into their roles their own
emotions. Aggression, which seems to have so much surplus
and non-useful energy, can often be channelled into a role in
a play or a competitive game. In this way aggression can be
dissipated without actual destruction or violence. Even here,
however, the thin line is often transgressed between aggression siphoned into ritual combat (which is always an action,
and controlled by the rules of the game) and aggression
expressing itself in violent behaviour against opponents.

Rituals and plays are designed as much for the onlookers
as the actors. 'Onlookers' is not a good description. A ritual
or play achieves its purpose when onlookers become par-
ticipants. The audience is caught up in the worlds of
meaning being represented in the drama or ritual context.
They too are able to externalize and channel into

non-destructive activity the aggression which is lurking within all of us.

I have dwelt at some length on aggression, to the neglect of other forms of behaviour. It has seemed important to do that because aggression, more than other types of behaviour, threatens all our efforts to become human.

Actions, activities and behaviour: all need consideration if we are to make sense of life. Experience, together with the hidden value-system each of us carries around within us, will lead us to make judgments about the weight to be attached to each. If, for example, our knowledge of ourselves, of our society and of human history lead us to believe that nothing can control the aggressive instinct, we shall conclude that life is largely meaningless. Similarly, if we feel insecure about our identity, or feel that reason is usually the victim of irrationality and futility, we shall feel little incentive to control our instincts. Mindless violence will become acceptable and even habitual. As I hope the preceding paragraphs have made clear, my own judgment is that behaviour can, with difficulty, be channelled into action, and some actions can glide into activity.

A cripple groping in the dark

Whenever we discuss action, we must be careful not to be naive. Actions can express evil as well as good intentions. An evil action can be as destructive as any wild outburst of aggressive behaviour. The law makes perfectly proper distinctions between, say, a calculated murder, a death resulting from a frenzied outburst of jealousy and frustration within a family, a killing caused by terrorism and a death caused accidentally. All, however, have in common the death of an innocent person. A society which does not react to the death of innocent people is morally bankrupt and has sown the seeds of its own destruction. So a society which is trying to nurture human values must enshrine in its legislation the moral intuition that the deliberate taking of innocent life is an absolute wrong. Similarly, social and political decisions have to be taken to limit conditions leading to the death of innocents from aggression and from accident. With respect to mindless violence and terrorism, it is not just a matter of fiercer social control, though that is a necessary immediate response. Also required is serious reflection on what prompts aggressive behaviour (frustration, injustice, insecurity) and what can encourage good action in its place. With respect to accidental death: what cost is society willing to pay to reduce, say, the 5,200 deaths caused each year in the UK by road accidents?

Not all evil actions lead to death. All evil actions, however, by definition undermine, diminish or threaten the dignity, identity and freedom of human beings. One of the puzzling things about our experience is that evil actions, like aggressive behaviour, can be directed against ourselves as well as others. Sometimes, indeed, our intentions towards ourselves and towards other people are good, but they are overwhelmed by irrational destructiveness. It then appears that our lives are hopelessly entangled in a process of evil which is beyond our control. This process operates in spite of our best intentions – individual and corporate. For the process of evil overwhelming us is not just an individual experience. It is also the story of our social history. Every nation and culture bears testimony to the fact that social well-being (security, prosperity, the advocacy of its ideals in the wider world) is not directly related to its moral seriousness. In those societies where moral endeavour has been given a high value and a religious sanction, it has been especially hard to accept that doing good does not lead to social well-being. That was a large part of Israel's struggle in pre-Christian times. Time and again the effort was made to interpret Israel's miserable history in terms of moral failure or disobedience of God's will. Eventually the attempt was abandoned. In its place was created a myth of a new era, beyond history, when the just would be rewarded and the wicked punished.

Politics and morality, then, are connected in an extremely complex way. Social life depends on moral foundations (e.g. the absolute wrong of taking innocent life); social life requires moral ideals if human beings are to flourish (justice, peace and freedom); but political wisdom cannot be judged by moral standards. Political actions which serve to maintain a nation's life and well-being must work in the realms of power, vested interest, calculated advantage and pretence. 'Who knows not how to dissimulate knows not how to rule.'[10]

This complex tension between morality and politics expresses our deepest human experience: we ought to do good actions; but the process of evil ensnares us even when we do good and threatens to displace order and meaning with chaos and aggression. To protect our lives and stabilize society we need political leadership, though its very existence represents some sort of trade with the power of evil which is so abhorrent to moral sensitivity.

Another way of expressing this dilemma is through the concept of 'alienation'. Alienation means that a part of our selves or of our life seems strange (alien) to the remainder of us; it is cut off from us. The alienated part of us appears to resist attempts to incorporate it into a meaningful life; or it even attacks us in a hostile and threatening manner. In moral terms, evil is an experience of alienation. The concept of 'alienation', however, has the advantage of being applicable to a broader range of our experience than what is normally included under the heading 'morality'. Karl Marx, for example, successfully deployed the concept to describe the experience of work in nineteenth-century capitalist industry. Work in the mines and factories of the industrial revolution in Western Europe was alienating. Men (and women and children) were required to engage in repetitive work which for them was without purpose. They were given no part in formulating the aims of their tasks. They were treated as addenda to machines, and thereby stripped of the freedom to perform actions. Work was cut off from the human meaning of their lives. Moreover, industrial workers were alienated from the products of their work.

In whatever ways industrial employment policies today have taken account of Marx' analysis, the experience of the alienation of work persistently rears its ugly head. In contemporary society it is frequently found among executives and managers, particularly in large industrial and commercial organizations. The firm requires a commitment which goes far beyond the formal job description. A manager must be instantly available to respond to the firm's rapidly changing needs; an executive must accept the pressure to perform at ever greater levels of efficiency. Work becomes obsessive. A manager becomes alienated from spouse and family. A profound crisis emerges as to where in this divided experience the quest for meaning and identity shall be focused. One thing only is clear: it is either one or the other, not both.

Psychology too has drawn helpfully upon the notion of alienation. I become aware that there are parts of me which seem disconnected from the rest of me. In our ideas-ridden, intellectualized society, men and women find it difficult above all to get in touch with their emotions. 'The habit of thinking prevents us at times from feeling reality, makes us immune to it, makes it seem no more than another thought.'[11] Sometimes we disown our emotions or repress them. That insight was no more confined to the generation of Sigmund Freud than was alienation through work confined to the period of Marx. It has to be re-learned in ever new contexts in each era. It may not be only the emotions from which we are cut off in modern society. One of the consequences of secularization may be that we are alienated from spiritual experience, represented classically by the mystic.[12]

More profoundly I may find myself alienated from my actions, or my actions alienated from myself. In the former case, I am carried along by fanatical participation in an ideology or cause. The party, the institution, or the campaign, contains everything meaningful. I am a dispensable cog in the system, a volunteer for kamikaze-like heroism. In the latter case I find my whole life in my interior being, with its rich patterns of thought and feeling. I am entranced by myself, and indifferent to what I do in the external world. I relieve myself of all responsibility for what I do. I therefore unleash all my instinctive behaviour. I feel myself to be whole and good; the world, however, perceives me as a sadist or a masochist.

We are now in a position to draw out briefly some of the themes which emerge from our discussion of evil processes and alienation discolouring all our actions and experience. I mention three. The first is *contradiction*. At the moral level this means that actions shaped by the highest moral intentions also stimulate in us (contrary to our conscience) actions to please ourselves. Outgoing love is distorted by self-concern. A commitment to serve a noble cause is tarnished by a secret delight when disaster befalls that cause. At the psychological level, the bits and pieces of our personality pull in different directions so that coherence is constantly threatened by disintegration.

Secondly, evil and alienation generate *failure*. Rational purposes are pursued, but the ends are not achieved. We end up wide of the mark, like the archer's arrow blown off course by a gust of wind. Things do not come out right. The gardener creates a vineyard in a promising location and nurtures it with skill and care. 'He looked for it to yield grapes, but it yielded wild grapes' (Isa. 5.1–2). As we have seen, that metaphor applies to conversations and to actions: they do not necessarily end well. Human wisdom and culture cannot create a just and peaceable kingdom. The best laid plans are subject to the vicissitudes of the unexpected; an organized life is disrupted by interruptions.

Failure and contradiction together constitute what Paul called 'the law of sin: that when I want to do the right, only the wrong is within my reach' (Rom. 8.21–25).

Third is *exhaustion*. A person sets his or her hand confidently to a task. Everything seems right for success: inner resources, attitude of mind, training and skills. Things begin to go well. However, after a time, in spite of a courageous negotiation of difficulties and disappointments, what seem like negative forces begin to take over. Skill, confidence and courage are undermined. The world seems strangely threatening, posing all sorts of questions to our hero's well-being. Things do not turn out quite as intended. Conflicts arise, leaving a deposit of resentment or insecurity, a feeling of having been bruised in a fight or of having acted badly. Stress at a destructive level is experienced: sleeplessness, anxiety about time-scales, a feeling of being without energy. The person begins to ponder whether the task is worth doing at all: does it merit this feeling weak, this uncertainty, a painful sense of isolation? He or she seeks out a parent-substitute, someone who will cuddle, soothe and hold, someone into whose arms he or she can escape for comfort and affirmation.

Exhaustion is an integral part of all human enterprises. Its ultimate focus is death, the ebbing away or the wrenching from us of life's energy.

Such an assessment of our experience often leads men and women to despair about life's meaning. Sin and death highlight life's absurdity and futility. That conclusion must be respected; any alternative assessment runs the risk of avoiding the bleakness of our human situation. In practice, however, most people go on living, planning, hoping and loving. They may see themselves as cripples groping in the dark. Meaning may be glimpsed only as shades of grey in the blackness of a subterranean cave. No sooner do we see something than we fall over, hit our head on a hard protrusion and feel dazed. We cannot regain our original vantage point. We cannot see even the greyness any more. Yet we start the search again.

In a world of evil we reflect on our story, we converse and we act. In a life dominated by death we write novels and poems, paint pictures, make music, act out drama and watch snooker. In a world fractured by violence we seek out the structure of DNA and the grammar of the Ugaritic language. In a world marked by alienation we struggle for justice and pray for peace, build communities, love and hate tradition. Deep inside us is a longing to make sense of our lives. Words and actions are the tools we use. Perhaps 'machines' would be a better description than 'tools'. Machines can be exceedingly complex; they often break down or, like computers, need debugging. But we cannot normally do without them.

3 Basic Resources: Feeling

Imagination and feeling

Father to young child struggling to cling to a favourite soft toy and at the same time to carry a too large chair into the garden: 'Why don't you let me take the chair? You carry Harry.'

Child: 'No! I've got a better idea. . . .'

However limited may be the child's coordination, physical strength and management skills, he has already the faculty which is basic to human life: imagination. The child can see potential situations in his or her head, and can evolve and evaluate plans of action. 'Imagination is the manipulation inside the mind of absent things, by using in their place images or words or other symbols.'[1] Imagination creates 'pictures' of wide scope, panoramic visions of how things are and how they might be. Imagination unifies disparate and varied bits of experience, creates order out of apparent confusion, recognizes continuities and discerns patterns. All sorts of hidden likenesses are suddenly noticed. All sorts of possibilities, relationships and difficulties about future scenarios can be contemplated before any one of them becomes a reality.

Archaeologists and palaeontologists seek to penetrate the mists of human history through fossil remains. They are attempting to piece together the complex chains of evolution and to identify when *homo sapiens* first appeared on earth. The fossil record is haphazard, incomplete and often difficult to interpret with certainty. Yet there is another clue, more powerful than the fossil evidence: the evidence of imagination at work. In the early Stone Age burial sites are found. They imply belief in some kind of survival after death. 'We must regard as *in principle fully human* any living entity to which such a world of ideas is to be attributed.'[2]

The usefulness of imagined pictures of the future depends upon how accurate the pictures are. I can imagine well what it would be like to live apart from my family for, say, six months because I have plenty of experience of living apart from them each day. In contrast, I cannot easily imagine what it would be like to be President of Syria because I am so ill-informed about Syrian politics and culture.

Even so, imagination can take me into extraordinary situations. So powerful, indeed, is imagination that it can create symbols, frameworks, relations – whole worlds – which owe little or nothing to the world we actually inhabit. Imagination can produce pure invention. This is the gift for generating fantasy and illusion.

Besides creating images of our world as it is, has been or might be, and of fictitious worlds, imagination can also operate on ourselves. We create an image of ourselves: a self-image. Self-images also can draw richly upon experience (the story-telling, conversation, activity and action of which the previous chapters have spoken); or they can be constructed as illusion and fantasy. Either way, our self-image is a holistic picture, a large hologram which expresses many dimensions of our personality – intellect, physical appearance, emotional sensitivity, our underlying values and convictions. Our self-image represents where we have reached in our search for an identity and a meaning for our lives.

When we imagine ourselves in some future situation, a very complex mental activity is taking place: we are constructing images of a future situation which are part real and part illusion; we bring to the imagined situation our self-image, which also is part real and part illusion. I envisage the interaction between me and the situation, but I have no way of knowing whether the imagined fears and pleasures are the result of real relating to real, illusion to illusion, or real to illusion. Yet there are few experiences as fascinating as imagining yourself in novel situations. So take time to imagine what it would be like if you were told that you had a terminal illness and a life-expectancy of six weeks; or if you were able to meet in private a member of the opposite sex whom you find very attractive. This is imaginative play, not very different from day-dreaming.

Inside the mind imagination can focus its 'energy' into two sorts of *activity*. One is logical reasoning, the habit of thinking and analyzing, of taking to pieces complex images and symbols in the search for what is basic and universal. Its finest flowers are the abstract theories of the scientist and the elegant theorems of the mathematician. The other activity is feeling. Thinking and feeling are opposite poles. They are not mutually exclusive, but temperament and upbringing tend to make us emphasize one and neglect the other. Most of us think too much and feel too little. The exception to that generalization is the artist; but we all know how marginal is the artist in technological society. This by itself justifies our giving more attention to feeling. My view is that feeling (balanced and complemented by thinking) provides a route towards the meaning of our life which cannot be overvalued.

There are two types of feeling – irrational and rational. The former is intuition. You walk into a strange room full of people you do not know; you 'sense' the atmosphere and the intentions of the group. This is a 'hunch', an inspired guess, an immediate grasping of the total situation which precedes all analysis and reflection. Rational feeling, in contrast, is a *considered* judgment on a situation. 'You've been a member of this college/committee/organization/club for a year now. Tell me, how do you *feel* about things?' The answer gives an assessment of the total experience – agreeable or disagreeable, comfortable or aggravating, good or bad.

Feeling is the capacity to grasp situations whole. It is not just an ability to see things on the large scale and in three dimensions (which is the gift of imagination); feeling also weighs and evaluates the raw material of the imagination.

Feeling assesses our self-image as well as an image we construct of an external situation. If we feel comfortable with our self-image, we normally say we accept ourselves. Sometimes, however, we feel negatively about ourselves, or we lack self-acceptance. On other occasions something happens to us and our response seems not to fit well with our self-image. This may challenge or question our acceptance of ourselves.

Rational feeling draws its stimulus from the emotions. In English we hardly distinguish between 'feeling' and 'feelings'. Yet there is a distinction, because emotions are involuntary and irrational responses to particular situations. Two examples will suffice. First, it is perfectly possible to feel angry about an event or a person (i.e. react with the emotion of anger) while feeling that the overall context (which includes ups and downs) is reasonably comfortable. Persistent and unrelieved negative emotions lead, of course, to a revision of feeling; we feel the situation has become destructive or worthless. Second, it is easy to imagine a situation full of pleasurable emotions (touching the untouchable object of our sexual desires?) which is however a situation about which we feel uncomfortable. The imagined situation may contradict our deeply held moral convictions. Goodness and happiness do not necessarily coincide.

We shall have more to say about the emotions in Chapter 7. Here we concentrate on feeling. There is a certain irony in what follows: we are analyzing and thinking about feeling.

Feeling and empathy

Feeling is a faculty which can be developed with practice. We talk about 'feeling our way into a situation'. This means that as our experience of a situation develops, as we become more confident in the situation so that we are more open to its constraints and possibilities, we regularly review our feeling about the situation. But more importantly, by simply making a habit of attending to experience with our feeling (as well as or even instead of our thinking), we become better at it. We say some people have a breadth, or depth, or complexity of feeling – about the world around them and about themselves. These are often called 'sensitive' people.

Sensitivity (breadth of feeling) is a skill necessary for empathy. Empathy begins by imagining what it is like to be in another person's role, or to be another person. (We start doing that quite naturally as very young children: we act out roles as soldiers, nurses, parents, etc.) Empathy includes also the capacity to imagine accurately how the other person feels. Empathy means literally 'feeling into', feeling from the inside of, someone else. Empathy, however, is an imaginative activity in which I retain my own identity and autonomy. I am not sucked into another person's problems or fears. Deep and lasting relationships make great demands on the development of mutual empathy.

Practice does not guarantee to make perfect. We need particular resources in order better to develop feeling and empathy. Art is the resource we need – both our own art, and the art of others (particularly of masters and geniuses of artistic creation). I am assuming here that 'art' refers to all sorts of invention, from cookery to sculpture, from flower arrangement to poetry, from pop music to architecture.

Art and meaning

There is no public agreement about what art is and how it works. I shall therefore have to describe a view of art which makes sense to me and, I believe, makes a vital contribution to our search for meaning in life. I do not want to suggest that other ways of thinking about art are invalid or worthless.

In my view, art involves three activities. First is a concentrated attention upon some portion of the world around us, in order to see it straight. One of my hobbies is sketching and watercolouring. From time to time I like to go away by myself for a day and find a subject to draw and paint. I have to gaze at the subject very carefully and notice details that normally are lost in general impressions. In the first instance I am trying to recreate on a page what I see. I find this a purging experience. I am taken out of myself. My concentrated energies of sight, hand-control, perception of colour and perspective are devoted to that which is not me. I am transformed in the process, unwrapped from my normal self-concern to a concern for the other. That 'other' might be a tree, a chimney pot, a gate or a building – something apparently inconsequential, but which becomes the object of a disinterested love.

Secondly, the artist must discern the feeling the situation has about itself. The artist is therefore going behind appearances into the unseen realm of self-awareness and meaning in the subject of his or her attention. The artist is practising empathy. Artists witness to the experience that empathy is possible not only in the case of other people but in regard to anything and everything that exists in the world.

People and objects do not readily or easily yield their feeling about themselves to the artist. When such insight becomes available it is usually experienced as a gift, a disclosure graciously entrusted to the attentive and loving artist.

> Someone . . . had once said to Tim, 'You painters must feel as if you are creating the world.' Tim never felt like that. He felt at his best working moments, a sense of total relaxation. Of course he was not creating the world, he was discovering it, not even that, he was just seeing it and letting it continue to manifest itself. He was not even sure, at these good moments, whether what he was doing was 'reproducing'. He was just there, active as a part of the world, a *transparent* part. Daisy, who hated music, had once said to denigrate that art, 'Music is like chess, it's all there beforehand, all you do is find it.' 'Yes,' said Tim. That was exactly what he felt about painting.[3]

Usually empathy (insight into feeling) comes like lightning on a dark night: unpredictable, short-lived, brilliant, rending the sky from top to bottom. All around is darkness and mystery. These flashes of light often shine through tiny fluctuations in the situation being addressed. The person who is giving undivided attention to the detail of what is going on is singularly alert to even the smallest perturbations. The artist notices the change and seizes on its significance. Like Alexander Fleming 'noticing' in his laboratory what many others before him had merely observed and noted: that in certain circumstances the cultures he was growing produced fungi.

For everyone else this spelt failure, and the impure cultures were thrown away. For Fleming, the keen and skilled watcher, the fungus was a significant deviation. He pursued the change, and penicillin was discovered. In a similar way, the artist recognizes that by a distortion of the image of what fills his attention its inner being can be revealed.

Often the object of the artist's attention displays no 'natural' variations. It is fixed and immovable, like a building or barren crag. The artist must then in the imagination *introduce* changes to what is being experienced with the senses. The artist adds to the situation or subtracts from it. In the imagination all sorts of experiments can be tried, introducing novel features, removing distractions, simplifying, highlighting, changing the context or tone of what is 'natural'. The trials and errors end when something 'inside' the situation is revealed. Art does not therefore merely describe and represent the world: through the artist's imagination, it adjusts and manipulates a portion of the world, to allow its mystery to be unlocked.

Thirdly, the artist pays attention to his or her own feeling. The feeling may be intuitive or rational. It will include the artist's feeling about the situation being looked at, listened to or touched. It will also involve the artist's feeling about himself or herself. Concentrated encounter with a subject involves the observer. The artist cannot remain detached. His or her self-image, meaning and identity come under scrutiny in the deep engagement (at the levels of sense and feeling). We say that artistic activity is self-involving. 'I do not believe in an art which is not forced into existence by a human being's desire to open his heart' (Edvard Munch).

Art fuses together the three activities we have just surveyed and gives them expression in a concentrated and memorable form. An example from poetry will clarify this. Here is William Shakespeare's Sonnet Number 116.

> Let me not to the marriage of true minds
> Admit impediments; love is not love
> Which alters when it alteration finds
> Or bends with the remover to remove.

O, no, it is an ever-fixed mark
That looks on tempests and is never shaken;
It is the star to every wand'ring bark,
Whose worth's unknown, although his height be taken.
Love's not Time's fool, though rosy lips and cheeks
Within his bending sickle's compass come;
Love alters not with his brief hours and weeks,
But bears it out even to the edge of doom.
    If this be error, and upon me proved,
    I never writ, nor no man ever loved.

The sonnet is about friendship. Friendship is a love-relationship of incalculable value which remains constant through all the vicissitudes of life, including the fickleness of the friend. ('Or bends with the remover to remove' means 'Agrees with the friend when he or she chooses to withdraw from the relationship.') Friendship in fact transcends time. Friendship is like marriage. Marriage is one form of friendship. Simply setting out the theme in this way illuminates what art provides in place of pedantic prose. My prose descriptions are doubtless true. But they have none of the vitality and sparkle of the poem. They feel abstract and detached instead of vivid, concrete and memorable.

The sonnet begins by making accurate observations of human friendship. Friendship does outlast the ravages of time. It is not dependent on physical attraction, even though beauty may trigger it off. We can all see that by looking around us. But now the second artistic activity mentioned above: reorganizing or distorting what is accurately observed in order to unveil something of its inner meaning. In lines 5–8 Shakespeare places alongside our knowledge of friendship another experience which is normally quite separate from our experience and discussion of friendship. It is a nautical experience – sailors finding their way by means of a lodestar. The poet makes this apparently unrelated phenomenon into a *metaphor* for friendship. The essence of metaphor is understanding and experiencing one kind of thing in terms of another.

To see our third theme at work, we turn to the final line of the sonnet. Here Shakespeare invests something of himself in the sonnet. He reveals his view about himself as a poet in just three words: 'I never writ.' Immediately the sonnet springs to a new level of interest. Shakespeare declares that the demonstration of love's transcending time is in the creation of poetry itself. In those three short words we, the readers, are caught up into Shakespeare's art and know directly what it is to be gripped by something that will hold its power from generation to generation. Art and love have the same eternal quality because art is the revelation of love – the artist's love for that of which he writes, paints, sculpts, composes.[4] Shakespeare again, more expansively, in Sonnet 19:

> Yet do thy worst, old Time: despite thy wrong,
> My love shall in my verse ever live young.

Responding and doing

Every artistic creation is a courageous statement on the part of an artist. The artist has seen a fundamental truth, and in his or her creative action has made that truth public. The artist is inviting everyone who sees or hears what is produced to check the truth conveyed in the artefact against their own experience. Shakespeare did that openly in the final clause of Sonnet 116: 'nor no man ever loved.' He was saying: 'If anyone has loved, he or she will know what I'm saying is true. Human experience will authenticate the theme of my poem.' A work of art, then, is a particular and concrete item which attempts to encapsulate universal human feeling, the common sense of the human situation. Human experience and human values are focused and illuminated in each great artistic creation. When I look at a Renoir nude, I see a particular woman with a unique personality, who stimulated the artist to discover and display something of himself and his self-understanding. At the same time I see something about *all* women of a particular age and the way that we males feel about them. The general and the particular, the historical and the contemporary fuse together.

It is worth exploring a little further what happens when we attend to a great work of art. Nothing at all happens unless we notice it, unless it causes us to stop what we are doing and give it our concentrated attention. It may simply puzzle us, or it may touch us straight away at a very deep level. In one way or another we find ourselves involved with the art. It seems to stimulate in us a whole range of memories of experiences which concern us. We are in touch with our feeling about ourselves. As we explore the work of art, noting both its precision of description and its distortion of what the world is like, we in a sense re-invent the artefact for ourselves – in our imagination, of course. We say to ourselves something like this:

'This book/picture/piece of music/play has brought to the front of my mind something I've experienced time and again – because I'm a human being, and this is part of everyone's experience. Through the eyes of the artist I can see the meaning of my experience more deeply and clearly than I've seen it before or in a completely fresh light.

I can also see myself more clearly. The artist's courage in saying something about himself or herself gives me the courage to do something similar. I haven't become Shakespeare by reading a Shakespeare sonnet; but as Shakespeare prompts me to reflect on our common experience of friendship he holds my hand so that I dare to look at my own capacity to love as a friend. I am more alert to what is required of me as a friend. I feel challenged to enter more deeply and authentically into the task of becoming a friend.'

In the performing arts it is obvious that dancers, actors and musicians have to discover for themselves the inventive imagination and the feeling of the choreographer, playwright and composer; and allow the work to inspire their own interpretation. What they do, however, makes it possible for the audience – in a different but none the less valid way – to participate in the same exercise. This process operates in every engagement with a work of art in every medium: re-imagining, remaking the art and infusing it with our own meaning and commitment. The only difference is that a play needs actors and a performance as well as an audience; a painting needs only someone to look at it.

If listening to music, reading a novel, or looking at a picture is in some sense re-inventing the art for ourselves, we ought to be encouraged to practise our own 'original' art. Searching for the meaning of life includes not only going to concerts, art exhibitions and the like but also painting, making music, writing and designing. Here we are inhibited and oppressed by the concept of the artistic genius. Few, if any, of us are likely to be a Picasso, Beethoven, Michaelangelo or George Eliot. We feel disabled and worthless in their company. In terms of impact on human history, this feeling expresses a true judgment. On the other hand, it seems to be a distortion of our experience to say that either we are artistic geniuses or nothing – with perhaps a nodding affirmation of 'First Division' performers whose works fill exhibitions and concerts in provincial halls and amateur gigs. Artistic creativity is integral to our humanness. It is part of our common quest for meaning because each piece of art marks an intersection between what is universally human and what is unique and individual. Only *my* art can represent my self-knowledge and express the complexity of my feeling about myself. So my art has validity, even though I show it to no one but myself.

We know that all sorts of things can go wrong in our fumbling attempts to create our own art. In the first place, we may have left undeveloped our skill of observing in detail what is going on around us. The most common result is that we devote so much energy to describing what is in front of us that we do nothing more. Learning to draw is a skill which assists painting but it is not to be confused with it. A young child can create art without being able to draw well, as every primary school testifies.

The next pitfall comprises focusing our attention on something less than universally human – an exotic toy, say, rather than a flower. Third, we may find it very difficult to dig out of our subject its inner meaning. It seems to resist revealing anything of itself, but remains simply an appearance, hiding from us its dark and silent mystery. So we lose patience and walk away. Alternatively we settle for an interpretation which we impose on the subject. Or we tint our observation with trivial sentiments and superficial emotions instead of deep feeling (in the subject or in ourselves). This often represents a refusal to recognize the realities of evil, alienation and death of which we spoke in the previous chapter. Everything is made to look glossy and successful. Finally, we compromise on the struggle to discern deeply buried meaning by washing our subject with conventional attitudes; we resort to cliché; we become mere purveyors of fashion. We allow the prevailing culture to rob us of our freedom to make a personal statement.

There is a fourth area in which all our artistic creativity may go wrong. We may not be able to master the forms and styles of the medium in which we choose to express our imagination and feeling. Music has its structures, colours and tones, painting its composition and its choices of surface and materials; ballet has its steps and figures; clothes have their cut and shape. It is a measure of the poverty of our education that we are so ill-informed on these matters. Our imaginations and our struggle for meaning are shrivelled precisely because we do not take it for granted that a fully human life involves copying, experimenting and adapting artistic forms and styles until we find a signature of our own. Of course, the search for a style can become obsessive, the be-all-and-end-all of life. Advertisers are notorious for packaging things 'in style', or for creating public images, which distract from their content and inner quality. Art is born when content, style and personal statement support one another. In great art they fuse. Something is brought into being which cannot be formulated in any other way. It cannot be translated into another form. It simply is – a communication of the truth of the human situation through a particular personality.

The fact that our own art will not be great art and will inevitably go wrong to some extent or other should not discourage us. All we are saying is that artistic creativity is an *action*. The content is formed from the breadth and depth of our imagination and feeling; the intention is to communicate; the action is the practical task of writing words, modelling clay, sewing clothes, carving wood, and so on. All actions are prone to go wrong – that is integral to our human situation. So we cross out words and try different ones; we crush our clay pot and start again; we cut too far into our material and have to build the mistakes into the final design. Eventually something emerges which is about life and about me – in spite of all its limitations and imperfections. The overwhelming sensation we feel as we look at what we have made is pleasure. Not unalloyed pleasure, but pleasure none the less.

The morning arrived, grey-blue, a morning filled with odours and street noises, and with variations in light that seemed to have been orchestrated by a single person; Proust, for example. Someone out there was directing the gigantic and naive world machine; someone was choreographing the clouds, winds, the horns of buses and the scents of lilacs, directing them with the adroitness, fervour and talent of a great artist. Edouard, who did not believe in God, found in this harmony proof of the existence of Art. Stretched out in bed, alone, he closed his eyes in perfect contentment. It was rare these days for his life – which seemed to be running off in every direction – to stop suddenly, then turn towards him and blurt out: Yes, I do exist, and Art exists, and Beauty and Harmony, and it's up to you to describe them and to prove to the world that we exist. A violent feeling, compounded of happiness and impotence, surged through him. He wanted simultaneously to thank Heaven that he was a writer, and to break all his pencils. At this moment, he wanted never to have loved, never to have been loved. He would have liked simply to be more intelligent, more sensitive, and to remain where he was, eager and attentive, ready to take it all down, understand, translate it into words. For himself first, and then for the world. Of course, his translation would in a sense be false, since words once assembled turn traitor. Yet his own arbitrary and unique way of assembling them would none the less help him to get to his own truth.[5]

Art and life

I hope it has become clear that creating art and responding creatively to the art of others (especially the masters) are very similar activities. Art is a metaphor for life. A consequence of this is that artistic creativity can spring from the contemplation of art as well as from concentrating on what is happening in the world around us. Usually artists respond to art presented in one medium by creating something in a different medium. Moussorgsky visited an exhibition of paintings by a friend, Victor Hartmann, who had recently died, in 1874. This inspired him to compose *Pictures at an Exhibition*. Similarly R. S. Thomas in *Ingrowing Thoughts* has set poems alongside modern paintings which have triggered his poetic imagination.

In neither of these cases is the artist simply translating the meaning of pictures into music or poetry. It is impossible to extract meaning from art, and then repackage it. If this were the case, art would be redundant. It would be mere decoration for statements of meaning which could be expressed adequately in straightforward sentences. Art, however, cannot be dissolved in this way. Moussorgsky's music and Thomas' poems are new inventions, with their own meanings, inspired by various pictures.

Because art is a metaphor for life, we conclude that our search for meaning will not end with a proposition, an ore which can be extracted from the seams and mines of experience. The search will never end, and countless new expressions of imagination and feeling are needed to light the way.

4 Broadening The Search

Science and technology

No exploration of our struggle to make sense of life in the modern world can ignore science and technology. Science is a thoroughly human activity. The first love of my own professional life was physics. I learned how to be a physicist at school, university and in my first job by being immersed in a community and tradition of physicists. Theoretical concepts and experimental techniques had to be mastered and used. The nature of the task, the procedures adopted, the language employed and the physicists themselves formed a sort of subculture. Within this community we knew almost instinctively what the aims of physics were and what was the area of experience with which we were concerned. We rarely, if ever, thought reflectively or systematically about such things; they were hidden assumptions. The task itself was all-absorbing, demanding skill, experience, creativity and accountability. Several writers have given vivid accounts of scientists at work: they show them embroiled in envy, competitiveness, disappointment, patience, striking inventiveness, single-minded dedication and extraordinary exhilaration.[1]

Science generates understandings of how the world goes. Sometimes the vast scope of scientific theories is breathtaking. Charles Darwin's theory of evolution stamped its authority on the scientific world not least because of the breadth of experience it encompassed – in zoology, botany and geology. The 'new' physics of the twentieth century unifies our understandings of the tiniest forces and building-blocks of matter at the sub-atomic level with the origins and development of the universe itself. The more comprehensive a scientific theory becomes, the more abstract is its formulation. Imagination has become wedded to logical reasoning.

Understanding the world takes away our fear of nature. Before the emergence of modern science, the world was the sphere of threatening supernatural powers, to which men and women responded with magic, fear and imprecation of spirits. To understand something is, literally, to 'stand under' it, to display the sort of confidence we feel in a well-built house: the ceiling will hold, it will not collapse and destroy us. Even simple scientific understandings de-mystify the natural world. Sophisticated scientific theories produce much greater confidence. However, no theory is absolute or final. In principle all scientific theories are provisional in character. That is why science is an unending task, accumulating more and more data and developing ever more comprehensive understandings.

In fact, science produces many, relatively independent, types of understanding of our world. Physics, chemistry, biology, economics, anthropology, psychology and sociology all have their different types of theory to contribute. All of them offer explanations which are the products of human research and invention. They make no reference to God. That point was finally secured by Darwin and his followers in their theory about human evolution through natural selection.[2]

Science cannot be isolated from technology. As Friedrich Engels pointed out, 'The object of science is to control nature through understanding it.' That is an important corrective to the ideal of a so-called 'pure' science, because it overcomes the dichotomy between theory and practice. Perhaps 'control' is too strong a word. Science tests the limits of the givenness of nature and society; it shows what can and what cannot be done with nature to serve human ends. Within these limits, technology transforms the world we live in according to the goals we choose. If society wants quicker and more efficient communication between individuals and groups, engineers and designers are encouraged to make the printing press, devise a postal system, invent the telephone and the telex link, and develop high-speed computers to store and give access to huge amounts of information.

Simply describing the story in these terms makes us aware of other factors in the situation. Science and technology generate their own momentum, which can be so powerful that it overrides political and social control. The transformation of society by science and technology then becomes a self-perpetuating end in itself, cut off from moral and social considerations. Many fear that this has already happened in the case of military research and development. It is certainly true that scientists and technologists have often been slow to accept their part of the responsibility that falls to us all, to shape our society according to our human ideals. 'If it can be done, it should and will be done' has frequently summed up their attitude.

Science itself is not a morally neutral activity. It depends fundamentally, for example, on what Bronowski used to call 'the habit of truth'.³ Equally basic is the notion of self-criticism. The formulation of a hypothesis or theory always derives from data; and every hypothesis or theory must in principle be capable of being tested experimentally. Indeed a scientist sets out not only experimentally to verify predictions from a hypothesis or theory, but also to look for ways of falsifying a hypothesis or theory. Progress in science hinges upon this constant interplay between theory and experiment, between imaginative thought and acute observation.

The critical spirit, embedded in the practice of science, has affected everything human in the modern world. It is now taken for granted that every appeal to authority, ideology or dogma must be subjected to critical appraisal. Only in this way can human beings be liberated from tyranny and irrationality. Each individual also, it is generally held, must become self-critical if his or her potential is to be realized and freedom secured.

Just how far this critical spirit must penetrate can be seen in the complex relation between criticism and the arts. The first task of a critic is to analyze and examine all sorts of factors in the background or context of a work of art (techniques and structures used, traditions drawn upon, social influences) to enable others who attend to the art to enter more deeply its world of meaning. Criticism gives us a point of entry into what otherwise might be baffling. But the critic also makes judgments. He or she assesses the authenticity of experience, and the depth and breadth of feeling, which an artefact or performance evokes in him or her. It is at this point that the critic needs to be self-critical and exposed to critical appraisal in wider society. Otherwise critics simply generate fashion. We decide to go to the cinema only on the strength of the reviews; or we spend as much time reading the programme notes as we do listening to a concert. The critic has then become the guru of taste and arbiter of success in the arts; we have surrendered our freedom to engage directly with the art and contribute our own critical appreciation.

With all its power and influence, are there limits to what science can explain? Clearly there are. Science is built on a few fundamental assumptions – that nature is intelligible, ordered and unified, for example. But science cannot explain why its own premises should be true – unless their truthfulness is assured by the fact that they work. Albert Einstein made the point memorably like this: 'The most incomprehensible thing about the universe is that it is comprehensible.'

Similarly, science cannot make sense of why anything should exist at all. It cannot contribute to discussions of any purpose that nature and society might be thought to have. These limits are exposed in a particularly sharp form when we reflect on ourselves as individuals. Science indubitably helps me to understand a great deal about myself. My self-knowledge would be unthinkable without the contributions of medicine, psychology, genetics, and so on. But this scientific knowledge has its limits. What am I to make of my subjective experience, that inner sense I have of myself which is inaccessible to scientific investigation? What resources and skills are available to me to understand and make sense of who I feel myself to be? (That is particularly ironic if my destiny and enthusiasm for life are located in science.) Science leaves me with the problem of how my inner life of belief, commitment, values and purpose connects with the objective world of nature and society which science so wonderfully defines and transforms.

History

Science has not brought into its control either art or history. As we saw in Chapter 3, art is a unique form of knowledge. History too has proved its independence. This is not to deny that history has been profoundly influenced by science. We take it for granted that one of the primary tasks of a historian is to sift fact and evidence from speculation and fantasy. The historian begins by tackling the question, 'What actually happened (at some specified point in the past)?' The technical name for this work is 'scientific or critical history'. We often forget that such a view of history is relatively recent. It was only in the middle of the nineteenth century that this task was rediscovered as being of crucial importance. The historians of last century took advantage of new skills and techniques developing in archaeology, geology, anthropology, sociology and the like. This generated enormous confidence that history could describe objectively not only what had happened but also the intentions and meaning of historical characters. History had been captivated by science, but in the process the past had been reduced to merely antiquarian interest, of little significance to the present. For those who were interested in such things, however, it seemed a marvellously refreshing change from what had been the case for a thousand years before. In the medieval period, for example, it was commonly supposed that the work of the historian was to tell the story of the past so that it was as edifying as possible to contemporary readers. That is why medieval 'history' owes more to legend than to fact.

We live today, however, in a culture where history is not subservient to science. We have had to recapture history as a distinctive tool used in the search for personal meaning. We have not simply redefined history. Instead we have drawn deeply upon classical views of history. In ancient Greek and

Roman society history attempted to fulfil various aims: to preserve men's words and deeds from oblivion[4]; to recount accurately what was said and done[5]; but primarily to discover and illustrate what were taken to be the guiding principles of life. One underlying principle was nemesis (retribution) – every act produces its necessary consquences. The historian provided a chronicle of events, and in dialogue with the philosophers, retold the story of the past so as to highlight from the flux of events their true substance and meaning.

The contemporary study of history is not dominated by the desire to elucidate general principles operating throughout all creation. In Chapter 1 we looked briefly at how history is now understood: we examined how we tell the story of our own lives. We saw that history is more than simply accumulating facts from the past, though the task of sifting fact from fantasy remains a crucial foundation to history. We construct a consecutive story from what seem to us *significant* facts and experiences, and in doing this we discover who we are. Our identity has taken shape through our personal life-history; but all history is coloured by our image of ourselves, our values and concerns.

We also noticed that story-telling scotches any picture of ourselves as lone and heroic individuals. Our lives and their meaning are enmeshed in a web of other lives, institutions and cultural influences. There is an interdependence between me and the rest of humanity; and only within that general context of belonging is my unique individuality secured. All historical writing has to confront the processes through which the individual and the collective interact. Either history focuses upon an individual, and must identify the social influences which affected that individual; or history tells the story of a group or institution, but must disclose how particularly influential individuals shaped that institution in distinctive ways.

Story-telling and contemporary historical writing not only nurture self-understanding. They also create freedom. In the first instance, freedom is secured from any sense of fate. When I explore the history of, say, the community in which I live, I quickly realize that in the past things have been very different from the way they are now. There is nothing fixed and final about the present situation. It can and will change, and change does not necessarily destroy identity.

This leads immediately to the second sense of freedom which history brings. We are free, to some degree, to create our own futures. Strictly, of course, the future is open. It contains unknown disruptions, hazards and opportunities. But the story so far has given us an identity and glimpses of meaning to life. History, laced with imagination, enables us to envisage new, realistic possibilities for ourselves in the open future; we can act to achieve these self-chosen goals. History itself does not picture any goal for us. But we can set our own aims and, so long as we know where we are now, we can make rational choices to assist our movement to where we wish to go. We can make plans for the future.

History can even assist us to identify our goals for the future. As we survey the past, we are free to choose critically from the wisdom and values enshrined in the experience of others. That is, we can sift from a wide range of traditions which outline ways of tackling life; and we can identify with one or more of them. Here is Alexander Solzhenitsyn making such a choice:

> There is a simple truth which one can learn only through suffering: in war not victories are blessed but defeats. Governments need victories and the people need defeats. Victory gives rise to the desire for more victories. But after a defeat it is freedom that men desire – and usually attain. A people needs defeat just as an individual needs suffering and misfortune: they compel the deepening of the inner life and generate a spiritual upsurge.[6]

If history does indeed bring us freedom, it is because history (in the modern sense) has demystified the past and the processes of change. We can explain why things turned out as they did, without appealing to magic or supernatural interventions. Not that explaining the past is an easy task. So the historian draws upon a whole range of explanations for the way things have gone. How, for example, can we understand the rise and decline of an institution like the Methodist Church in the United Kingdom?[7] We might make much of the contributions from outstanding individuals (John and Charles Wesley, Hugh Bourne, Jabez Bunting and Hugh Price Hughes, to name but a few); we could trace the effects of their gifts, skills and psychology. Or we might make use of social and economic analysis, emphasizing the appeal of early Methodism to the oppressed classes in a period of rapid social change (the enclosure movement; rapid industrialization and urbanization); they sublimated their grievances into religious fervour and upward social mobility (i.e. they became a group of respectable shopkeepers, teachers, and the like). Again, we might explain the story as a struggle to find and affirm a corporate identity (the transition from a holiness and renewal movement within the Church of England to an independent ecclesiastical institution taking its increasingly bureaucratic place in the family of churches precisely when all were shrinking under the ravages of secularization).

There is literally no limit to the sort of explanations which history can draw upon to understand the past. History draws on the sciences (e.g. psychology, sociology and economics), but is not captured by science. History indeed asserts its independence and authority over science by devising a history *of* science (and indeed a history of art, and a history of anything else we care to name). History is one of the principle means we have for making sense of life because of its breadth, but also because it witnesses to something integral to *all* reality: everything without exception is locked into time and change. There are beginnings, disruptions and endings for everything that exists. Science may discover the unchanging forces and laws which explain why things move and change as they do; art may give intimations of eternity (see p. 46 above); but only history talks about birth and death, and makes us confront the unpredictable ruptures in the way things go. History is wisdom about the complexities of human existence, even if it is wisdom after the event.

The limits of history

(*i*) History is a parasite. It draws endlessly from every conceivable sort of explanation (psychological, social, economic, political, etc.) to make sense of the past. Each sort of explanation is satisfying as far as it goes. But the past remains forever elusive. We can pile up the ways we understand the processes of change, but we cannot exhaust the past of its significance and meaning.

(*ii*) History cannot convince us that the past is wholly susceptible to rational understanding. Here we encounter again the tragic experience of evil, brokenness and alienation, which mocks all our analytical skills. The human can sink to the bestial. Who or what can make sense of Auschwitz?

> Evidently evildoing also has a threshold magnitude. Yes, a human being hesitates and bobs back and forth between good and evil all his life. He slips, falls back, clambers up, repents, things begin to darken again. But just so long as the threshold of evildoing is not crossed, the possibility of returning remains, and he himself is still within reach of our hope. But when, through the density of evil actions, the result either of their own extreme degree or of the absoluteness of his power, he suddenly crosses the threshold, he has left humanity behind, and without, perhaps, the possibility of return.[8]

In the light (or should we say 'darkness'?) of such phenomena, we must give up any lingering notions that history reveals progress or displays the hand of providence. Evil and death also set limits to what we can expect of rational plans for the future. Human actions, we must keep reminding ourselves, can go wrong, can evoke unexpected reactions, and can trigger off consequences which were never envisaged.

In pre-scientific times, people frequently resorted to mythical ways of thought to focus attention on (and try to come to terms with) the unexpected and the horrendous. They envisaged supernatural beings intervening in the course of history.

Human beings were often the unwitting pawns of conflicts and campaigns in an invisible heavenly world. No wonder human actions produced no reliable consequences.

There is no reason to think that human experience in pre-modern times was any less complex than is ours today. One difference between the ancients and ourselves is that we have many tools to explore this complexity (art and criticism, and the sciences), but they had few. Myth was a bit of a catch-all, which had to do service for what we assume are distinct activities. Myth is to modern historical methods as the eighteenth-century rural clergyman is to a contemporary parson. Oliver Goldsmith's clergyman was the resident schoolmaster, magistrate, financier, health adviser, politician, counsellor and father-figure as well as preacher, celebrant of the sacraments and rites of passage, and advocate of Christian morality and discipline. His modern counterpart is an almost redundant occasional visitor struggling to find a role, an amateur in a world of professionals.[9]

We have noted above the use of myth to explain the capricious way things go in the world. Two other functions of myth in ancient history are worth noting in passing. The first was the use of myth to express imagination. Myth was the normal material in which the ancients clothed their dreams, imagined worlds and freely chosen future goals. Further-more, as we saw in Chapter 3, art is created by distorting what is observed, so that inner meaning can be uncovered. It was taken for granted in pre-modern times that *history* could unlock its mysterious meaning only if its story was distorted. Historical story was above all material for artistic creativity, and myth was adopted imaginatively to manipulate history.

Second, we must consider what I call 'pure myth' (as opposed to mythical history). Pure myth was pure invention. It described an imaginary world in the primordial past ('Once upon a time, long, long ago') when the gods gave to nature and society their fixed forms, structures and purposes. Pure myths were recited time and again, and enacted in cultic rituals. Myth and ritual combined to create an anti-historical atmosphere. They were intended to inhibit or undo historical change, to recreate the past in spite of all that had happened. Pure myth turned people's attention backwards, and made the future an undesirable threat to life's meaning and purpose.

(*iii*) Historical study is bound up with culture; it is not a universally valid tool for making sense of life. Already in this brief chapter we have noted how different understandings of history emerged in different epochs and cultures. In the ancient world there were mythical views of history, history told to illustrate a principle (nemesis), and, in medieval times, history proclaiming an edifying message. In the modern era, the nineteenth century saw history as a scientific tool of enormous power, sifting fact from legend, and recreating the story of the past as the progress of civilization. Today in European thought history is neither an art nor a science; it is its unique self – an elusive and mysterious story of change, largely but not completely susceptible to explanation; it is the story through which we make sense of ourselves, and through which our beliefs and values impinge upon our neighbours.

How then do we in *our* culture *truly* understand the past? A culture gives us a pair of spectacles with a unique tint and a unique focal length. Only through these spectacles can we see anything at all. How can we take off the spectacles given us by our contemporary culture and put on the spectacles of a different world-view? How can we get inside strange ways of thinking and feeling, and begin to see as significant what they instinctively regarded as significant? The primary model we use is the one outlined in the first chapter: *conversation*. Such a cross-cultural conversation requires enormous imagination, the more so as one 'partner' to the conversation is not another person but historical writings which often spring from an alien (mythical) culture. Their silence is an invitation to listen more attentively. And notice the implications of using the metaphor of a conversation. The past can speak to us, can change us and challenge us, can help us to see ourselves and the meaning of our lives more clearly. Conversations open up the possibilities of discovering shared understandings.

One of our current difficulties is that, even among those

who think about these things, a truly contemporary understanding of history has not been readily grasped. Many are still living with nineteenth-century ideals. When they read an historical text they expect it to yield an 'objective' meaning, which we (the modern readers) can ponder in a detached, uninvolved way. This is the philosophy of John Ruskin: 'Be sure you go to the author to get at *his* meaning, not to find yours.' In line with this, academic and scholarly exegetes are considered to be authoritative guides. We defer to them because we believe they can truly tell us what an ancient text means. All this, however, is illusion. There is no 'objective' meaning which can be abstracted from the past. The scholar does have a crucial role to play: he or she delineates a probable context for the text, and suggests some of the meanings which might have been intended by the author writing as he or she did in such a context. From that point on, the struggle for meaning is a shared responsibility, in which we all undertake to converse with the text, to question it and listen to it; and when some light dawns for me I must initiate a conversation with you about the light that has dawned for you. The seminar or discussion group aided by a resource person better represents our effort to understand the past than the omniscient lecturer purporting to tell us what our ancestors thought and believed.

We conclude with a well-run theme. Every conversation is a risk, exposed as much to failure as to success. Some conversations leave us puzzled; others set us ablaze with fury. Yet somehow the effort seems worthwhile. We have all met the shallow person who thinks that only what is thoroughly modern can be meaningful.

II The Point of Pastoral Care

5 Pastoral Theology

Pastoral theology: its tasks

Pastoral theology began in Chapter 1. It has been making its way throughout the first four chapters – even though no reference has been made to God! Pastoral theology begins with the search we all make for meaning in life. Pastoral theology takes with complete seriousness every struggle we engage in to understand ourselves, our culture, and the functioning of nature and society; and the connections between them. Pastoral theology incorporates our conversations, and the narrative we tell of our lives and their significant moments; it embraces our actions and reactions, our activities and behaviour (including the irrational, the outrageous and the destructive); it encapsulates our imagination and feeling, and therefore our art; it digests our science, technology and history. A pastoral theologian appears to live in the first instance as if there were no God. He or she is glad to be what we all are in reality: human beings grasping challenges and discoveries, exploring our personal identities, values and purposes, discovering our contexts in nature and history and puzzling over that mysterious relationship 'I' have with the world. I am enmeshed in the world, its product, dependent on it; and yet I am unique, a person, with a mysterious centre of power transcending the world, able to change the world or destroy it, enhance the lives of others or 'pinch the life out of [my] neighbour's buzzing glory.'[1]

What more is there to say? Most people in the contemporary Western world have concluded that there is nothing to add.

We are all children of the secularizing process. Among those schooled in science and technology there has been an almost joyful discarding of religious faith; such boldness has gradually affected most of society. A few, particularly those who value greatly and explore critically our cultural traditions and recognize how deeply in the past they have been intertwined with religion, note the demise of religious faith wistfully and painfully. For them, religious faith has seemed like the light on the back of a train disappearing into a dark tunnel, just at the time when night is falling and the whole landscape is becoming dark and murky. Or religious faith has appeared to be a flickering candle around which gathers a tiny fraction of the human family in a locked room. No amount of effort or sympathetic imagination seems to open a door into their private world of meaning.

A pastoral theologian, however, works on the assumption that more can and must be said. A religious faith is faith in God. Whoever or whatever 'God' is, faith in God involves the conviction that a coherent meaning can be discovered for life *as a whole*. God is the ground of the unity to life's meaning. A pastoral theologian attempts to show that the fragments of puzzling meaning which we explore and vaguely grasp are authentic outcrops of an underlying and unifying meaning to life. We normally scour the beach for shale to extract drops of oil; religious faith claims to sink a well and draw oil from the reservoir below.

In the contemporary secular world, religious faith can be entertained as a possibility only through history. That a religious past should be able to transform our contemporary life is in principle not particularly striking. History is made up of significant events. To be sure, as time proceeds, we reassess what is thought to be significant in our life-story. So the idea that there will be *one* pivotal epoch whose significance will outlast every reassessment in succeeding eras is not a foregone conclusion. Such a possibility does emerge, however, if an historical event could force us also to treat it as a work of outstanding art. This is because, as we have touched on the notion in Chapter 3, great art in some sense can transcend time. Every antique dealer wants to sort out the classic (which lasts for ever) from the period piece, from the trash. What could ever displace a Stradivarius violin? Made at one point in time, its significance has outlasted reassessment in succeeding eras.

An historical event of significance in its own time gains this ability to transcend and transform when it is in itself a creative work of genius. The invention of the wheel illustrates this. The conclusion is that if there should be a historical life of unparalleled significance which somehow gave coherent meaning to the whole of life, and which was simultaneously a creative work of genius, then God would be revealed. The Christian tradition claims to point to such a unique combination in Jesus of Nazareth. In the light of this, the second task of a pastoral theologian becomes clear. It is to establish a 'conversation' between: on the one hand human beings seriously struggling towards meaning, values and purpose in life, confronting our dilemmas of achievement and destructiveness; and on the other hand the Christian tradition.

St Mark's Gospel

This is not the place to examine systematically the phrase 'the Christian tradition'. None would dispute that it includes as its primary ingredient the Bible. So we may illustrate possibilities opened up by the Christian tradition by investigating – critically – a fragment of the Bible. The Gospel of Mark will serve our purposes.

The Gospel of Mark is written in a form that requires two readings, not one, if its meaning is to be discerned. Both readings are difficult for us because Mark wrote in a culture vastly different from our own. It requires an enormous effort of the imagination to put ourselves even approximately into the shoes of Mark's first readers. This effort, however, is no greater than is required in reading almost all literature from the ancient world; and critical scholarship provides resources and guides for such a flight of the imagination. A crude guess at the context in which Mark's Gospel was produced is the following. Take yourself to Galilee in the last third of the first century AD. Galilee has a mixed population: mainly Jews but also many people whose way of life is indebted to Greek culture and religion; and a smattering of Roman influence from the long years of imperial occupation. In the midst of the complex mosaic of religious movements in Galilee, there are small groups of Jesus-followers. They are almost invisible to the public eye because they are small in number and they meet more or less in secret in homes; and they are being driven underground by Jewish persecution. But they have inspired a number of enthusiastic itinerant missionaries. Mark's booklet has been produced for use both in evangelism and in the house-church meetings.

The booklet has a grand title: 'The gospel of Jesus Christ the Son of God' (1.1). Like most titles of books, it is eye-catching but hardly self-explanatory. Presumably its meaning will emerge as we read through the booklet.

We notice quickly that the author of this anonymous pamphlet (it is only for convenience that we call him Mark) takes for granted a particular view of society, nature and history. It is a complicated genre, but well established in the literature of the time; it is known technically as apocalyptic. It assumes that there is an unseen supernatural world, populated by supernatural forces of evil and good. Our so-called 'real' world of nature and history is in some sense a replica of the invisible world, which is the 'power behind the scene'. This world we familiarly inhabit is the battleground where the conflict between the invisible forces of the hidden world is enacted. That is why our place in society, and the quality of our insight into life's meaning, seem puzzling and arbitrary. In a significant sense, such things are outside our control. We, of course, have our experience of freedom, but it is a severely curtailed freedom, circumscribed by struggles of which we know nothing. (Though presumably those beings who inhabit the supernatural world know what's going on.)

Mark, like all apocalyptists, assumes that history and nature are flowing towards a crisis. The one utterly transcendent God of love and goodness, whom the Jews worship, will reveal his hand at a moment of his choosing. This will provoke a final challenge from the powers of evil; but inevitably God will defeat them, and in the process he will destroy all in nature and history that they have tarnished. God will then create a new world where his justice, peace and freedom will rule unopposed, to the eternal joy of his elect.

Now for our first reading of Mark's booklet. We may imagine ourselves as non-Christian Galileans. The story is about Jesus, a figure of recent Galilean history, together with his disciples. The persistent question posed to us as the story proceeds is: Who is this Jesus (8.27–28; also 3.21–22, 4.41, 6.2–3, 14–16, etc.)? He is baffling beyond words to his own disciples. On the one hand is his awesome supernatural authority (1.16–20, 2.5–12, 11.27–33) and knowledge (2.8, 9.33–37), expressed in miraculous cures and stunning ripostes to hostile questioning. On the other hand is his closeness to his disciples, to the outcasts (2.15–17) and to his Galilean environment (6.1–6). On occasions the disciples, or at least some of them, glimpse something of Jesus' meaning and significance – what Jesus himself refers to as 'the mystery of the kingdom of God' (4.11; also 9.2–8); though it remains a mystery as to why *they* should be among the few to see anything. Such insights, however, are like dry sand in the hand, or flickering images on a screen: they are no sooner here than gone. So the disciples find themselves shrouded in ignorance and confusion, drawn to following Jesus they know not why or how (6.51–52, 8.17–21, 9.31, 10.32).

If there are hints in the story about how the fate of the disciples can be changed, it is in those passages which point to Jesus' forthcoming struggle and defeat, which are presented as a divine destiny for Jesus (8.31, 9.31, 10.33). He at least seems to know where he is going and for what purpose. As we move towards the narrative of those climactic struggles, we begin to identify more readily with Jesus in his suffering. He seems to be increasingly stripped of his suggestively supernatural powers and insight. We see a man struggling in the garden in Gethsemane in a battle of wills – his and God's. We observe a Jesus stripped naked on the cross in more sense than one – stripped to a raw conflict with a faith which must now incorporate his becoming a victim, intense physical pain (15.23), and an experience of being abandoned by God (15.34). Jesus is now indisputably locked into *our* history, and into our experience of contingency and death (15.37).

Precisely there the puzzle is solved – about God, about Jesus and about history. About *God* in 15.38 – 'And the curtain of the temple was torn in two from top to bottom.' This is probably a reference to the curtain in the Jerusalem temple separating the Holy of Holies (the innermost sanctum into which no one was allowed except the high priest, and he only once a year) from the rest of the temple and certainly from profane eyes. God's presence is no longer locked up in religion; God cannot be contained in the sacred and excluded from the profane. God has disclosed himself to all creation in Jesus and from a cross.

The puzzle about *Jesus* is resolved in the very next sentence: 'And when the centurion who was standing opposite him saw how he died, he said, "Truly this man was a son of God"' (15.39). A gentile grasps who Jesus is in the manner of his death: Jesus is God's representative for all humanity because of his obedient plunging into the depths of the human enigma, of confusion, pain and death. The centurion responds in faith to a God who unveils his rule in Jesus and from a cross.

Finally there is the puzzle about *history*. For this we move to the mysterious ending of Mark's booklet (16.1–8). There a story is told of the stone at the entrance of Jesus' tomb having been rolled away, of the tomb itself being empty, and of an angel proclaiming Jesus' resurrection. The intended meaning of the narrative is clear: in Jesus God's kingdom has overcome the kingdom of evil and death; the new era of God's love and justice has arrived not at the conclusion of history but as part of history; the new age of peace and freedom can be experienced by human beings. But are such claims credible? In response to such a question, Mark's narrative is at its most subtle. No historical event (not even a miraculous event) or any assertion (not even from an angel) convinces the women. They run away terrified, disobedient and awestruck. The clue to Mark's conviction is in verse 7: 'But go and give this message to his disciples and Peter: "He is going on before you into Galilee; there you will see him, as he told you."' Those who wish to know the truth of history's transformation will discover it only by active participation in history, in particular by becoming disciples of Jesus.

From very early times the ending of Mark's booklet has baffled its readers. A number of attempts have been made to add what has seemed to some to be more appropriate endings; others have given up the unequal struggle and settled for the concept of a 'lost ending' to the Gospel. In my view it is probable that Mark intended to finish at verse 8, precisely to reinforce and develop the themes in this final paragraph of his book. His purpose is to drive the reader back to the beginning of the Gospel. 'Read it through a second time, now from the perspective of a disciple following Jesus in Galilee' is his concluding message. Only such a re-reading of the Gospel can clarify Mark's understanding of history in the light of the resurrection of Jesus. Mark 1.14 and the following verses form the natural corollary of Mark 16.7–8!

Since Jesus, God discloses his kingdom to those who follow Jesus as obedient disciples. Becoming and remaining a disciple does not in itself drastically change the world in which we are set; we operate in the same culture, with its continuing constraints, puzzles and ambiguities, and its familiar struggles between good and evil and between meaning and nonsense. The disciple, however, can make the choice of trusting Jesus and giving up everything in his service (1.16–20, 2.14, 10.17–31); he or she will see who Jesus is, if only gradually and fitfully (8.22–26), and will participate both in Jesus' mission (6.7–13) and in his suffering (8.34–38). It is just this incorporation, in breadth and depth, into the life of Jesus which introduces the disciple to the experience of resurrection life – God present and ruling, and life becoming open-textured enough for the obedience of love (12.28–32). Strictly this is a *provisional* and flickering experience of resurrection life, of meaning and purpose appearing for our human existence in the course of our own history but from beyond history.

However, Mark's discipleship, in spite of all its mysterious enigmas, opened up for him such a depth of renewal that the future seemed auspicious. Discipleship included the gift of hope. This he expressed, in the mythology of his culture, in the imminent expectation of the Last Day and the consummation of God's kingdom beyond history and nature (9.1, 13.3–37).

An initial conversation

Our words and deeds, our art, science and history are statements. Statements attempt to express meaning. What, however, is the precise connection between statements and their meaning? That question has puzzled philosophers over the centuries. This is not the place to pursue the question extensively, but I mention here in an absurdly simplified form three important answers which have been influential.

The first was one of several ideas propounded by Plato (d. 347 BC). He suggested that meaning was a reality of a completely different kind from any sort of statement. Meaning was absolute and eternal; words were culture-bound and changed over the course of time. Words were like signposts on a journey: they pointed you in the right direction, but the building or community to which they pointed was not a bit like the sign itself. Or, words were like a telescope: you looked through them towards a distant and mysterious island, to try and glimpse some of its prominent features.

The second view was strongly advocated at the end of the nineteenth century, under the influence of scientific method. Here words were supposed to be like wrapping paper around Christmas presents. When a present is put into our hands, before we take off the paper, we try to guess what is inside by touch and shape. All we know for certain is that the present is not like the paper; but the paper can convey to us some inkling of what is inside.

The third view is the one I wish to dwell on. It has been made famous by Hans-Georg Gadamer.[2] For him words are symbols. A symbol (like the cross in the Christian tradition) enables us to recall repeated patterns of experience, and associated with these patterns are familiar responses – emotion, feeling, moral sensibility and intellect. A symbol *suggests* meaning to the imagination; it does not contain meaning. But a symbol, unlike a sign, does not point from a distance to that which it suggests and evokes: in some sense it participates in the meaning. If we were used to the culture of the Eastern Orthodox churches, we would say that words are icons of meaning; an icon is a window into heaven. So imagine we are standing outside a building with dim lights inside and frosted glass in the windows. The window has an identity of its own, but is also part of the building; at the same time, it lets people see a little into the rest of the building. If the building is like the meaning of something, the window is like a symbol.

This latter illustration enables us to go one stage further. Words and statements do not necessarily express meaning clearly. But words can be manipulated – a noun can be clarified with an adjective; a sentence can be rewritten or edited. Words can be negated. We sometimes say, almost in despair: 'I may not be able to make myself clear, but at least I can tell you what I don't mean!' That is coming close to our smashing the frosted glass in the windows, so determined are we to see more clearly the murky shapes inside the building. Even then we should not see everything: through a window with no glass we cannot see, for example, what is on the inside of the wall in which the window-frame is set. Meaning is like what you can see in some respects, but not in others. Meaning transcends all statements. In this sense, every symbol is a sort of metaphor (p. 45).

In Gadamer's view, then, meaning cannot be cut off from statements; and without statements there can be no meaning. And by 'statements' we do not mean just words! Actions, hobbies, art, scientific theories, history – all are the necessary means by which meaning is disclosed to us. In the first four chapters we saw how fitful and problematic those meanings are, dogged by our experience of evil, death and things not coming quite right.

There is, however, a profound link between the nature of all language and the message of Mark's Gospel. Jesus on the cross revealed that God is enmeshed in our world of history and nature. God cannot be cut off from our existence; he is necessarily immanent (Mark 15.38). Jesus on the cross was a *symbol* of God. More strictly, the historical life of Jesus was a symbol of God. But he revealed God most clearly by being manipulated, challenged, plunged into aggression and evil, and destroyed (Mark 15.39). In this he shared most fully in our human experience. The crucifixion of Jesus thus became *the significant* event of world history, with universal implications and validity. Finally Jesus was also a *metaphor* of God. God was disclosed on the cross, but he was not contained there, locked up in the death of Jesus. God calls men and women from a death to life. He calls us into an unknown future as disciples of Jesus, that is to create a new world of love and justice, confronting irrationality and the evil powers in suffering and powerlessness. Disciples step forward in hope, convinced that human history has a goal, God's kingdom (Mark 16.1–8, then 1.14ff.).

It was another early Christian writer who crystallized the message of Mark's Gospel in the statement, 'Jesus was/is God's Word' (John 1.1–18).

Mark and the Christian tradition

All I have tried to demonstrate is that a conversation is possible between our secular human struggle to make sense of life and the Christian tradition as represented by the Gospel of Mark. But how representative is Mark's Gospel? This is yet another huge question we cannot explore fully here. I wish only to sketch a few items of importance. Mark's Gospel has its place in the Bible, which forms the core of the Christian tradition. The Bible is not a uniform book, as Christians have always noted by referring to Old and New Testaments. Within each testament there are considerable varieties of literature (poetry, letters, community sagas, law codes, history, collections of traditional wisdom, and much else). There are diverse authors, contexts and aims for the different documents in each testament.

Within the New Testament however, in spite of many permutations, there does seem to be a common thread of understanding about history: in some sense God's new age has arrived with Jesus; and yet the final purposes of God for his creation have not yet been revealed. From that point of view Mark's Gospel is typical.

One of the ironies of Christian history is that the fundamental insight, 'Jesus was/is God's Word', was born into a world where *Plato's* theory about language and meaning was taken for granted. This led to a most profound distortion of the biblical tradition. It went something like this. The meaning to life as a whole (God) is separate from our world of nature and history: he is pure transcendence. He has an eternal and absolute Reality, completely different in kind from any reality we can know or experience. The most we can hope for in this world are flickering images of the supernatural world. These may be granted to us in moments of intense ecstasy or when we are 'taken out of ourselves' in experiences of concentrated pure thought (i.e. detached from worldly cares and constraints). Some of the consequences for Christian discipleship were these:

(*i*) The unique and pivotal revelation of God in Jesus became a major problem. The doctrine of incarnation addressed directly the problem caused by God's absence from the world in heaven.[3] Incarnation is not the same as immanence. Immanence means that God is always in everything that exists, though hidden; incarnation talkes of a supernatural Being becoming a human being.

(*ii*) Christian spirituality became other-worldly. A heavenly world, fairer and juster than this one, which awaited the faithful after death became the object of devotion. Christians enfolded themselves in the church, which was conceived as the entrance vestibule of heaven. Church and world (notice the terminology – as if the church were not part of the world!) became separate compartments to existence, and Christians held back from too deep an involvement in art, politics, sexuality, conflict and science – the warp and weft of historical existence. In brief, faith was an alienating experience.

(*iii*) Theology became the preserve of the intellectual. Attention shifted from the concrete and practical affairs of living to the abstract and speculative. Christian theologians saw as their natural companions the most sophisticated philosophers and metaphysical thinkers of their day and of preceding generations. Theology was reduced to propositions and abstract structures of thought, at times verging on 'metaphysical mystification'. Creeds, doctrines and dogmas became the norm of Christian identity, that is to say orthodoxy (right thinking).

Here is an illustration of how far things shifted from the concrete to the abstract in the early centuries. When in the fifth century AD Christians wanted to affirm their identity by recounting the Christian story, they recited a creed (the Apostles' Creed or the Nicene Creed). An enormous gap had thus opened up between the form of the story and the fears and joys, the confusions and discoveries, the goodness and brokenness of day-to-day existence. Contrast that with, say, Psalm 77. The psalm begins with a deep exploration of feelings, hurts, puzzlement, anxiety and despair (verses 1–10). It represents a perspective on life which all can immediately identify with. Alongside that human experience is placed the story of faith, the Exodus from Egypt (verses 11–20). And the whole psalm is poetry, a work of art which is 'graceful, strong, and afraid of nothing.'[4] Here history and art intertwine, and there is nothing like that to rekindle religious faith.

For centuries the intellectual edifices constructed in medieval Christendom have been crumbling. The sixteenth-century Reformation played its part; so did the religious wars of the seventeenth century; then came the Enlightenment, the French Revolution, the birth of democracy, industrialization, and the emergence of a secular society. Yet through it all some assumptions have remained largely unquestioned in the church: that theology is correctly defined in terms of abstract thought, and that the agenda for theology devised in the post-biblical era of doctrine and dogma remains inviolable.[5] In other words, theology as classically practised has survived, dinosaur-like, into the twentieth century. Contemporary men and women have long recognized its impotence in engaging with their experience of themselves and of our world.

Pastoral theology is not anti-intellectual or unintelligent. What it refuses to do is to idolize the intellect. It pays more attention to art than to philosophy. It attempts to engage the breadth of human experience and to assist men and women to make sense of their lives in the only world we know and have – this one. There have, of course, been pastoral theologians at work throughout the church's history, even though they have sometimes been neglected.[6] More importantly, pastoral care has continued throughout the church's life, even though its scope may have been limited and distorted by prevailing theological and philosophical assumptions. And Christian instinct and imagination time and again burst through the artificial constraints of the so-called theologians to recover a more authentic spirituality – thank God for Francis, Benedict, Dominic, the Reformers, Wesley and Bonhoeffer!

Thus the Christian tradition needs to be evaluated critically. It is not a question of the Bible *versus* the rest of the tradition. The Christian tradition after the Bible is far richer than the rarified intellectualism of the theologians. It includes poetry and hymns, art and architecture, wisdom and proverbs, community rules, prayers and liturgies, stories of faith and martyrdom, of individuals and institutions serving the world and being corrupted by it, succeeding and failing in the struggle to follow Jesus. Here is a vast seam to be mined, a companion with which constantly to converse as we attempt to live well in the world.

6 Pastoral Care: Purpose and Aims

The purpose of pastoral care can be stated like this: to assist men and women and boys and girls to live as disciples of Jesus. This purpose is sought by trying to achieve the four aims of pastoral care.

Aim 1: To encourage people to make their own sense of their experience

Pastors frequently declare how important pastoral care is in their ministries; it is often put top in the list of their priorities. In practice they devote only a relatively small proportion of their time to pastoral care. Doubtless there are many reasons for this mismatch between intention and achievement. One of the reasons is uncertainty about the tasks, or loss of confidence in the tasks. It is not uncommon, for example, to hear people involved in pastoral visiting to talk angrily about their having to 'waste time talking to old dears'. That and similar expressions of despair seem to betray considerable confusion.

Much of the time set aside for pastoral care will be used up in meeting people and relating to people going about their life in the world. The early chapters of this book have devoted quite a lot of space to the basic resources by which we make sense of life, precisely because they are basic. Most of the time, pastoral care means encouraging people to talk about themselves – their life-history, particular crises or joys, significant encounters or losses, their families, friends and communities. And then listening to their story. Pastoral care also means conversation. The topics may or may not be ones which immediately interest the pastor, but often they excite, challenge or puzzle the other partner in the conversation. Pastoral care is about finding enough imagination and love genuinely to share someone else's hobby, or to become engrossed with their favourite toy. Pastoral care may involve sharing a task with other people, acting collaboratively to change things in the world (usually on a minute scale). Pastoral care includes facing up to the way people behave – often atrociously – and working with them to accept what has been done and its consequences. Pastoral care is affirming people where they work, in their responsibilities as parents, citizens, voters and the like. Pastoral care is the privileged entry into other people's creativity: it therefore calls for authentic appreciation of what they have written, cooked, knitted, carved, built, redesigned, decorated, grown or played on a musical instrument.

None of this can possibly be wasted time once we have seen what these words, deeds and feelings seek to achieve: by them people make sense of life, find identity, grope towards life's meaning and purpose, and contribute to human history.

Certain qualities are required in a pastor in order to encourage other people to make sense of their experience. Trust and confidence are most important. So are respect for people as human beings, and acceptance of people for what they have become and the values they have espoused. A bigoted or narrow-minded pastor is no good to anyone. But where there is in a pastor a breadth of human sympathy and a secure reliability, people find the courage to become open to themselves (and also, in passing, to the pastor). That can encourage a whole range of explorations which may be vital to a person's self-acceptance and well-being. The repressed emotions, the unmentionable subject, the intensely private fear or achievement ('I've never shown this to anyone else before') are made the content of conversation, reflection and action.

It is obvious that the pastor does not dictate the agenda. The other person's or the group's life provides the raw material, the lived experience which must be teased open, questioned and put in perspective, if its fragmentary meanings are to emerge. The pastor, however, is not simply 'there' as a passive enabler. He or she must become committed in two fundamental ways.

First is the issue of seriousness. A pastor has a duty to challenge people who are being trivial or evasive, who live in fantasy and illusion, or who seem so withdrawn that they cannot make any point of entry into their own lives. Sometimes a pastor feels a bit like a doctor: everyone or every group he or she meets has a problem, a concern, a crisis to work through. At other times, however, a pastor feels like a visitor to a sterile laboratory: everything seems cold, lifeless and uninviting. The pastor must then initiate something, open up what is hidden away. And always the question of truth is on the pastor's agenda.

Second is the matter of mutuality. A conversation is necessarily two-way, so that a pastor conversing with another person must contribute as well as listen, be questioned as well as question, and share responsibility for the success or failure of the conversation. More generally, however, a pastor can fairly encourage others to make sense of their lives only if he or she is willing to do the same for himself or herself. The pastor's openness and vulnerability here come up for discussion. The pastor's *own* story, concerns, strengths, art, hobbies, and so on – and his or her acknowledgment of failure, tragedy, ambivalence and the irrational, inscrutable power of evil – are added to the agenda. The very fact of a pastor openly sharing life with another person is not only an encouragement to the other; it is also a witness to a fundamental reality – the interdependence of our lives in our quest to be human.

A conclusion to be drawn from the previous paragraph is that a pastor cannot be a highly professionalized person. (Throughout this book I use the word 'pastor' to refer to anyone who practises pastoral care. It is not a description exclusively of an ordained minister or an authorized church visitor.) To be professional means to engage in a relatively detached way in a limited area of human experience where one is confident because of accredited training, knowledge and public accountability. Doctors, solicitors, teachers, and so on, are rightly professional. The pastor's first calling, however, is to be human, to work with risk at an agenda that is as wide as life itself. This calling leads to enormous confusion among those few pastors in the church (principally the ordained) who do perform semi-professional ecclesiastical roles in society. In the last generation they have tried to resolve this confusion by adopting stances drawn from professionals such as counsellors, to give shape to their pastoral care. This has been a false and damaging move. In the final chapter of this book I shall explore other, I believe more fruitful, models of self-understanding for all pastors, ordained and lay alike.

To deny the possibility of a pastoral care *profession* is not to deny that pastors can profit greatly from, say, the human sciences. Chapters 7–13 will try to illustrate that. What is being denied is the notion that the first aim of pastoral care can be fulfilled in any way but by being open to and honest about life in its kaleidoscopic dimensions. The pastor's humility before the mystery and fascination of life is underscored when he or she recognizes that human beings without number contribute alongside the pastor to the fulfilment of this first aim. In fact, everyone does it, and many do it with enormous sensitivity and care without adopting a title or self-conscious role.

Aim 2: To disclose Christian meaning in life

Every pastor is a witness to Christian faith, and to the sense faith makes of life. In the Christian view, the meaning of life is love. However much we refine and illustrate such a sentence, we are in danger in such words of reducing to a cliché our human turmoil and ecstasy. A cliché discloses nothing, except the poverty and laziness of the imagination. So how can we break through the hackneyed phrase and the conventional kindnesses which pass as Christian love? Authentic conversation can help. Conversation invigorates self-criticism and integrity. A pastor may speak blandly from the perspective of faith, but can helpfully be brought up sharp by a bewildered look or searching question which will expose what is trite. In moving on from that challenge, better words may emerge to disclose Christian meaning.

Jesus, we may note, was an artist before he was a conver-sationalist or philosopher. Parable and theatrical action were two important vehicles for his creative imagination. A parable is a particular form of invented short story. It is a story of ordinary life set in the culture of those who are listening. A parable contains symbols. All words are symbols, of course. What we mean here are socially powerful symbols, symbols which represent in a whole culture common and deeply felt experiences – relationships between parents and children, rich and poor, powerful and oppressed. The story is long enough for the listener to recognize these characters and events: they refer to himself, and suggest familiar memories and feelings. The listener identifies with the story as it proceeds. It is about people just like him in his world. Or the parable sums up those people who are most unlike him, those who always provoke negative feelings. It is as if the parable is projecting on to a screen what is deeply embedded in the inner life of the listener. Before long the listener begins to anticipate how the story will turn out. He has seen these conflicts and dramas so often in 'real' life. Just when he is lulled into a complacent sense of anticipation, but before he loses interest, suddenly there is a twist in the tail, a demonstrably absurd conclusion. A question mark has been interposed against the listener's ability to predict the future. Out of the blue there is an *open* future, full of marvels. Who can describe what possibilities lie before him? But can he grasp this vision, see it as an invitation to hope against hope and turn it into concrete actions? Dare he let go of the assumptions and the hard-won wisdom which may have closed down his imagination, to be sure, but which at least enable him to control his life?

Parable is a fundamental art form for disclosing the Christ-ian gospel. Mark discovered that, and his short Gospel with its surprising, unpolished ending is constructed in parable form. The pastor is often called upon to invent a contemporary parable, if Christian sense about life is to be disclosed and lead to discipleship.

Jesus also used theatrical action. Washing the disciples' feet (John 13); placing a child in the midst of grown men arguing about status (Mark 9.33–7); and, I believe, enacting outside Jerusalem a comical mockery of a typical Roman triumphal procession (Mark 11.1–10)[1] can only be described as drama. Jesus has become an actor playing out his own improvised comedy.[2] His audience was drawn into imagined worlds, and we know the possibilities which that presented for their seeing themselves and their 'real' world differently (pp. 46–7).

Dramatic gestures and mini-plots are crucial resources for the pastor wanting to disclose Christian meaning. They are not, of course, scripted and rehearsed. They are spontaneous creative actions. A pastor was sitting silent in a room where everyone else was moaning about life: the government was inept; the weather was unfailingly foul; money was tight; the news contained nothing but violence and corruption. It was late afternoon, in early winter. The gloom was gathering. She could feel the heaviness seeping into her own soul, sucking her into despair and defeat. Without forethought she suddenly leapt up from her chair and started to perform a Scottish dance.

Parable and drama are focal elements in Christian witness because better than anything else they liberate men and women to welcome the future in new ways, marked by hope and love. Faith is always the acceptance of a responsibility for the future, a decision to act as kingdom-people in shaping the future.

Pastors, however, cannot always expect high levels of inspiration. Inventing parables and creating drama are rare highlights. Complementing and undergirding them must be a spirituality (i.e. way of life) which is nothing less than structured discipleship. A pastor needs a reliable framework of understandings and a predictable pattern of actions which can operate whatever may be his or her emotional state or personal circumstances. These understandings and patterns of action must be shaped by love. They are the *cantus firmus* of pastoral care, on top of which exquisite tunes and novel harmonies can be built through parable and drama.

Defining this solid core of pastoral actions which represent faithful kingdom-life is so important a task that it occupies Chapters 7–13. Ideally those chapters belong here. It is only the constraint of needing a sensibly structured book which has necessitated their postponement to the next section of the book. Here I shall make only two comments. The first is that pastoral actions which predictably shape our loving response to a whole range of situations we can anticipate remain *actions*. They are exposed to all the complexities and hazards of which I wrote in Chapter 2. No pastoral action can unambiguously achieve our best intentions even when it has been refined and critically assessed time without number. I have made dozens of bereavement visits; I have thought about grieving as carefully as I can. But I have no guarantee that I shall not make a mess of my next visit to a recently bereaved person.

Second, I want to clarify what I shall seek to set out in Chapters 7–13. They are working models for pastoral care. Perceptive readers will notice their indebtedness to Jung, Erikson, Bion, Fowler and many other important authors. Each model could be developed analytically with endless discussions from psychology and sociology. I shall not, however, go down that path. I present these models because, from my own experience and the experience of students, I believe they give Christian form to pastoral care. Faced with what seem to be overwhelmingly complex and confusing human issues, they attempt to help us to experience what is going on and to act in Christian ways. Faithful discipleship always carries the possibility of disclosing Christian meaning.

Aim 3: To stimulate men and women to engage in their own conversation with the Christian tradition

Pastoral theology is everybody's privilege. Unlike traditional theology, it is not the preserve of the intellectual or the ordained. The Christian tradition is rich enough in imaginative resources to provide stimulus and insight for anyone who seriously wants to engage with it, from whatever context they come. It is also crucial to stress here that pastoral care *necessarily* involves encouraging people to converse with the tradition. So often it is wrongly supposed that there is a hiatus between caring and being 'interested in theology'. Nothing can be more destructive of the heart of the matter. There are a number of ways in which pastors can help themselves and others to re-integrate caring and theological reflection.

(*i*) A pastor encourages people to start from the questions and discoveries that genuinely concern them. There is no prescribed agenda. A person's experience of life creates his or her own initial agenda. So a pastor invites people to respect and work with what deeply fascinates or puzzles them – about themselves (and their self-image), about their role or vocation in life, or about their underlying values, meanings and purposes. Sometimes a crisis provokes deep self-questioning; on other occasions new experiences in unusual situations throw up new insights and challenges; or there may be issues that have lurked in the mind almost in a subterranean way over a long period.

One particularly demanding aspect of a pastor's ministry in this regard is the following: pastors do well to encourage people to *start* their conversation with the tradition from the bleakest or most guilt-ridden of their concerns. None of us likes getting in touch with the pains and hurts that fester in the deepest recesses of our souls. We play endless games of self-deception and public image-making to avoid acknowledging even their presence. The pastor, however, must not collude with this avoidance mechanism. Nor must the pastor see his or her role like that of a nurse or doctor, to take away pain. The pastor must encourage people to confront their hurts and anxieties (and support those who find such honesty with themselves almost more than they can bear), and so to discover that depth of healing which integrates them into the rest of life. The reason is this: the heart of the Christian tradition is the story of a crucifixion. There more than anywhere lies the potential for seeing things whole, for experiencing a way of life which includes and transforms pain, and for discovering the God who is really present everywhere though usually hidden. Only our pain can connect deeply with the pain of Jesus, so that shared meanings can emerge.

(*ii*) A pastor makes available resources from the Christian tradition. Sensitivity and breadth of imagination are the virtues which enable a pastor to place in the hands of an individual or group the right book, Bible passage, prayer, picture, hymn. . . . More often than not, what is required is the patience and courage for trial and error. This is impossible if the pastor is colluding with a picture of himself or herself as omnicompetent or omniscient (a fantasy to which the ordained, in particular, are prone).

(*iii*) A pastor dare not assume that in this secular world men and women will instinctively want to converse with the Christian tradition or to find God. Most of the tradition seems alien, strange and irrelevant. Enormous effort is therefore required to stimulate curiosity about something which has become marginal to society's life. People will not fall in love with something which is unattractive or which seems dead. It is beauty and mystery which draw from us deep feelings of fascination, and the willingness to become involved. I use the metaphor of 'falling in love' because it seems to fit best what it is the pastor must encourage: a conversation (between things that concern us deeply and some fragment or other of the tradition) which is part and parcel of a tempestuous love affair. Pastoral theology is not a polite tête-à-tête. It is passion, feeling, alert mind, struggle, a no-holds-barred demand to get at the truth of things. (Psalm 89 is worth reading here; and see p. 63 above.)

(*iv*) Conversations between lovers are a basic constituent of their relationship. Conversations may give way to shared actions; they may lead to a point of shared silence in mutual wonder or fatigue. But it is difficult to envisage a situation where lovers will not want to talk to each other again. Pastors will draw the conclusion that pastoral theology will be a recurrent item on their own agenda and on the agenda of those to whom they minister.

What happens in a fruitful conversation between our deepest self-questioning and the Christian tradition is some sort of inductive leap. A spark leaps across the gap, creating not just one more shared understanding but also a sense of being grounded in something, of having one's fragmentary bits of meaning fall into some sort of pattern. And yet it is but a lightning flash. We sense that behind the dark and threatening clouds which fill the sky there is a world of light; but it remains a mystery. An inviting mystery, however. That stimulates us to dig deeper into the tradition, or to explore a part of it not tried before. It simply will not do for pastors to persuade people each day to read a portion of the Bible (with notes) interminably, in order to stress that encounter with the tradition is an unending exploration. People's needs, like the pastor's, demand infinitely more sensitive, broad-ranging and imaginative counsel. Growth is more significant than routine.

Aim 4: To encourage holiness

In each moment when faith is born we stand on the edge of the future, facing in a new, particular direction. This is because, in Mark's view, 'discipleship is the only form in which faith can exist'.[3] Other New Testament authors use different metaphors for this experience. Paul, for example, thinks of the preaching of the gospel as an opening of a door from one room to another (in Adam/in Christ), and an invitation to walk towards the now open door. Saying 'Yes!' to the invitation and involvement in the initiatory rite of baptism effect our transfer to a new life in Christ. Luke, contrariwise, thinks of gospel preaching as being like a gale-force wind (Spirit) suddenly blowing up but turning us round so that we can breathe freely again. In fact, each author uses a variety of suggestive images. An underlying concept is freedom, or salvation. Freedom is 'the passage from fear to trust, from hostility to love, from ignorance to self-knowledge, from passivity to creativity, from self-centredness to concern for others.'[4] This clarifies what discipleship entails: it requires us to take responsibility for actions of love and justice which will transform every facet of existence. Holiness is the commitment to infuse with love (as we understand it from Jesus) our interior lives and external world, individual relationships, corporate structures and the whole life of society within the natural environment. Holiness is both a private commitment and a glad cooperation with all others who perceive their discipleship in approximately coordinate ways.

Chapters 7–13 will offer some models by which we give structure to our quest for holiness. They will attempt to show the 'givenness' and the fluidity within both ourselves and society which love and justice must work with. Our stress here, however, is a little different. At any particular moment, the risen Christ who calls us into the future as his disciples will be only dimly perceived. We follow him in puzzlement, doubt and confusion, with a lamentable grasp of what kingdom-life is actually like. We see God and we don't see him; the kingdom is both present and yet to come. Holiness is therefore a commitment to have our understanding of love transcended and transformed in the course of discipleship. There is no known or fixed concept of Christian love which we simply apply more and more thoroughly in the course of our discipleship. Rather, holiness is openness to an ultimate *mystery* of love, coming to us from the future and challenging every notion of love which we are seeking to express.

To return to an earlier analogy to do with words and meanings (pp. 74–5): We discover a new word. We grasp what it means as best we can. We hear the word being used, or we see it in sentences; and we look it up in a dictionary. But, as every teacher knows, 'There's no impression without expression.' So we are called upon to *use* our new word. We include it in our own sentences. We listen to its sound. We play around with it, adding adjectives or adverbs, or putting it next to words which have not been associated with it before. We grasp new nuances and meanings. At some point, however, we exhaust its meaning. Then, on very rare occasions, we find all our skill with words and our total vocabulary brought to a halt by some indescribable experience. Only a new language will do. So Shakespeare painted a fabulous picture of Cleopatra's procession down the Nile, letting word tumble after word. But when it came to Cleopatra herself: 'For her owne person, It beggerd all description.'[5] In the face of that beauty, a new turn of phrase had been invented – to beggar description.

There are two particular areas in which a pastor's encouraging of holiness will be severely tested. The first concerns those perplexing issues we explored in Chapter 2: irrational behaviour, particularly aggression, and the sense we have of being locked into alien powers of evil, brokenness and death. Mark 12.1–12 was designed to provoke reflection on such themes. Jesus is portrayed as telling a story about escalating violence. The stakes are progressively raised, but nothing can break the spiral. In Matthew's version, Jesus provocatively goads his listeners into active participation: 'When the owner of the vineyard comes, how do you think he will deal with those tenants?' (Matt. 21.40). The answer is inevitable: he will crush the opposition. Now Jesus' comment. It was not moralistic ('Thou shalt not!'). Instead he drove his listeners to puzzle over an enigmatic text from their scripture (Mark 12.10–11 = Ps. 118.22–3): God chooses something that has been thrown away to be the corner-stone of his temple. There must, presumably, be some completely different set of values and way of living (which is largely ignored and little admired) which might transform human instincts to punish, defeat enemies and meet violence with greater violence. The 'alternative' way of living is kingdom-life: forgiveness, reconciliation, patience, kindness and gentleness. (See also texts like Gal. 5.16–25; Eph. 4.16–5.5; II Tim. 3.12–13; James 4.4; I John 2.15–17.)

Jesus' paradox typically challenged the hearers to take responsibility for the way they lived. He made no promise that kingdom-life would solve the problems of violence, evil and death. His mission was to indicate possibilities of *hope*, even in the most intractable ugliness and absurdity of life. Only kingdom-life can present human existence with a future beyond our bestiality.[6] Discipleship cannot involve turning our backs on violence, circumnavigating it, or supposing we shall not normally be contributing to it. Holiness, however, is the courage to enter the ravages of evil protected only with love. The holy disciple follows Jesus himself to a cross – 'nakedly follows the naked Jesus'.

No pastor can glibly encourage others to a holiness which

costs so much. Encouragement can come only when pastors participate with others in the depths of human degradation and destructiveness: they must know what is in their own hearts, and they must not avoid the demanding task of empathizing with others as they explore the murky and violent depths within themselves.

Now the second particularly hard area for a pastor trying to encourage holiness. It relates to Christian people making new sense of their past. Discipleship is primarily about embracing the future in love and hope: not, however, in a way that disowns the past. Faith changes none of the facts of the past, least of all the uncongenial ones. Faith, however, invites disciples to re-interpret their past, to put it in a new perspective. Faith looks back to all those marvellously rich gifts and those achievements won from immense struggle and courage which we call the fragments of meaning we glimpse in life (Chapters 1–4). Now they are perceived as gifts of *God*, shadowy images of divine self-disclosure. Faith looks back on the past as a life grounded in a hidden, immanent God. Traditionally this reinterpretation of the past was known as the search for God's providence.

Of course, the past never fits exactly any unifying reinterpretation. Life is far too elusive, subtle and puzzling for that. The impenetrable facts of irrational evil, alienation and death remain as brute obstacles. We are often tempted to ignore these realities, and pastoral responsibility once again must hold on to honesty and truth. There is nothing easy or pleasant in being the person who must keep the unanswerable and the unintelligible on the agenda.

Also in the way of a too easy reinterpretation of the past are our own evil actions. The pastor is then confronted with the issue of guilt. He or she encourages growth in holiness by enabling people to hear their God offering forgiveness. This is exceptionally hard. To begin with, the Christian tradition is clear that divine forgiveness cannot seep into the depths of our past except by our practising forgiveness of others (Matt. 6.9–15; I John 4.7–21). Allied to that, all pastoral experience demonstrates that divine forgiveness is dependent upon our freedom to forgive ourselves, to accept ourselves truthfully. That is difficult for us all, because there is always some degree of mismatch between our self-image and our 'real' self. When a person's self-image owes a great deal to fantasy, or is hopelessly inaccurate, a pastor needs enormous patience, integrity and kindness to help that person to face even small amounts of reality about himself or herself. The commitment of time may seem too great a price to pay; we are talking about months and years, not hours and days. Mediating forgiveness of the past frequently becomes one of the most demanding tests of a vocation to pastoral care.

Achieving the aims in practice

I should like to focus the four aims of pastoral care in a concrete situation. Here they flow together into a complex set of feelings, decisions and actions. I will leave the reader to make the connections between the case I shall describe, and the analysis given in the preceding paragraphs.

Gill was asked by her minister to call on Mavis Smith, aged about fifty-five. Mavis' husband Joe had died at work the previous day. He had suffered a massive heart attack. There had been no hint of Joe's heart trouble before his death. Neither Mavis nor Joe were churchgoers. The minister was able to give Gill only the sketchiest briefing of the family background. Conquering her natural reserve and nervousness as best she could, Gill rang the doorbell at 23 Long Street, and Mavis invited her into the small and rather gloomy front room. Gill explained who she was and expressed conventional condolences.

Without really paying too much attention to Gill as a person, Mavis poured out a wide range of stories, memories and feelings – about Joe, about herself, and about their marriage. Gill didn't interrupt, even though some of what was said made little sense to her. In any case she couldn't sort out fantasy from considered judgment. It puzzled her that sometimes Mavis spoke as if Joe would be home for tea that afternoon. It disturbed Gill that Mavis' narrative was interrupted with bouts of wailing, crying and coughing. What was this doing to Gill's emotions? Her heart went out in sympathy to Mavis, but Gill was struggling to recall anything in her twenty-three years when she had felt even remotely as Mavis must have been feeling.

Gill felt paralysed. She was ill-at-ease in this strange environment. She was young enough to be Mavis' daughter, and yet she was being talked at as if she belonged to the era of Joe and Mavis. In her inner silence she felt a heavy cloud descend on her spirits. She was beginning to sense what this bereavement visit might entail for the future: visit after visit, hour after hour of repetition about Joe, an emotional strain. What would it all be for?

After a while – Gill had no idea how long, and she dared not look at her watch – she felt the time had come to go. Up to then she had said virtually nothing. What to do now? She offered to say a prayer with Mavis. How she wished she had thought about this in advance! Mavis consented; so Gill found herself thanking God for Joe's life and the happiness he had brought into the world, commending Joe into God's safe-keeping, and praying for God's love and comfort to support Mavis and her friends. She ended with the Grace, which she invited Mavis to join in. How embarrassing! Of course, Mavis couldn't possibly know what the Grace was. So Gill pressed on herself, unaccompanied.

Gill rose to leave. At the door, she fumbled in her pocket and produced for Mavis a small card. On it were printed two or three texts from scripture, a cross and a picture of some Spring flowers. Gill didn't know how to say farewell in the circumstances. So she put her arms round Mavis' shoulders, hugged her and said she would call again in a day or two.

Gill certainly knew the rudiments of pastoral care, though she would be the last person to acknowledge it confidently. Perhaps she should have listened to the voluminous thanks with which Mavis let her go.

III   *Structures for the Tasks*

7 A Map of the Terrain

'For the commandments are all summed up in the one rule, "Love your neighbour as yourself"' (Rom. 13.9). Love of others becomes effective when we love ourselves. Self-love, which is very different from selfishness, depends on self-knowledge; for only knowledge disperses fear and opens up the freedom to love. The first four chapters of this book have indicated the principal ways in which we grow in knowledge of ourselves. Story-telling, conversation, activities, action and reaction, art and creativity all point to symbiotic understandings of human existence. The quest for self-knowledge is pursued in association with others. It is therefore radically different from an individual pursuing an ego-trip or indulging in 'navel scratching', that is, isolating him or herself from the collective.

Figures 1 and 2 are schematic representations of a human personality at any moment of time. The stress must be on the word 'schematic'. The figures are not like a still from a film, extracted and blown up; nor are they like sections of tissue which the biologist looks at through a microscope. These things display what is actually there on a different scale. In contrast, figures 1 and 2 highlight only crucial functions and relationships that mark out our human personalities. In the remainder of this chapter I shall be describing what these diagrams attempt to represent. (In chapter 8 we shall see how to use them in pastoral care.) However, analysis of personality must never prevent us from keeping sight of the individual as a whole. The individual is more basic and is larger than the

Figure 1

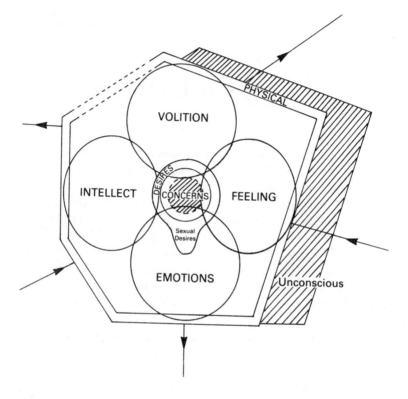

parts into which we may analyze him or her. Each individual is unique; he or she has a name and an identity which confirms that person's uniqueness. An individual is *never* an illustration of a theory. As the schoolteacher put it, 'I do not teach mathematics; I teach John mathematics.'

Figure 1, except in the shaded areas, represents the conscious personality. We shall examine the details by moving from the margins of the diagram towards the centre.

Environment The individual personality is amazingly sensitive to its environment, both the immediate and the larger environment.

By the immediate environment I mean a wide range of factors like temperature, noise levels, the nature and intensity of the light, the decor, the sense of space or the degree to which one feels hemmed in. That in turn may be much affected by the weather (bad weather forces many people, e.g. the frail and the elderly, to stay inside). Littering the immediate environment will be reminders of responsibilities carried, unfinished tasks, or jobs that need to be done which in anticipation seem threatening or particularly uninviting (and may be no more than an unintelligible or illegible form from the Inland Revenue). All in all, the local environment is so important in terms of various degrees of comfort, in the nature and level of challenge presented, and the feeling of being in familiar or unfamiliar surroundings that it feels as if it has a personality of its own.

The larger environment is a web made of things like: buildings and their lay-out (all that town and country planners deal with); relationships to concrete and tarmacadam on the one hand or land and organic systems on the other; relationships to natural rhythms of the days and seasons or to man-made divisions of time (shifts, timetables, etc.); levels of pollution; and access to resources such as shops, decision-makers, bureaucrats, leisure, networks and systems. The larger environment is also made up of social and political issues – safety and security in a community, justice and freedom. Chapter 13 will explore these further.

Relationships These are indicated on the diagram by the straight lines moving out from and into the personality. They represent relationships with individuals, groups, institutions and communities. Chapters 11, 12 and 13 will give more attention to these. At this point we note two factors. First is that the arrows point in both directions on the 'relationship lines'. Relationships are to do with giving and receiving. The web of relationships represents interdependence. Second, in each individual the number, quality and strength of the particular relationships will vary enormously.

Physical   Each individual receives information about the external world through the five senses: sight, hearing, smell, taste and touch. The 'physical' portion of figure 1 represents these, which may have various levels of functioning (impaired eyesight, acute hearing, etc.). Indeed, 'physical' summarizes the whole range of issues which affect the well-being of our bodies: health, fitness, and any handicaps or disabilities. Also included here are: skills we are developing or have mastered; and the memory, that incredible store of information and experience which can be recalled rapidly to consciousness.

The face is a prominent feature of our bodies. It communicates so much about our personalities, including many facets of the 'physical'. That is why if we want to know what someone looks like, we search for a picture of the face: the face alone is sufficient. In the face, the eyes are unquestionably the most significant feature, as every portrait painter and photographer knows. The eyes are almost an extra faculty for touching people and things. So we say, 'He ran his eyes over everything in the room'; or 'Her eyes were glued to the television.' The face and eyes also reveal emotions.

Emotions   Emotions are involuntary inner agitations provoked by current situations or memories. Something is said and we feel upset or uptight. Emotions surge up from some unfathomable depth. They are positive and negative, good and evil. Gratitude and pleasure are intermingled with fear, jealousy and anger.

Emotions are charged with energy. Augustine of Hippo (354–430) called them the feet of the personality, that is to say, the principle of movement which can lead the soul towards or away from truth. Figure 1 illustrates that intensive (or high) emotional states can probe very near to the centre of the personality, making contact with our deepest concerns.

Religion flourishes in the context of strong emotions, whereas severely cerebral control of the personality is the kiss of death to religious sensibilities. However, as we shall see in the next chapter, the intimate relationship between faith and emotion becomes dangerous when emotion is believed to be the sole avenue to faith: 'Often the step between ecstatic vision and sinful frenzy is very brief.'[1]

Similarly, intense emotional or heightened psychological states have often been confused with religious faith. Some of our deepest emotions are connected especially with sexual desires, as figure 1 shows. There is a very narrow divide between the explosive rapture of 'letting go' in sexual intercourse and the sudden birth or renewal of religious faith. But they are not identical.

Feeling   Chapter 3 has already explored this capacity of the personality. Here we are concerned principally with the rational faculty of feeling, the judgment we make about the comfortableness of an overall situation as presented to us by our imagination. Feeling, like the emotions which overlap so much with feeling, probes deep into the heart of the soul. It was Friedrich Schleiermacher (1768–1834) who emphasized this insight. He defined religious experience as a *feeling* – of absolute dependence, on something outside and apart from the self (i.e. God).

In Chapter 10 we shall look further into various sorts of feeling which we habitually experience, for example, trust, shame, guilt and worthlessness (and their opposites).

Intellect   This represents the capacity we have for reason and analytical thought. Intellect enables us to think clearly and abstractly, to draw conclusions from arguments and premises, and to learn from our mistakes. The thinking person is the hero of mathematics, science and philosophy. Rene Descartes (1596–1650), the father of modern philosophy, grounded certainty about anything in a connection between our capacity for thought and human existence itself: *Cogito, ergo sum* ('I think, therefore I am'). Since the Enlightenment in Western Europe, the intellect has been increasingly honoured as the jewel in the crown of human personality. Because intellectual capacity can be measured (IQ), educated and examined, it has come to dominate our image of the personality. Other human potentialities have been downgraded, particularly emotions and feeling.

As figure 1 illustrates, one of the noteworthy features of the intellect is that for all its truly amazing achievements in de-mystifying the world and human history, it cannot dig very deep into the central portion of the personality. The intellect remains a bit detached from our desires, concerns and spiritual capacities. Luther summed up this characteristic in a typically memorable way: 'Reason is a whore who will serve any master.' (See Chapter 4 and p. 68)

Volition   Volition is what translates ideas, feelings, desires and intentions into actions. Volition includes the capacity we have for concentration on a task, for consistency in tackling a problem, for the ability to stick at something no matter what may be the cost or the pain. Volition provides sturdiness, steadiness and single-mindedness. It is the backbone of the inner life.

Desires   Desires and volition interact in an intimate way. If we want something badly enough, we often find ways of getting it. Strong desires stimulate imaginative actions and resolve. That has been human wisdom from time immemorial: 'Ask and you will receive; seek, and you will find; knock, and the door will be opened' (Luke 11.9).

Our desires lie very near the centre of the personality. Some desires are instinctive (e.g. hunger and sex), and they lie in the realm of the unconscious (see figure 2). Other longings, wishes and ambitions are often hard to bring into focus; they lie hidden and we find it very difficult to get in touch with them.

Desires are good and evil. We want to be compassionate, for example, but that longing is sometimes muddied with the appetite of lust. As we have noted above, sexual desires are an incredibly important component of our wishes. That may have been taken for granted since the pioneering work of Sigmund Freud (1856–1939); the complexities caused by this acknowledgment are none the less difficult to manage.

Concerns   Desires merge into concerns and it is sometimes hard to distinguish one category from the other. Desires and concerns together form the *Self*, the organizing centre (or heart) of the personality. Strictly, concerns are those realities which matter to us, in the sense that our identity and stability seem to depend on them. Concerns are therefore constituted of the underlying purposes, the fundamental aims, the non- negotiable values and the basic meanings of our lives. These are largely unconscious. Chapters 1–4 have illustrated with what difficulty we identify them. At the core of our concerns are those ideals on which we stake everything, the content of religious faith. The focal point of these transcendent ideals is what we call the God within us.[2] There is no direct way of getting in touch with the God within. Our faith is mediated through religious symbols, stories, rites and rituals – a tradition of faith.

There is not necessarily a God within (what Paul Tillich called an ultimate concern). The heart of the personality can be an incoherent jumble of desires and concerns. Moral values often co-exist as contradictory opposites. It is only our infinite capacity for self-deception, for example, which calls wastefulness generosity, in order to make us appear consistently kind. When there is confusion in the heart rather than a coherent spiritual centre, we speak of anxiety. 'Anxiety is actually nothing but the consequence of lies' (Dostoyevsky).

General comments on figure 1

(*a*) The diagram represents schematically the interconnectedness of the items of the conscious personality. Input into any one component has a 'knock on' effect in all the others, to some degree or other. One familiar way of describing this reality is to refer to the human personality as a psychosomatic whole. But the level of inter-connectedness is not the same everywhere.

Emotions and feeling overlap and interpenetrate to a large extent. Emotions, feeling and volition probe deep into the Self; intellect, however, is not very Self-involving. Emotions and the physical characteristics of our bodies also inter-relate particularly closely. Hands, eyes, facial expressions and complexion express our emotions, sometimes against our wishes. Conversely, hormonal imbalance and vitamin deficiency can cause significant emotional distress (e.g. premenstrual tension in women).

(b) Each component of the personality has its limits and boundaries. Without too much trouble we can measure the limits relevant to our bodies, our health and our intellectual capacity. In a more diffuse sense there are in each of us top and bottom limits to our capacities for emotions, feeling, volition and desires. Recognition of limitations to any or all of our human qualities provides no basis of judgment on our worth as persons. A person is a gestalt, a whole larger than the parts. The infinite worth of each and every person is an insight of love, not a conclusion drawn from the measurement of the parts.

Granted that our worth as persons is not dependent on physical strength, IQ, and so on, it remains a fact that our potential as persons is related in part to our pressing to the limit each of our faculties. (Potential and fulfilment relate also to the coherent interrelationships within the personality and between the individual and the external world. To this we shall return.) Most of us live much of the time with unnecessarily restricted perceptions of our capacities. We rarely test our supposed limits. Though when we do, we need the wisdom to distinguish what can be changed from what cannot be changed, and the grace to accept the latter.

(c) Sometimes our views of our capacities (physical endurance, self-control, intellect, creativity, dependability) are fanciful – inflated beyond all the evidence. Here we rub up against the difference between our self-image and the reality that others see in us. Our self-image is distorted by our limited knowledge of ourselves. Particularly in our modern society, our self-image is blind to our emotions, their strength and their (often disruptive) impact upon all our dealings with one another. This is the result of our culture emphasizing unduly the physical side of our personality (e.g. modern surgery, high-tech medicine, etc.) and the intellectual aspects (through the education system, particularly secondary and tertiary education).

(*d*) In figure 1 I have given the personality an arbitrary and angular 'shape'. We often think of personality as having shape ('I'm a square peg in a round hole'; 'I don't fit in here'). I am wanting to suggest that the shape of a personality is only approximate. It is not fixed, but malleable. In some people, or over particular periods in all our lives, changes of shape take place imperceptibly slowly; in others, or at memorable moments for us all, the shape of our personalities can change dramatically quickly. I have represented this flexibility by means of the dotted portion of the personality's contour.

The shape of a personality can be analyzed in a number of ways. The physical shape is basic – female or male,[3] tall or short, fat or thin. Beyond that the shape of a personality can best be described by the balance of opposing tendencies or characteristics in each individual. For example, the balance between what the Chinese call Yin and Yang.[4] Yin is a clutch of interests like receptivity, passivity, contemplation, protectiveness of life, tenderness, flexibility, cooperation, and the acceptance of the therapeutic value of simple routine jobs. Yang is a different bundle of interests: analysis, organization, reasoning things out, achieving results, initiative and adventure, and independence.

(*e*) Beneath the conscious personality in figure 1 lies a shadow, the unconscious. The linkages between conscious and unconscious, and some reflections on the unconscious are represented in figure 2. Figure 2 is to figure 1 as an elevation is to a plan.

Any discussion of the unconscious must be treated cautiously. By definition the unconscious cannot be known; any pictures we have of it must be speculative and indeterminate. A good example of the difficulties concerns psychic studies, which include telepathy, clairvoyance, precognition and psychokinesis, near-death experiences, evidence for survival beyond death and reincarnation. Scientific study of such phenomena is notoriously difficult: most people discount psychic phenomena altogether; a few are so deeply involved (for example, with Satanism and black magic) that they lose touch with rational perception of the world and themselves.[5]

The following broad categories attempt a very simple description of some fundamental structures in the unconscious. We may leave open for our purposes what is confined to the personal unconscious and what belongs to what Carl Jung (1875–1961) called the collective or racial unconscious.

Figure 2

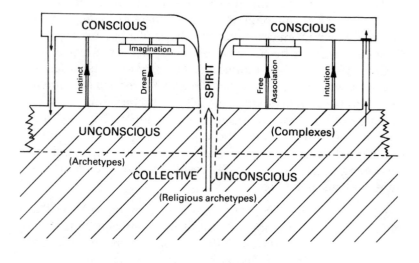

The boundary between them is fuzzy and imprecise. They merge into one another in a way that represents how our individuality is a unique entity, yet has roots which spread out into our culture, the web of lives which interconnect with our own and ultimately into all human and evolutionary history.

What is naturally in the unconscious We noticed earlier that each of the components and faculties of the conscious mind has its limits. This is true of the five senses. There are limits to what we can see and hear, both with the unaided eye and ear and with any amount of magnifying equipment. It is probable that many signals which are so weak or short-lived that they never register in the conscious mind enter directly into the unconscious. Such subliminal experiences are stored there and may affect behaviour.

The unconscious seems also to be a vast repository of the struggles for survival and meaning to life in which the human race has been involved throughout history. Nothing is precise. When something from the unconscious does somehow force itself into our awareness, it is like a set of footprints in very wet sand (which allows us to say only that something or someone has passed that way before us); or like the pyramids, representing levels of imagination and technology which we notice and admire but which puzzle us because we cannot emulate them. In particular, the unconscious stores collective experience and wisdom in these forms: innate drives or instincts, a capacity for intuition, and what Jung called archetypes. We have touched before on the instincts, particularly aggression (pp. 29–32), and on intuition (p. 40). Here we can develop a little our understanding of archetypes. These seem to be coded representations of some of the most intractable dichotomies and contradictions which affect our human existence. The archetypes signal antinomies between, say, life and death, sex (procreation) and destruction, good and evil, male and female (or father and mother), terror and peace, victory and defeat, authority and submission. Over the centuries the archetypes have been forged out of experience, and now act as guardians against simplistic, naive or unbalanced understandings of life (see pp. 109–13). Their power is rekindled whenever human beings rediscover and share with one another something of the vast store of folklore, myths, magical practices, customs and rituals which have circulated from time immemorial.

I do not want to be misunderstood here. I am not romantic about the distant past; nor am I suggesting we can pretend to see and feel the world as ancient people saw and felt it. But we do ourselves a disservice if we despise the past and its cultures. Our contemporary world is shrivelled because it does not have taken-for-granted ways of symbolizing deep-seated confusions and paradoxes. Art and religious traditions have a great responsibility of representing these insights so that they are not merely archaic.

What is put into the unconscious In each of the components and faculties of the conscious personality there seem to be holes into the unconscious. All sorts of things can fall down these holes without any conscious decision or effort. So the unconscious has a store of lost, much neglected or filed away thoughts, feelings, emotions, desires, concerns and impressions. We say they are in limbo. They are not easy to recall; but occasionally something happens to us which forces them back into consciousness, often to our great surprise. We had no idea of what had long been lost to consciousness. Conversely these 'holes' in the conscious mind can prove very frustrating: we have a name or idea 'on the tip of our tongue', when suddenly it slips away; no amount of searching can retrieve it, and we are left feeling embarrassed.

There are other holes in the conscious mind (I speak, of course, in metaphors all the time) with lids on them. Here we hide away life's rubbish. We repress uncomfortable or unacceptable thoughts, feelings, emotions, desires and concerns. We firmly bolt the lid, and live as if the repressed entities never existed. They are skeletons in the mind's cupboard. Unfortunately there is no incinerator in the unconscious. Repressed these things may be; they are not, however, non-existent or ineffective.

What is made in the unconscious The basic structures and resources of the unconscious combine with what is put there from the conscious mind to create complexes. An 'inferiority complex' will serve as an illustration. A person with such a complex has a self-image as someone who is strong and competent in most situations. Reality is different from the self-image. In truth, he or she is severely inadequate in some particular way. The conscious mind cannot accept this inadequacy, so the idea and the strong emotions associated with it (fear, shame, insecurity) have been repressed. In the unconscious, the repressed emotions, as it were, encounter the archetypes, those silent witnesses to life's ambivalence and many-sidedness. Thus an unconscious conviction is born which overstates the person's inadequacy (the inferiority complex). The complex counterbalances the unrealistic *conscious* picture of competence and resourcefulness. A complex is thus a sort of hidden intense energy source waiting to burst into consciousness to put back on the agenda what cannot forever be avoided. A complex is like a coiled spring in the unconscious; or like a tender spot just below the surface of consciousness. With the slightest perturbation in the system, the latent energy gushes forth, charged with emotion.

Activated complexes produce predictable and memorable patterns of behaviour. Characteristically, the public expression of an inferiority complex is defensiveness (to protect what is thought to be excessively tender or vulnerable) or open aggression (to deflect attention from the inadequacy and to overcompensate for it).

The behaviour patterns which are typical of activated complexes (overcompensating for unbalanced attitudes in the conscious mind and repressed emotions) are an integral part of human existence. Throughout the ages they have been identified in legends and fairy tales. Particularly prominent and powerful are sexual complexes, and these have generated the richest store of legends. The Greek legend of Oedipus, for example, seems to illuminate many aspects of maleness and some of the hidden feelings and irrational reactions men have towards their parents. Oedipus was abandoned by his parents and reared by the King and Queen of Corinth. In later life he became a hero of male intellectualism by solving the riddle of the Sphinx, but unwittingly killed his biological father in a roadside quarrel, and married his mother. When the truth of what he had done emerged, Oedipus blinded himself in remorse.

Other legends identify common, but none the less intense and passionate, affairs of the heart between women and men. From ancient Greece comes the story of Psyche, a beautiful woman loved by Eros (Cupid in the Roman tradition), the god of love. Psyche was forbidden to look at Eros. Eventually she did so and he left her. It was only after a long and painful search that Psyche was reunited to Eros in heavenly marriage. In German legend, the Lorelei are water nymphs whose singing enchanted sailors beyond all reason, but lured them to their death.

From unconscious to conscious   Seeing a symbol out of the corner of an eye can be a sufficient trigger for powerful complexes to be activated. A phallic symbol can stimulate all sorts of erotic fantasies and sexual desires. More commonly, something happens which seems a perfectly manageable event, but we are thrown off balance by a massive emotional disturbance which is out of all proportion. Only subsequent reflection can suggest a linkage between the triggering event and the activation of a complex. Parents who are carried away into a wild frenzy by a child's behaviour regularly have to sit down, drained of energy or still shaking with rage, to think out what it is in *themselves* (the imbalance in their life, or repressed emotions, or simplistic views about interpersonal relationships) which has generated such destructive energy. A persistent unresolved conflict in the unconscious can lead to a neurosis, whose emotional effects (e.g. phobias, extreme depression) or physical effects (e.g. hysteria, paralysis) cause deep suffering.

On other occasions whatever is locked away in the unconscious seems to force itself into consciousness like water seeking the cracks and fissures in a dam. Aggression, for example, has a propensity to release itself in association with heightened sexual desires. More gently, dreams and free association are pathways used by the unconscious.

The capacity for recalling dreams varies enormously from person to person. Some can remember dreams vividly and in great detail for a long period, and can readily identify recurring dreams. Others have fleeting and haphazard recall of their dreams. Some cannot remember dreaming at all, though like everyone else they wake up sometimes with a vague feeling or mood permeating the whole personality, or conscious of having suffered a bad night's sleep for no apparent reason. Schools of psychology founded by Freud and Jung have concentrated on the analysis of dreams.

Free association was formally invented by Freud as a route for the self-disclosure of the unconscious. In a relaxed context, with the controlling influence of the intellect scaled down, our rambling or disconnected speech unveils something of what is churning away in the unconscious. Informal parallels are very common in daily life. We are travelling in a train, lulled by the rhythmic movements into a sort of day-dreaming or inventiveness which allows fresh light to flood upon complicated issues unsolved for months or years; or we sit back and begin fantasizing, because in a train we are anonymous persons, relieved of our formal responsibilities in life and of a public image which needs cultivating; or we doodle on a piece of paper and discern unexpected patterns and designs in the jumble of hieroglyphics. On other occasions we are oppressed by a difficult problem; we put it to one side for a period (we may 'sleep on it', as we say); when we return to the problem its solution is clear and simple.

Dreaming and free association (both informal and formal) are the seed-bed of artistic creativity. An artist has a relaxed and well-practised knack of crossing the gulf which normally separates conscious and unconscious aspects of the personality. The rich archetypal images of irreconcilable opposites coagulate in ever new combinations in the unconscious; from here they resonate with external situations and relationships, stimulate imagination and feeling in fresh ways, and generate artistic invention. Indeed, noticing anything in the public world (in the sense of being seized by it in some measure, and finding our attention and enthusiasm focused on it) – this is the first stage in all art – is probably the fruit of our unconscious powers itching to affect our personality. Why do I turn my head to look twice at *that* woman rather than this one? It is because the image of a perfect woman which I carry in my unconscious to counterbalance my self-image as a male suddenly resonates with some of the features in the actual woman my eyes have observed. This mechanism is not only the beginning of art; it is also the way in which relationships are born. More generally the unconscious at work behind the conscious means that human observation is usually a richer but more problematical engagement with a subject than the neutral (though objectively accurate) observation of a scientific instrument.

We have summarized so far two sorts of movement from unconscious to conscious: external symbols or events activating complexes or resonating with archetypal codes; and the gratuitous release of the unconscious in dreams and free association. There is a third mechanism, to which we shall return in Chapter 11: projection. A projection occurs when what is pushed firmly down into the deepest parts of the unconscious is so abhorrent to us that when it comes into consciousness we disown it. The only way we can cope is to believe that someone else has and expresses the emotions which to us are intolerable.

Drawing together the threads of this section, it becomes clear that the unconscious is an ambiguous facet of the personality: a fount of creativity and love, a rich store of experience and wisdom; but also a disgusting cauldron of unmentionable chaos burbling with poisonous energy. The unconscious is to the conscious as the sea is to dry land. That is the testimony of many ancient cultures (e.g. Ps. 69.1–3, 14–15, 107.23–32; Mark 4.35–8; Rev. 8.8, 13.1, 19.20, 20.10, 13–14; cp. 21.1) and contemporary writers:

Another world was anchored below her mind and lay

shimmering there like a great lake, its waters silken and seductive, waiting to engulf her in its mysterious depths. She could turn from it and walk away along the firm dry land whose every contour she knew or she could summon every morsel of courage, draw herself up and plunge in, to swim or to sink.[6]

The gift of the Spirit   The Christian tradition is full of images and language which address the hidden and transcendent God within us as Spirit. The tradition also regularly uses images of depth for the Spirit in the heart. Hence Paul: 'The Spirit you have received . . . makes us sons, enabling us to cry "Abba! Father!" In that cry the Spirit of God joins with our spirit' (Rom. 8.15–16). Again he writes, 'For the Spirit explores everything, even the depths of God's own nature. Among men, who knows what a man is but the man's own spirit within him? In the same way, only the Spirit of God knows what God is. This is the Spirit that we have received from God' (I Cor. 2.10–12). Charles Wesley better than anyone expresses these themes in his hymns. He speaks of the heart in an act of faith (see also Gal. 3.14) abandoning itself into the Spirit, as into an infinitely deep sea – so deep that only God himself can measure it.

> Plunged in the Godhead's deepest sea,
> And lost in thine immensity.   (*Hymns & Psalms* 282)
> God through himself we then shall know
> If thou within us shine;
> And sound, with all thy saints below,
> The depths of love divine.   (*Hymns & Psalms* 469)

There can be little doubt that religious faith is one facet of our getting in touch with our unconscious. That is why the symbolism is so similar.

Although the psychological dynamic of religious faith is not unique, the release of energy into the heart of the personality (i.e. Spirit) is not to be confused with anything else – the activation of a complex, say, or the revelation of a dream, or the upsurge of an intuition or instinct. These things are sufficiently similar to religious experience that discrimination is often difficult (Chapter 8). Ultimately, however, a concern for God is a surrender of the very Self into the unfathomable depths of the unconscious in a way that releases an utterly new quality of life – spiritual life.

> Send us the Spirit of thy Son.
> To make the depths of Godhead known,
> To make us share the life divine.
>
> (C. Wesley, *Hymns & Psalms* 300)

This becomes possible because in the unconscious the symbols, stories, metaphors, rites and imaginative drama of the Christian tradition leave *their* coded marks. They reside alongside but, as far as content is concerned, distinct from the archetypes of accumulated human experience. Many external stimuli resonate with these 'religious archetypes' and release in the heart the energy of the Spirit, which is pure grace. Prominent among them are verbal and enacted presentations of the gospel message, images of Christ and relationships infused with Christ-like love.

8 Inspirited to Love

Pastoral care as spiritual counsel

Much more than knowledge is required for us to love ourselves. Our fumbling efforts towards self-knowledge highlight imbalances in our inner selves (intellect *v.* emotions, for example), contradictions, confusions and a pervasive sense of alienation and evil. In the Christian view, there is no way of overcoming the anxieties and sin which constantly threaten disintegration and nonsense but by going to the centre of the personality. 'The first [commandment] is, "Hear, O Israel: the Lord our God is the only Lord; love the Lord your God with all your heart, with all your soul, with all your mind, and with all your strength"' (Mark 12.29–30). The clear implication of this text is that the journey inwards towards the heart and to God is itself to be a movement of love. Gentleness and patience with ourselves are more likely to be fruitful than rigorous asceticism or brutal self-criticism.

None of us can make the journey inwards by himself or herself. We are not isolated individuals with innate powers of introspection. We are members one of another. Each of us needs pastoral care if he or she is to find God within. This has been recognized throughout Christian history. In some parts of the tradition, those who exercise pastoral care of this kind are called spiritual directors, or (to use a less authoritarian metaphor) soul friends. In other parts of the tradition, members of a small group have exercised a ministry of this kind to one another (e.g. the Methodist class meeting). But we need not confine this facet of pastoral care to formal offices or structures. It is an integral component of all pastoral care, formal and informal.

The objectives of pastoral care as spiritual counsel are:

(*i*) To support and encourage someone who wishes to get in touch with the centre of his or her being. This recognizes that movement towards the centre involves confronting much pain and turmoil; and that faith in God is a decision which costs everything.

(*ii*) To encourage explicit expression of inner anxieties which, if left as ideas and feelings running around inside the mind, aggravate a sense of confusion and hopelessness. 'She'd asked herself these same . . . questions in the past so often – and so vainly, since she could never bring herself to ask them aloud – that she'd given up looking for the answers.'[1]

(*iii*) To bring a wise and critical perspective to someone's journey inwards – honesty in the face of self-deception, reality for fantasy, and challenge in place of demands for collusion.

(*iv*) To work with someone else to identify landmarks on the journey, to collaborate in discussions about when to stay and struggle through difficulties and when to move on, and to keep the general direction of the movement towards the heart. This requires not only a clear sense of the goal we all seek, but also makes heavy demands on the capacity for feeling and empathy. It is the skill of seeing the wood as well as the trees.

(*v*) To point towards appropriate symbols and images (including those of the Christian tradition) which might help another person to explore their journey more fully.

Pastoral care as spiritual counsel is both an awesome privilege and hugely dangerous. On the one hand there is a sense of being trusted to accompany someone on a private journey which is deeply serious, leading to a point which evokes reverence. 'One feels that one has touched something central to another person, or to a subject, and one feels silent and grateful in a sort of way, because one was allowed to penetrate a layer of understanding which remained impenetrable to others.'[2] On the other hand, the relationships established in this facet of pastoral care, and the deep and mysterious powers released from the inner recesses of both partners to spiritual counselling can overwhelm and destroy. 'Even if you are as virtuous as a hermit in a hair shirt you cannot resist them all. When a woman bares her soul to you, she is much more dangerous than when she simply slips off her blouse and skirt. The ones you reject spread scandal. The ones to whom you yield so much as a gesture of affection become as voracious as maenads.'[3]

It stands to reason that no one can exercise this form of pastoral care without travelling inwards towards his or her own heart and God. 'The difficult task of knowing another soul is not for young gentlemen whose consciousness is chiefly made up of their own wishes.'[4] Moreover this quest for painful self-knowledge and for the God within requires each pastor to *receive* pastoral care. We shall examine in Chapters 11–14 some of the contexts in which this happens, and discuss where pastoral care/spiritual counsel can be a mutual giving and receiving, and where it cannot.

Pastoral care as spiritual counsel is an important but nevertheless limited resource for people interested in finding and loving God. The inestimable value of conversation, and of having someone willing to listen to our stories and to empathize with our deepest hurts, perplexities and questions must never be forgotten. However, it is of the essence of the matter that my journey inwards must be mine and mine alone. The journey must therefore contain space and time for solitude as well as for support and guidance.

In our aloneness there are many resources in the Christian tradition which may be drawn upon in addition to pastoral care. Temperament and experience will colour individual choices of what is creative. Finding appropriate resources can often take a lot of time, and it is probably best to begin by tasting all sorts of things in a fairly dilettante fashion to find what is helpful. It is evident from Chapter 7 that psychoanalysts have much to offer. It is also important to remember that psychology was not invented by Freud. Many of the greatest playwrights and novelists who predated the turn of the century, as well as many who are the direct heirs of modern psychological insights, have probed deeply into the human mind. To reveal a personal predilection, I would suggest that George Eliot's novel *Middlemarch* become compulsory reading for those who are serious about understanding what goes on inside a person and its effects on human relationships and behaviour.

Furthermore, the greatest theologians and pastoral counsellors throughout Christian history have explored various psychologies and the relationships between psychology and the imaginative resources of the Christian tradition. As with everything else, we espouse these with a critical spirit, but also with a respectful sympathy. Augustine, Gregory the Great, Julian of Norwich, Ignatius Loyola, Teresa of Avila and John of the Cross are but a few of the giants on whose shoulders we may climb to peer at distant horizons.[5]

The journey into the heart and all that flows from an encounter with God in the mysterious depths is a large part of what we mean by private prayer. Prayer is a much larger concept than 'saying prayers'. However, prayer articulated in words has its place, and the prayers of others which have stood the test of time are an invaluable additional aid on the journey. Prayers which combine psychological insights and the language of faith are the most useful. The Lord's Prayer, many of the weekly collects used in the church's public worship, the rosary from Roman Catholicism and the Jesus Prayer from the Orthodox tradition are the best examples. They are most useful when they are committed to memory. This makes them more accessible and more capable of undistracted, meditative reflection.

From the edge to the centre

There is no means of getting quickly or easily to the unconscious ocean of life at the centre of the Self. We have to start at the outer perimeter and move inwards. This sets a rough agenda of priorities in the pastoral care of individuals. I stress the word 'rough'. What I set out now are a few bands or coagulations of issues which belong in a certain order. We have to move through them in order if we wish safely to arrive anywhere near the God who truly concerns us.[6] Moving in this order is appropriate for both a one-off pastoral visit and a long sequence of pastoral counselling.

Band A: Approaching from a distance

Each of us is a unique individual. Before there can be any useful exploration into the centre of our lives, or any concentrated attention given to one part of our personality which persistently blocks or deflects our struggle to find ourselves, there must be a recognition of our unique personhood. We need to see ourselves whole, from a distance. Each of us needs to be affirmed and respected simply because he or she is alive, as a unique human being, no matter what may be the record of achievements, failures, sicknesses or phobias. We gain this perspective on ourselves through others – family, friends and pastors. They greet us by name. They notice even small changes in our appearance (dress, complexion, hair style). They enquire about our general well-being, how we feel. They engage us in gestures which are meaningful at many levels and which at that moment focus their undivided attention on us as unique individuals. All this is taking place when a pastor meets someone with a handshake expressing warmth, a look straight in the eye and a friendly greeting by name; and blocks off all other concerns sincerely to enquire, 'How are you feeling today?'

Each individual lives in a natural and social environment, and is part of an organic system, an ever-changing web of reciprocal relationships. For most of us most of the time, nature and society are simply 'there', an almost neutral backcloth to our lives. It is only when something in the environment leaps out at us and involves us that it becomes a stopping-point on our inward journey; or when a relationship becomes significant to us, for good or ill. A deep concern about the morality of nuclear weapons, for example, or about famine in Africa; joy at the birth of a grandchild or anguish provoked by the breakup of our parents' marriage – these sorts of experience draw otherwise colourless items out of the environment and engage us deeply. At the surface of our personalities there is a meeting between something coming towards us from the outside and energy surging out from within us.

Band B: What is on the surface

Even before we can give attention to people and issues which concern us, and reflect on their meaning for our lives, we must deal with matters in our immediate environment and to do with our bodies which challenge our continuing existence. Our primary need is to survive. We must therefore take responsibility for the surrounding temperature (every pastor knows the threat of hypothermia to the elderly), for weather-proof shelter, for food and diet, health and fitness. If, because of great youth or great age, severe disability or profound shock, an individual cannot take that responsibility, it must become the priority of pastoral care. Much pastoral visiting of the housebound involves practical tasks to sustain life in moderate comfort; pastoral visiting of the newly arrived begins by helping them to get their bearings and find their way to shops, doctor and dentist, garage. . . .

There are some issues to do with our bodies and our immediate context that are exceedingly difficult to manage, even with support and expert advice. Safety and security in communities where burglary and street muggings are relatively frequent is one example. Another is health care in the case of severe handicap, disability or terminal illness (Chapter 9 looks further into this). Almost as paralysing can be an immediate environment which is overwhelming in its demands: a garden too large to control; a house too expensive to maintain; piles of unanswered letters or half-completed tasks.

Even these fundamental needs to do with survival and self-management can take us beyond themselves into our inner lives. Sometimes, for example, people lose interest in looking after themselves or live in chaotic surroundings because their self-image does not match the real circumstances of their lives. (Someone may picture himself as a very important person in society; another as someone with little energy and few administrative skills.) Here, as everywhere else, it is crucial both to deal with practical problems, and also to go behind the immediate issues to the emotions, feeling and volition, aroused by the issues. These are the means by which the Self is involved, and engagement of the Self overcomes the alienating sense that our survival and management problems somehow or other do not belong to us, that they can be glibly pushed aside as of little account.

This brings us back to those issues from outside which impinge upon us sharply and evoke strong feelings. We need to allow appropriate full expression to our emotions – anger, joy, fear, outrage, jealousy and so forth. We need to recount the stories by which events have taken hold of our lives. We need to talk them over with someone who cares enough and is wise enough to help us make sense of them. By these means something of our inner desires and concerns becomes clear to us. We begin to notice what might be in our heart: the anxiety of confused and contradictory concerns, or the secure peace of a coherent commitment to transcendent ideals, purposes and meanings.

Band C: What comes to the surface

'*Something* of our inner desires and concerns . . . which *might* be in our heart': yes, but not much more! There can be no firmer knowledge of these things until we allow into consciousness what is repressed in our unconscious. Here we must deal with the unmentionable and with powers charged with overwhelming emotion. It is a frightening area to unleash. It threatens our stability and self-image. We prefer to keep our public image neat, clean, respectable and cared for, and to hide away our rubbish and filth. Social norms reinforce this set of values, encouraging suburbanites to create neat gardens and freshly painted houses, and to hide away what is unacceptable behind net curtains. Presumably this is one reason for the deep prejudice in our society against gypsies. They reverse our life-style, leaving their rubbish on public view all around their caravans, which inside are spotless, neat and greatly loved. The journey inwards is an invitation to become a gypsy. We resist that transition. We play endless games of avoidance and self-deception to defend ourselves against such a change.

A familiar form of avoidance and defensiveness is intellectualism. We transmute every issue to a cerebral discussion, and thereby detach ourselves from it to a considerable degree. Feelings, commitments, and self-involvement are pushed away. We dehumanize ourselves to become embodied brains; if we could, we would become disembodied brains. I have noticed that this is specially prevalent in people who work in academic institutions, and in women who in childhood were pressurized by their parents to succeed academically at almost any cost.

I should not wish to imply that there are no occasions when clear intellectual discussion is part of pastoral care as spiritual counsel. Some issues and our reactions to them are bewildering until we can understand with our minds what is going on. That type of searching for intellectual grasp has a clear authenticity: it is born out of pain and enables us to return to our pain. Similarly there are some forms of intellectual discussion which are highly appropriate precisely because they release deep emotions. Sometimes they signal major changes in spiritual convictions. 'We are particularly hostile to truth that is just beginning to impress us and, in our reluctance to admit the need to change an attitude, we want to land a last blow out of perverse loyalty to the ideal we know we are going to surrender.'[7] All this is very different from escapist intellectualism.

More positively, how can we find the courage to allow the cracks to show in our self-defence? The following conditions seem basic. We need to be in a context which relaxes us, free of distraction and of threatening or judgmental attitudes. (Even our physical orientation to a confidant is important. A face-to-face arrangement is oppressive; an invisible presence behind us is threatening. Most productive is a pair of easy chairs of the same height and style set at about 120 degrees to each other and with no barrier like a table between them.) We need confidence in someone or something. It must be a confidence which has been thoroughly tested. Often we provoke someone artificially and outrageously on a theoretical or tangential issue which might be expected to shock, in order to check the reliability of that person should we choose to reveal the horrendous sunken wrecks, flotsam and jetsam which pollute our hidden lives. We need to be with someone who will value us as persons in spite of everything, who will give us esteem and acceptance even when our self-worth has disappeared in shame, guilt and faithlessness. We need someone who will not be swept away by the strength of our passions, the depth of our inner pain or the violence and promiscuity of our dreams and fantasies. We need someone who will remain true to himself or herself because he or she has passed through this sort of purgative experience already – and has survived.

It might seem that only God can fulfil our need when we wish to travel inwards through our repressed pain and failure. Some indeed conclude that only in total privacy can they pour out their souls to God. No other human being must ever be privy to their inner darkness. Such an approach must never be despised. It is, however, exposed to self-deception. There is a danger of creating a God who will be satisfied with the twilight, or, rather, allow us to confuse twilight with pitch darkness. On the other hand, if we find someone who will stay with us in critical support through our inner journey, we run the risk of identifying him or her with God – a fantasy which many pastors find it comforting to collude with.

It is probably fortunate that few of us have the time to contemplate these possibilities at leisure. For most of us, entry into the dark recesses of the unconscious is sprung upon us unexpectedly, as events overtake us. A crisis occurs (a bereavement, a spouse walks out without warning, an accident cripples us for life) or a complex is activated, and we are stripped bare emotionally. We break down; our defences are swept away. We are then glad of any friend or pastor who will stand with us and hold us secure; and we are amazed at what rich resources of wisdom, stability and trust are graciously offered to us by those to whom we would never dared open ourselves in leisured spiritual conversation.

Band D: Towards the centre

Words are inappropriate or need to be sparse if they are to capture possibilities here. Silence is everything, cultivated perhaps by a quiet hobby (see p. 28). Only church attendance officers ridicule the person who claims to be close to God in a garden – or while fishing, knitting, painting, rambling. . . .

Towards the centre of our lives we touch our deepest longings, those yearnings and wants which, if all else was lost, would sustain what there is of identity and purpose in life. In travelling towards the centre of our lives, we have probed deeply into the story of our life so that our identity and meaning have become known to us. With that knowledge comes some measure of anxiety. No one's heart is pure. There remain strong desires which forever threaten to tear us apart; there are dislocations and inconsistencies between the various parts of the personality. This makes us naturally egoistic. 'I am a selfish man – the more so because I am frightened of the cracks and divisions in myself.'[8] In some instances egoism appears in an intense form – narcissism, or the worship of oneself.

Towards the centre of our hearts, appearing from the unutterably mysterious depths, we meet the God who concerns us ultimately. For us soaked in the Christian tradition, God meets us as Christ and his energy and values spring up as Spirit. Prayer becomes an imagined conversation between us and the image of Christ which is implanted in our hearts. We are exploring how our deepest wants relate to what our God wants, and we are pondering what it would cost to want nothing but what God wants. 'Abba, Father, all things are possible to thee; take this cup away from me. Yet not what I will, but what thou wilt' (Mark 14.36).

Abandoning ourselves unreservedly to God's will is a sort of death. We surrender whatever confidence we have in whatever our Selves amount to, in favour of we know not whom or what. Faith is a plunge into a mystery, inspired by the gospel (pp. 70–3). In choosing faith we do not deny or destroy the identity and meaning we have struggled towards. If anything, we affirm them – but in a context where their significance is radically relativized and re-evaluated. Before, they were the rock on which we stood for safety in the surrounding quagmire; now they are pushed aside like a pebble so that we can sink into the inviting quicksand, which silently rises to envelop us (and the pebble) like an elixir of life. God's grace gives us a new being. (Read Phil. 3.1–11 as a classic example of this.)

As A. N. Whitehead pointed out, religion is what a person does with his or her solitariness. However, even at the point where knowledge of ourselves is abandoned in favour of the darkness of faith, we are not isolated. The web of relationships, culture and organic rhythms in which each of us is set continues to nourish and challenge us, if only through the collective unconscious. The literal presence of a pastor can also be extremely beneficial to witness to the following point.

When we choose faith we need a critical conversation with the Christian tradition which has brought us to this decision. For the God to whom we give ourselves cannot be guaranteed to be the God of the tradition. In practice the picture of the God whom we meet in our hearts is profoundly affected by our self-knowledge and self-image. God is the transcendent focus from whom flows the answer to our own deepest questions and the ideal who unveils the undreamed of possibilities in our personal lives. Our discernment of the divine will cannot be absolute. At best it is partial, needing amplification and correction; at worst, it is a demonic perversion, or a fanciful dream. That is why the Gospel of John stresses not only the Christ dwelling in us but also our need to dwell in Christ, that is to say, to be immersed in an ambience where the dialogue can continue with the tradition about the way we picture God (e.g. John 15.1–10).

From the centre to the edge

Almighty God,
to whom all hearts are open,

all desires known,
and from whom no secrets are hid:
cleanse the thoughts of our hearts
by the inspiration of your Holy Spirit,
that we may perfectly love you,
and worthily magnify your holy Name;
through Christ our Lord.   Amen.

O God, since without you we are not able to please you,
mercifully grant that your Holy Spirit may in all things
direct and rule our hearts; through Jesus Christ our
Lord.   Amen.

The Spirit works from the still centre outwards, seeking to
infuse everything with the energy of joyful love (Gal. 5.22–3).
Every facet of the personality is encouraged by the Spirit to
exercise its powers by becoming an avenue of divine love. The
Spirit is itself the content of our ultimate concern, and from
that base the Spirit invades our values, priorities, choices and
desires. The Spirit fires the imagination, strengthens our
capacity for volition, stirs up deep emotions and encourages
their expression. The Spirit gives us the confidence to trust our
instincts and intuitions, releases creativity and encourages us
to respect a new complexity and depth of feeling about
ourselves and our world. The Spirit stirs the intellect from
indolence, makes it bold to question, enquire and criticize
everything in the quest for understanding – but keeps it
appropriately humble. The Spirit enlivens the body, making
us sensitive to our responsibilities for our own health and
fitness. The Spirit makes us aware of ourselves, open to
ourselves, and therefore unafraid of the mysterious deeps of
the unconscious. Instead of being a fearful whirlpool over
which we seem to be perilously poised, it becomes like the
North Sea – a turbulent ocean, but one in which we can fish
and from whose bed we can extract oil and gas, resources for
life.

The aim of the Spirit is to create harmonies in the personality. Inspired by the Spirit, all the facets of the personality
interconnect, attending to one another in mutual sympathy,

creating a coherent and richly-textured sound like a well-rehearsed symphony orchestra. Love is the power to unite in genuine freedom things which prize their independence, or pull against one another, or want to relate to one another in master/slave or parent/child relationships. Love creates order out of chaos, and music out of noises.

An inspirited personality whose every potentiality is realized and where all the parts freely cooperate to produce harmonies is one of the goals of Christian wholeness, or holiness (see pp. 89–93). This goal is never reached. It stands before us as an image of Christ, alluring us, beckoning us to grow and mature (Eph. 4.13). All growth is painful and slow. There are limits to what can be achieved. In the Spirit we become more, not less, aware of the corrosive and dastardly forces of evil, alienation and death throughout human existence.

It seems to me that the principal implications for the pastoral care of those who wish to grow in faith and love are these:

(i) A programme of *Christian nurture* must be devised which starts where people are and develops all the facets of the personality. Time and resources are needed for growth in many directions, for a reconstruction of values and life-style. New converts and the young often set about this with great enthusiasm. They cry out for responsible tasks to do (to demonstrate and test their reliability and loyalty); from the perspective of their newly discovered ideals and intellectual vitality, they criticize tired institutions and experienced Christians who have been compromised by the world; they demand a vigorous group-life which is usually strong on prayer and joy but thin on anger, silence and the gruesome complexities of life.

Pastoral care certainly involves being sensitive to these needs and affirmative of the growth they generate. But, as always, a critical spirit is appropriate. New life is always infinitely fascinating; it takes courage to sustain growth when the initial glamour has faded, when limits have been encountered, and when an unbalanced programme has produced curiously lop-sided attitudes, prejudices and fears. Everyone loves a baby, but who wants to know a loud-mouthed and fickle adolescent? Pastoral care, however, must always hold out the ideal of growth towards wholeness. In personal conversation and shared actions as well as in groups a pastor must seek to correct imbalances, open up what is closed, integrate what is disintegrating, and help people to confront, own and absorb what is alien. (See further, Chapter 12.)

(*ii*) Pastoral care must be particularly honest about those *parts of the personality which most resist the Spirit*. In Chapter 6 I mentioned aggression and guilt. Here I highlight the emotions and ingrained habits.

There is no easy way of digging into those desires and emotions which stubbornly remain repressed. Activated complexes usually catch us out, shock us with their virility and depress us with feelings of shame and guilt. Christians in families, as much as everyone else, have the most horrendous arguments, threaten their children, become violent, abuse and vilify one another. Christians have extra-marital obsessional passions, become depressed and suffer from psychiatric illness. Self-control seems a distant ideal. It is not for nothing that over many generations and in many parts of the church, it has been thought the only hope for holiness lies in abstinence from sexual activity, and in a structured life of obedience to authority which minimizes self-will. But as the Reformation made clear, when chastity and obedience are required as conditions of holiness (rather than seen as one possible form of its expression), the life of the Spirit has been defeated.

In parenthesis, we must note that there is a fundamental difference between, on the one hand, things like repression, neurosis, disciplines of self-denial imposed by force, self-flagellation and the like, and, on the other hand, *suppression* of powerful desires and feelings. Suppression is a rational choice by which the free energies of an integrated personality are focused in a concentrated way, so that the fundamental purposes of the heart may be better achieved. Sexual intimacy, for example, may be suppressed in an extra-marital friendship of great warmth, in order to retain the integrity of a marriage which is understood by its partners to require sexual exclusivity. (See I Cor. 7.3–5; Matt. 19.10–12.)

Hazardous as it may be, a 'whole' life has to accept explosive emotions, unpredictable moods and passionate desires, and weave them into a pattern whose controlling theme is love.

Almighty God, who alone can bring order to the unruly wills and passions of sinful men and women: give us grace to love what you command and to desire what you promise, that in all the changes and chances of this world, our hearts may surely there be fixed where lasting joys are to be found; through Jesus Christ our Lord.   Amen.

Cultivating new habits is part of what we do to achieve such an end. One new habit which the Spirit inspires is *self-recollection*. We take time habitually to reflect on those tiny annoyances which make us 'blow our top'; on issues which release in us levels of anger and passion quite beyond what they merit or which leave us cold and uninterested when intellectually they seem worthy of commitment; on people and events which leave us exhausted and depressed or which excite us almost uncontrollably. We stop and ask ourselves 'Why?' We talk over our experiences with someone we trust.

A second new habit is *positive thinking* – consciously filling the mind, imagination and memory with 'all that is true, all that is noble, all that is just and pure, all that is lovable and gracious, whatever is excellent and admirable' (Phil. 4.8). Christians may bemoan the generally negative, violent and destructive tone of, say, many popular newspapers. That, however, is part of the reality of human existence, and morbid fascination with it is a feature of the fallenness of the race. It cannot be avoided and doubtless the media frequently exploit that fact. But even here there are stories of heroism, goodness, humour and beauty. Anyway, we are not victims of the media. We *choose* what we read, reflect on, look at and talk about. Very occasionally we are able to influence the tone and mores of the advertising and news media.

A third habit to cultivate is a *rhythmic interchange between solitude and acting*, between journeying inwards and inviting the Spirit to drive us outwards. The journey inwards is not something we do once. It is a journey to be undertaken time and again. It is never the same on any two occasions because we are always growing in experience, changing our awareness of ourselves and delving more broadly into the Christian tradition. We need to find and entrust ourselves to a new God from time to time, and God needs to start again to recreate us in his image. Without a periodic return to the depths at the centre of our being, our struggle for wholeness fades away into fatigue, despair or depression. There are no rules of thumb about how often and in what way each of us finds a rhythm of renewal. Pastoral sensitivity is about encouraging individuals to be exploratory and flexible in devising a creative pattern of rest and work, to affirm whatever 'habit' is eventually settled for, and to keep on the agenda a review of what is habitual, to overcome staleness.

New habits challenge the grip of old habits. Ingrained habits die hard. Years of fascination with power, wealth and the seduction of intellectualism; long periods characterized by confused or compromised values, self-gratification and self-protectiveness – these leave deep scars. Especially in old age, the habits of a life-time may produce a most unattractive character now stripped free of the veneer of social politeness. Pastoral care must be utterly realistic about the constraints and limits imposed by old habits on the movement towards holiness. It is crucial not to despise the day of small things.

(*iii*) Pastoral care deals gently with *the fragility of Christian character*. None of us can safely expect not to have painful crises to deal with. They can create havoc with our growth in wholeness. A tragic blow can in no time at all displace love and joy with bitterness, wild behaviour and inner confusion (see Chapter 9). The integration of the personality in love is a fragile achievement. Pastoral attitudes of judgment or censoriousness say more about the pastor than anything else: they may suggest an unconscious pretence that the pastor's own life in the Spirit is strong and well-integrated; or they may reflect a feeling of guilt when a pastor cannot attain an impossibly high ideal which he or she has set for himself or herself. Christian care is comprised of gentleness and compassion – that 'rare virtue, founded on the admission that each hides in his own heart the weakness that he damns in his fellows, and that pain or thwarted desire may drive him to greater excesses than they have committed.'[9]

Compassion, however, is more than an acknowledgment of reality and shared vulnerability. It is a release of love which encourages reintegration and stronger new growth; and envelops experience in hope. What is the basis of hope when Christian character seems so fickle? It resides in the crucial distinction between faith and character. Character is the rebuilding of the inner conscious personality which the Spirit does in love. Faith is as different from character as darkness is from light. Faith is the abandonment of the deepest recesses of the soul into the unfathomably deep void whose ground is God. Faith can remain a still centre to life in the same way that the bottom of the ocean is at peace even while gales lash the surface into wild turbulence. The pastor stands alongside the broken and distressed Christian and nurtures hope by affirming the security of faith. Psalm 130 makes the point well, but is perhaps surpassed by the majestic hymn of Martin Luther, 'Out of the depths I cry to thee' (*Hymns & Psalms* 429).

When the Spirit of God surges with energy and love from the unconscious depths at the centre of the personality, refreshing and uniting in harmony everything from the centre to the edge, it does not stop at the edge. Individuality exists in relationships. The Spirit's love must now infuse those relationships. New life in the Spirit necessarily shows itself in loving *actions* (Matt. 7.15–21; James 1.27, 2.14–26). Actions of love do not wait for the holiness of the subject. They spring directly from the intentions of love which the Spirit plants in the heart. We love others even while we are being transformed inwardly. Petition and intercession are prayed together. We shall pick up this extending story in Chapter 11.

9 From Night to Morning

Caring for the bereaved

When I arrived home I noticed a message on the telephone pad: Vera's mother had died. This was no surprise. The old lady had been housebound for years, and her last illness had been long drawn out though not unduly distressing. On several occasions I had visited her and Vera, her only child, a spinster and busy professional woman. I now went straight to Vera's bungalow. Vera said, 'I'm not at all upset. I did my mourning long ago while mum was dying.' Part of me recognized the sense of what Vera said. In the depths of my being, however, I felt Vera was hiding from something. I was drawing on my own experience. My own mother died from cancer of the liver; her 'dying' went on for weeks and all the family used the time to come to terms with her leaving us. Nevertheless, when the telephone rang one Saturday afternoon and I was given the news of her death, I sat down and wept. An appalling sense of hollowness almost paralyzed me, certainly made it impossible to carry on with any work. I was left dazed and confused. I knew therefore that part of my ministry to Vera would be to encourage her to mourn.

Many pressures in contemporary society discourage mourning. This makes for a great deal of misery and unnecessary stress. Christian pastoral care encourages mourning, in private and in public. In private we have to confront the English disease of the stiff upper lip and the distaste for showing strong emotions. Bereaved people need to be given a secure context of acceptance and understanding in which they can weep and wail. Men find this particularly difficult. When friends and relatives urge bereaved people to stop crying, be brave, pull themselves together, look to the future and the like, they betray their own anxieties as being more powerful than the needs of the bereaved. There is no pain like the death of someone close to us (a spouse, child or parent). Not to cry and mourn is to store up trouble for the future.

In public, it is tragic that death has become a taboo subject, unmentionable, or kept at a distance from the rough and tumble of life like a disinfected operating theatre. We have left few public symbols which signal our grief, like wearing black. Social pressures make us think we must valiantly carry on living as if nothing untoward had happened. We return to our daily work at the earliest possible moment, wearing gay summer clothes – a travesty of the hurt and pain which is felt deep down, and which is being artificially thrust from consciousness. Colleagues may acknowledge once that a death has occurred; after that, the subject is closed. All this flies in the face of human experience throughout history and in all cultures. It is part of Christian pastoral responsibility to question anaesthetized forms of minimal grieving which are becoming indigenous in our society. We need to pioneer a new and more honest set of social conventions and symbols within which patterns of grieving can be worked through more thoroughly.

A reconstruction of social habits which encourage mourning must be based on fairly precise knowledge of what happens to us when we grieve. Figure 3 is a highly schematic representation of some of the predictable features.[1] It is vitally important to stress immediately that this graph describes exactly *no* one's particular mourning. Grieving is not a mechanical process; it is an incredibly complex personal experience coloured by features in our individual history and context which cannot be calculated. Vera and I reacted differently to the news of our mothers' deaths. Grieving highlights our solitariness and our uniqueness. Yet even here we remain locked into a web of interconnected lives and griefs. Beneath the particulars of my individual grief, provoked by the severance of a unique relationship, there are echoes of shared human experience. The diagram attempts to point to the underlying common threads which we often do not notice because we are besotted by the surface colours and textures of the individual grief in which we are clothed.

The death of a loved one produces a profound shock. We feel numb. We cannot take in the awfulness of what has happened. Sometimes we even refuse to accept the bare facts of the tragic loss. We feel as if we have dropped to the bottom of a very deep ditch: we are in the dark, bruised and battered, but the pain has not yet surfaced; we cannot easily get our bearings. We wander about, surprised sometimes that we do not feel more upset than we do (Vera again). This feeling of being in limbo can often last for about a week. It is during this time that we have to attend to a great array of formal and technical matters. We are busy dealing with the doctor, undertaker, registrar, insurance agent, and minister of religion. We lay plans for the funeral (notices in the

Figure 3

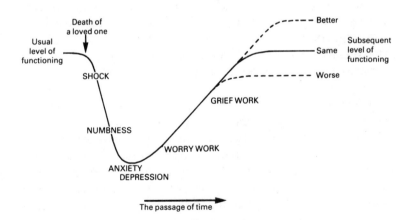

local press, letters to friends and relatives, arrangements for accommodation, preparations for the post-funeral wake, buying clothes). It is a period almost of suspended animation, which the funeral service often brings to an end.

During the period of initial shock there are often outbursts of intense anguish, anger and panic. The reality of what has happened and the indescribable feelings of hollowness, loneliness and anxiety that are part and parcel of the dawning realization are still to come. The second week after a death is often much worse than the first week for a bereaved person. Now he or she is at the bottom of the ditch and knows it. But perhaps that is too easy a metaphor. It is more like this. I have indeed fallen suddenly into a very deep and very dark hole in the ground. I have had time to come to. I am shaken and afraid. I cannot make out much of where I am. I have the sense that I have come to rest on a narrow and fragile precipice. The slightest movement on my part and I shall be plunged into – who knows what? A bottomless pit? My own death? I am petrified. I am utterly alone. I hear voices and sense presences somewhere vaguely nearby, but they are like ghostly things, flitting through the air, unable to touch me or I them. (It is impossible to stress too much the need for those who exercise pastoral care physically to hold the bereaved.) I am poised on the edge of the abyss which is at the very heart of my personality (pp. 113–14). What is brutally exposed is my capacity for faith in God, or an underlying, insoluble anxiety about collapsing into chaos.

Towards the end of the previous chapter, I wrote about the pastor needing to affirm the reality of faith when life and character seem to have been swept away by a swirling flood. Words are not always a helpful medium for communicating that truth to the bereaved. More important are the inner security of the pastor and the nature of the relationship he or she offers to the bereaved. It needs to be *quiet, stable, listening friendship*. Every bereaved person needs a friend: usually a non-relative is better at this than a relative, and preferably someone of a similar age and experience. A friend is called upon to fulfil tasks like these:

At least in the early stages of grieving, to be flexible enough to be available at a moment's notice, at any time of the day or night.

To stay loyal to the bereaved through thick and thin over many months, sometimes years.

To be a presence – not a domineering, activist or threatening presence, but an unshakeable resource of quietness and serenity.

To resist strongly the temptation to take over and direct the life of the bereaved.

To be willing to assist with any number of mundane chores, and above all to be a listener. Bereaved people tend to tell the same stories over and over again. They are pouring out from the depths of their souls vast stores of memories, fears, insecurities, hurts, past bitterness and joys. In this repetitive story-telling they are making sense of life – a shared life which has now come to its end (Chapter 1).

Being with a bereaved person is a great test of patience. Is it worth the strain? Persistent loyalty as a friend is one of the most significant and therapeutic pastoral ministries imaginable. Close relatives are too involved emotionally to perform this task effectively. But when a friend from outside the family circle remains fixedly and tenderly beside a bereaved person, he or she becomes a symbol of God. This is a situation which may provoke for both the bereaved person and the friend the issues of faith and divine love.

From Mark's Gospel we recall Jesus on the cross. Jesus has borne so much suffering and agony that he *feels* abandoned by friends and family, by the universe and by God himself. Yet he clings to God even though he has gone beyond all thought and feeling about God (Mark 15.34). 'I am convinced that there is nothing in death or life . . . nothing in all creation that can separate us from the love of God in Christ Jesus our Lord' (Rom. 8.38–39; see also Ps. 23).

Pastoral care of a bereaved person who is lost in the depths of depression does not always work out well. Some grieving people find that whatever it was on which their lives were built has collapsed under the strain. Faith was a fiction. This can lead to pathological depression, aggravated by many earlier experiences in life. (To this I shall return in the latter part of this chapter and in the following chapter.) Others find that the God within them does enable them to survive; but their God is not the Christian God. They are reinforced in their commitment to other values and ideals.

On the other hand, in the critical experience of being stripped to the root of existence, some bereaved people become conscious of a latent faith or discover a new or refined faith. It is not at all uncommon for a pastor visiting the bereaved to be the privileged recipient of a rich store of unreflected encounter with God brought out – perhaps for the first time – from the unconscious depths of the heart of the bereaved. They talk eloquently and seriously about God, the meaning of life and human destiny. The sensitive pastor attempts to draw from within himself or herself imaginative resources in the Christian tradition which interpret and develop the hitherto unreflected experience of the bereaved (pp. 86–9). Inevitably (and in the tradition of Mark's Gospel), the rich symbolism of Christian hope becomes a prominent part of the conversation of those who are trying to make sense of God and of themselves in the face of death. Sometimes the bereaved, precisely because they are confronted with the darkness and insecurity at the core of their own being, make radical adjustments in the values, purposes and meaning on which their life is to rest, or espouse Christian ideals for the first time. They discover new life in the Spirit.

It would be wrong to suppose that the possibilities for spiritual growth touched on in the previous paragraphs necessarily or ordinarily take place rapidly, while the be-reaved person is in the 'trough' of figure 3. Questions of faith are certainly posed when grief drives us to confront the possibility of nothingness at the centre of existence. Their outworking may take place gradually, or in fits and starts, over many months; faith must be related to, and hopefully integrated with, every other facet of our human existence.

Adjustments and changes are also taking place simultaneously at many other levels, in response to a significant loss. In the depths of depression it is common for the bereaved to feel disturbed in every aspect of the personality, even shattered into separate fragments. The memory is frozen; the brain seems paralyzed; emotions are confused and unpredictable; the body does not want to eat, feels pains in unexpected places, and is drained of energy to such a degree that sleep (itself fitful) cannot refresh. Feeling is suspended, choices cannot be made; and if there is a desire to do something, there is no power to achieve the intended goal. Sometimes utterly wild and dramatic gestures are contemplated, or enacted. The bereaved person decides on the spur of the moment to cut off all his or her connections and move to a new house in a completely unknown locality. Or there might be lapses into bizarre and uncharacteristic behaviour patterns, as repressed anxieties flood to the surface of a disorganized personality. Pastoral care is about accepting all these things as a *normal* part of grieving, but holding a secure boundary within which they can be contained without too much damage to the bereaved person or his or her relatives, friends and neighbours.

From the bottom of the 'trough', there is a long and painful climb back towards normal functioning. This can often take eighteen months or two years. It is not a smooth climb. It feels like climbing up a cliff-face with many jagged edges cutting into us as we grab them to haul ourselves upwards; or with many loose stones and sandy ridges on the cliff-face which give way as we put our weight on them, so that no sooner do we seem to gain ground than we find ourselves back at the bottom of the dark hole. Certain moments in the period of lengthy recovery almost always undermine the 'worry work' and the 'grief work' of recovery: like the first anniversary of the death, and the birthday or wedding anniversary of the deceased.

'Worry work' is the incessant talking through the emotional and spiritual distress caused by the death of a loved one. Loneliness, anger (against life, against God, against whatever or whoever may be supposed to have caused the death) and ferocious criticism of those who support and care (for not caring enough, or for being intrusive) are common. So is an almost obsessive searching for the person who has died. The bereaved person wanders round the house expecting to see the dead spouse in one of the rooms, or imagines his or her voice calling from the kitchen or the garden shed. Sometimes a visit is made to a building or location soaked in affectionate memories (a holiday home, or honeymoon hotel), to rekindle a lost presence. Photographs of the deceased long stored away in folders and cupboards are retrieved and given a prominent position. But the searching is as much for an explanation of the death as for a 'living' person. Why did Jack die? Who was to blame? What *exactly* happened in those last days and hours? Could anything different have been done (by the doctors, nurses, and above all by me) which would have prolonged life or made the last days more comfortable? Accusation and guilt impregnate vivid memories.

Eventually the nervous energy of the 'worry work' is dissipated. The bereaved person has now let go of the deceased; or, more exactly, he or she has refined an internal image of the dead lover which has been tested against memories, conversation and pictures, and is not dominated by the final moments of earthly life (which can often be distressing). If the 'worry work' has been done well, this internal image is now strong. It is not sentimental or fanciful, but realistically incorporates achievements and failures. It resides safely in the inner being of the bereaved, and he or she is confident that it will not fade or vanish with the absence of the dead person's physical presence.[2] (It goes almost without mention that overhasty or selective 'worry work' produces an internal image which is one-sided, unbalanced and imaginary. Any challenge to it with facts is met with ferocious defensiveness and hostility.)

Now is the time for 'grief work'. This is best done in silence. Some measure of solitude is also appropriate; but because the bereaved person is still feeling depressed, it is important that he or she is not left alone too long. In grief work the bereaved person is adjusting his or her self-image to fit in with the new situation which has now been realistically grasped; and is working out the consequences in a new life which has to be painfully constructed. New ways of using the living accommodation have to be worked out, or a decision made about moving to a new home. New financial arrangements are necessary. New skills have to be developed (to fill the gaps left by the person who is now dead). Existing close relationships (with remaining relatives and friends) have to be renegotiated to take account of the changed circumstances; new relationships, new interests, hobbies and activities have to be explored, and where successful, incorporated into a new lifestyle.

Every aspect of grief work is difficult, and many trials and errors have to be accepted. Eventually the bereaved person will assert his or her new self. A new life has been created. Figure 3 leaves open what might loosely be called the 'quality' of the new life which emerges at the end of the grieving process. Some people remain permanently, or for many years, crippled or handicapped. They do not resume the levels of autonomy, creativity and wholeness which they enjoyed before death struck. This usually means that some aspect of the internal crisis has not been worked through fully, or some dimension of its long-term significance has not been accepted realistically. Those who care pastorally for the bereaved should not necessarily blame themselves if this end-result appears. Reduced levels of functioning may be due to the residual, intractable effects of crises much earlier in life which have distorted the current grieving process, as much as to inadequate care in the recent bereavement.

Figure 3 suggests, however, that for some the grieving process may lead in due time to personal *growth*. This possibility is not to be grasped glibly. Growth beyond bereavement does not mean that some people forget the past more adequately than others, or falsely reinterpret what was a loving and nurturing relationship as a prison from which they are now glad to be free. Growth is about spiritual maturity, complexity of feeling and a patient working through of tortuous emotions. It involves acceptance of the permanent sorrow that all humanity is diminished by the death of each individual; it looks death and one's own mortality straight in the face; it surrenders all this pain to a God who holds within himself forever every detail of every living entity ('Are not sparrows five for twopence? And yet not one of them is overlooked by God. More than that, even the hairs of your head have all been counted,' Luke 12.6–7); and from that deep centre allows God's Spirit to stimulate new and larger possibilities for discipleship. (These possibilities spring precisely from a truer incorporation of the painful ambiguities of life.) In brief, a death can generate hope. An end can create the conditions for a thrust forwards. 'Tears may linger at nightfall, but joy comes in the morning' (Ps. 30.5; see also Ps. 126).

All losses are griefs

> From famine and disaster;
> from violence, murder, and dying unprepared,
> **Good Lord, deliver us**[3]

The loss of one's own life is the ultimate challenge we face to a meaningful life. Recent research has suggested that the news of a terminal illness is a crisis which initiates an inner process not unlike that portrayed in figure 3. A form of grieving takes place which may release in some the incentive to adjust all sorts of debilitating attitudes and negative relationships, and produce rich growth towards holiness. In others, of course, negative and depressing consequences may flow; though wise pastoral care can even here uphold those who rush towards their death in fear and anxiety. Sudden death robs us of the opportunity to prepare well for our dying.

In fact, however, we are in a sense preparing for our death from the moment we are born. Every significant loss is a crisis whose emotional and spiritual consequences to some degree or other mimic what happens when we confront the profoundest crises in life – bereavement and the news of our imminent death. The depth of depression, the ferocity of inner dislocation, the distance we travel towards oblivion and God, the time-scale of recovery, the possibilities of reconstructing a genuinely changed life – all these factors will vary from one sort of loss to another. The process, however, albeit on a reduced scale, feels remarkably similar. Concentrated, reliable and skilful pastoral care is therefore required for events like: serious injury and illness; unemployment, redundancy and retirement; a young person leaving home for the first time for work, study or marriage; the breakdown of an important friendship or a marriage; a removal from a community in which an individual or family has established deep roots, respect, clear social roles and many rewarding relationships, to a new home; an outstanding loss of self-control or temper; a disturbing challenge to our self-image; a deep questioning of our understanding of God, or of our underlying values, meaning and purpose in life.

So painful are experiences of loss and separation, especially when they are inflicted on us without warning, that we naturally fear any hints of future crises involving loss or major transitions. Anticipated separations or the news that what is safe and nurturing will one day come to an end appear to us as profound threats. Instinctively we put up defensive barriers. We play all sorts of (largely unconscious) games to stabilize situations and minimize change. If, however, this becomes an entrenched attitude, it is life-denying. Life requires movement and change. Not that life is a naive openness to the future. Evil, sin and death are powers that must always be taken with the utmost seriousness. Change is not in itself an inherently good thing. Some balance has therefore to be struck between change and stability, openness and containment, vulnerability and defensiveness. The origins of this dilemma go back to the earliest months of life.

A new-born child begins life in the closest possible physical contact with its mother. The organic bonding within the womb is broken at birth, but replaced with a relationship which imitates it as closely as possible in the new situation. The child nestles in its mother's arms, feeds from her breast, is fondled by her caresses and is cocooned in her bodily warmth. But mother cannot be, indeed before long chooses not to be, the child's environment every moment of every day. The mother leaves the child. The child sleeps and wakes without its mother being visible. The child cries when it is hungry, and if its cries are not soon heard and answered, has unmistakeable ways of expressing frustration and anger. It is perhaps not too fanciful to suppose that already the child is being confronted with primal experiences of loss and separation. The child is alone, and soon this feeling moves towards one of abandonment. The question for the child is whether the situation in which it finds itself stimulates, challenges or destroys its capacity for trust in its mother. The dilemma between trust and mistrust perhaps remains open in the short term. Mother comes: she leans over the cot, lifts the child up to herself, and the child gazes upon its mother face to face. Mother addresses the child by name. The child is fed by mother's milk, is fondled, cared for and cleaned. The child is made to feel at home in the world. In a fundamental way, the child is being educated to handle all future experiences of crisis, change, aloneness, bereavement and death. For all those tragedies which are sure to come, when life cruelly rips away those people, places and institutions in which identity and security are nourished, has the child learned enough to trust itself, to trust God and to trust the future?

I do not want to suggest that a child's earliest relationship with its mother determines for the rest of its life its capacity for trust or fear, openness or defensiveness. It does seem to be the case, however, that this earliest relationship can significantly *affect* future developments for good or ill. Like a building, a good life needs a secure foundation. As the child grows, the question of trust and mistrust is posed in new forms and new contexts, which we shall look at briefly in the following chapter.

It is impossible in adult life to tell accurately when particular experiences in the past may have damaged or enhanced an individual's courage to trust. None of us negotiates completely successfully all the opportunities for trust which life presents to us during our upbringing. For us all, therefore, trust and fear coexist and compete. The question remains: which is characteristically dominant, trust or mistrust? A pastor is bound to be particularly concerned with this problem. He or she wants to encourage in men and women a trust in God which is so liberating that it flows naturally into an appropriate openness and confidence towards people, ideas and the unknown future.

It is not too difficult to discern a life which is shrivelled when mistrust is vastly more prominent than trust. Two thumb-nail sketches can highlight some typical features. Jacky has a small circle of acquaintances, but only a tiny number of very close friends – one or two at the most. She is a fairly withdrawn young woman. She makes little attempt in her dress and appearance to be attractive to men. She thinks of herself as plain and uninteresting. She fears long-term relationships; she is convinced they will end in hurt and her being let down. She has an intense wish, of which she is hardly conscious, to destroy all efforts by others to show her love and care. So people give up. This confirms Jacky in her suspicion that it is always her own fault. She sees herself as a failure. Jacky has little sense of humour.

Henry is a fairly intense and serious sort of person in midlife. He has often tried kicking the habit of smoking twenty-five cigarettes a day, but the slightest disappointment drives him back to the addiction. Henry is married to Fiona. Henry is very possessive of his wife, intensely jealous of any independent thought or activities she might enjoy apart from him. When he is with her, Henry unconsciously blocks out of his mind all other claims on Fiona's time and attention. He is not a little selfish. He rarely shares with Fiona his feelings or needs. He expects her to know these things instinctively, and becomes quite violent when she fails to discern the fears and expectations which are locked up deep inside him.

Attitudes of these kinds rob life of a lot of its joy and serenity. Jacky and Henry are also typical of those who find bereavement and other significant losses particularly disruptive, destructive experiences. The 'normal' processes of grieving are distorted. The period of initial shock, for example, may be extended over weeks or months; every imaginable device is used to hold up the passage of time, and to deny any sense of being on the edge of a dangerous precipice. Or, they cultivate and cling to a wholly romanticized picture of the deceased, fearful that any balanced image (incorporating weaknesses as well as strengths) will demonstrate again – and now in a way beyond redemption – their own introverted loneliness. They fear a realistic picture will say: *No* one can be relied upon absolutely; all dependency is a recipe for self-inflicted and well-deserved hurt.

A Christian pastor in such circumstances is often tempted to despair. His or her concerns for reality in place of illusion and for wholeness in place of emotional paralysis seem blocked. In reality, however, the human personality is a highly complex living organism. It is malleable, even if change and adaptation come imperceptibly slowly. (Sometimes, after a long period of fierce resistance and defensiveness, a depressed and fearful personality collapses altogether. This is frightening, and normally pastoral care must be assisted by specialized medical and psychiatric help.) This in itself is a good reason for pastoral care maintaining a long-term commitment. A trust-worthy kindness which stays loyal through any amount of emotional trauma, fantasy, denial and energetic withdrawal from the friendship holds out some hope, however small, of growth in trust and security.

In the Christian view there is another reason for faithful pastoral care of those whose normal stance to life reveals more of mistrust than trust, and those who are comatosed by loss and separation. It is the grace of God. Divine grace is the unpredictable, surprising surge from transcendent depths of a regenerative love. Christian conviction is that God's love is ever present and unfailing; but it is normally hidden, holding us in the unknowable depths beneath the heart. From time to time God's Spirit gushes upwards, presenting us unexpect-edly with radical new possibilities for our lives. In Matt. 13.44–6 two brief episodes illustrate the experience. The first is about a farm labourer working in a field, digging or ploughing. Quite unexpectedly he strikes something hard. It is an earthenware pot buried beneath the soil – in first century Palestine a familiar way of hiding treasure. The labourer's heart starts pounding with excitement. Suddenly he can see a vision of a wholly new life for himself and his family. Without more than a moment's delay he knows what he has to do, however high may be the stakes with which he is playing. He sells everything and buys the field. Now legally he is in a position to lift the treasure from the earth and have it as his own.

The second episode focuses on someone who deals in pearls, precious stones, jewellery and the like. Over the years he has gathered a great deal of experience and expertise. He knows a good stone when he sees one; he can value things accurately, and make a living buying and selling. He also knows that noticing one very rare stone or one perfect pearl could make his fortune. One day his dreams come true. There before his eyes was a pearl in a class of its own, of outstanding value. 'So he went and sold everything he had, and bought it.'

Both episodes hinge on an assumption about how people behave: given an unexpected chance to be fabulously rich, or to own something of superlative value, we will grasp the lucky break, even though it means risking everything we possess. By analogy, the kingdom of God is experienced as divine grace. If we recognize God's grace for what it is, the incalculable cost of discipleship seems as nothing. The kingdom comes therefore as an offer radically to reconstruct life. The pure, transcendent love of God is disclosed with such startling richness that it becomes the meaning of life; it wins our heart, and changes everything. Mistrust is displaced by the capacity for trust. A distorted, crippling and imprisoning form of grieving is converted into a normal healing process, which through its pains and struggles opens up the hope of personal growth. A fearful adult can, perhaps for the first time, relax into an experience akin to what most of us go through in our earliest days and weeks with our mothers: of trusting life even when we are alone because that trust is not abused and we are not abandoned to hunger and fear. 'I tell you, whoever does not accept the kingdom of God like a child will never enter it' (Mark 10.15).

Stable, unflinching pastoral care of those whose grieving is 'abnormal' provides the context within which God's grace can operate in its sovereign freedom. The pastor holds a situation which seems blocked and despairing, but he or she remains alert to any inner flashes of energy and creativity in the bereaved which may be interpreted as divine grace. No interpretation that the pastor suggests at such moments will ring true unless two conditions are fulfilled. First, the pastor's constant and much tested attitude to the bereaved person must have expressed authentically the hidden, unfailing love of God, of which the event of grace is seen to be a startling appearance. Second, the pastor's deepest longing (i.e. his or her prayer) for the terrified, clinging soul or radically withdrawn human being will be exposed: is it for a permanent relationship of dependence on the pastor, in which the autonomy of the bereaved is written off? Is it a secret desire to escape and be rid of all the trouble and time soaked up, uselessly, on this 'case'? Or is it for the discovery by the bereaved of grace, faith, love and hope? A verse by Charles Wesley expresses well what a pastor has to pray on behalf of those who cannot pray it for themselves.

> Give me a new, a perfect heart,
> From doubt, and fear, and sorrow free;
> The mind which was in Christ impart,
> And let my spirit cleave to thee.[4]

10 From Birth to Decay

I am in my early forties, married, with three children. That snippet of autobiography is important. It suggests something of the framework in which I interpret experience. Without question, as I have been writing this book, I have had in mind my own struggles to make Christian sense of life. I have been speaking primarily (though I hope not exclusively) to men and women in the middle years of their life. We see things in characteristic ways. I am also conscious that when I was younger the world and God seemed very different from the way they do now. In this chapter, therefore, I want to attempt a simple survey of the typical ways in which human beings search for God, pray, give and receive care at different phases in life.

Some introductory comments:

(*i*) This chapter is not an autobiography. As I write I shall silently recall particular incidents from my own life-story; and as you read I hope you will bring to mind significant encounters, conflicts, events and relationships from your story. Primarily, however, I want to stand back in this chapter from the quest for meaning through personal story-telling (Chapter 1). Instead I want us to notice regular patterns underlying all human growth and development, from the cradle to great old age. We are trying to summarize a more or less 'scientific' record of how Christian discipleship is structured in successive periods in our lives. This is related to vivid autobiography as a description of the slow movement of the tide is connected to the experience children enjoy of splashing around in the waves at the seaside.

(*ii*) Human growth and development is an exceedingly complex process, and it takes place at different rates and under different influences for each aspect of the personality. Some well-known facets of these developments I shall not touch on at all – for example, physical growth and intellectual development. I shall concentrate on how, at different ages, we experience the deeper things of life, how we organize emotions, feeling and concerns to make sense of ourselves and of life, that is to say, how faith and discipleship take shape.

(*iii*) I shall divide the discussion into six sections, three for childhood, one for adolescence and two for adulthood. This is a rough and ready guide. In reality all life is more subtle and interesting than any scheme can suggest. The six sections, if you like, are themes for a symphony. I introduce them in the order in which their principal statement appears in the score. To the discerning listener, however, there are throughout the symphony ingenious variations of each theme following its formal statement, and even hints and innuendoes in advance of each theme's introduction. This means that childhood, adolescence and adulthood are not watertight compartments. A full human life incorporates continuing openness to every aspect of experience covering the whole age range. None of us can truly live in isolation from others, or even simply with our peers. We flourish most in human communities in which children, young people and adults of all ages inter-relate in pastoral care for one another. Figure 4 represents the substance of this paragraph in a schematic way.

(*iv*) Between each of the six sections there is a significant transition. It is impossible to tie each transition to a precise age, though before adulthood each transition is usually linked to an identifiable short period in the life-cycle of a few months or years. Some transitions are extremely painful to negotiate. They introduce into the spiritual life perturbations which feel like grieving processes (Chapter 9).

Figure 4

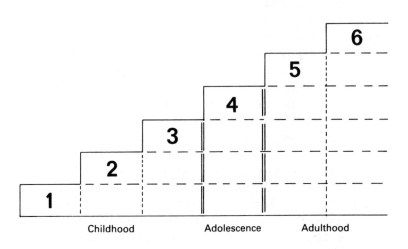

(v) To state the blindingly obvious: I am a male. I want to be sensitive to the fact that, at several points, the experience of men and women may be significantly different. I shall touch on this issue when considering the later sections; it deserves much more thorough discussion, from girls and women.

Growing in faith and love

1. *Trust and mistrust*　In the previous chapter (pp. 143–4) I sketched how the basic dilemma of trust and mistrust is experienced by a very young child in its relation to its mother.[1]

2. *Power and fragility*　By about two years of age a child is beginning to discover the power of speech. Language is limited, but imagination is rife. Meaning and reality in life are communicated through fairy stories, dreams and imaginative make-believe. The child is not yet able to grasp connections

between causes and effects, nor has it the capacity for rational reflection. An appeal to magic and mystery suffice to describe how things relate to one another.

The child is also aware of developing physical skills (holding things, walking, building piles of bricks, etc.), but these are not fully under the child's control. Nor does the child have resources to assess adequately what is possible and what is not. The child identifies with heroes whose strength and size are legendary (dinosaurs, medieval knights and space explorers). Revelling in its own new-found energies, the child asserts its independence. There are no limits (the child imagines) to what can be done or to what may be explored, investigated and tried. Every child is a Goldilocks. Unconsciously, however, the child's security rests on the reliable love and care of its parents. If a parent is just one minute late meeting a child from school, the child becomes profoundly anxious; if a parent is away from home for only a short period, the child fears he or she may be dead.

In the three or four years up to about the sixth birthday, this framework of meaning remains more or less the same. Three highly significant sorts of experiences take place in this context which deeply affect the child's continuing capacity for trust, and indeed which colour all subsequent self-images and metaphors for God.

(a) Shame   A child attempts to do something which everyone else appears to achieve with effortless ease: walk across the room. The young child, however, falls flat on its face. For ever afterwards this becomes the dominant metaphor for shame. It represents public humiliation, a feeling of inferiority and self-doubt, and looking a fool.

Another source of shame springs from the inevitable intervention of parents into the child's world of independence and exploration. Sometimes parents want to help and encourage, to be greeted with 'I'll do it myself'; sometimes they want to guide and suggest, to be confronted with 'You can't make me do it'; sometimes they must prevent or limit, for safety's sake, as little Red Riding Hood's mother ought to have known. Conflicts arise. The child is no match for a disapproving gaze, a parental ticking off, or a firm 'No!' The child collapses in confusion. Daring and spontaneity seem of little worth when judged against an adult (and to the child, unintelligible) rationality.

Parents see their young children mastering all sorts of tasks. They invite a child to cooperate ('Tidy up your toys, please, John'), but often misjudge what the child is capable of in terms of concentration and application. Parents become upset and angry, a response made easy by the inevitable exhaustion which child-rearing produces at this period (and aggravated by the demands of other children in the family). The child is shamed by its failure to please.

Few experiences are more painful than shame; few experiences are so indelibly etched on the memory. In its shame the child ventilates its rage, throwing tantrums, lashing out at those it imagines are the cause of its humiliation. Then the child hides away, covers its face, blots out the stern disapproval, creates a private area where it can be itself without parental criticism, caution and constraint. If all this should be ground for further parental disapproval ('John, don't be such a naughty boy'), the child may swing to another extreme: pleasing mum and dad at any cost, disguising from itself a painful insecurity and a ferocious anger turned inwards.

(b) Guilt As a child's self-control and experience develops, so do its capacities to weigh consequences of actions in advance, to make plans, and to devise rudimentary connections between cause and effect. Boundaries around acceptable behaviour are made increasingly firm; expectations of obedience are heightened. Punishment or reward is meted out by parents, even if the rationality of their decisions is sometimes a puzzle to the child. A child eagerly tests the limits, but transgression of them provokes guilt. Conscience is being formed. The child acts out this new faculty in endless battles between 'goodies' and 'baddies', but often has to refer to adults to decide who are properly to be identified as one category or the other.

Guilt and shame are often intertwined ('I'm ashamed of you, John; I thought you knew better than that!'). In itself guilt is not particularly difficult to deal with. Forgiveness is never far away. Guilt combined with shame, however, is a far more intractable problem.

(c) Sexuality   During this phase of life a child increases its ability to differentiate intimate relationships. Mother and father are distinguished, but the relationship between them is also noticed by the child as being something significant to both mother and father but distinct from the relationship either parent has with the child. Siblings and the maze of relationships each has with mother, father and the child come into focus, often provoking intense rivalries in the claims on parental attention. A child notices its own gender, and takes very seriously the differences between boys and girls in its circle of friends.

The first inklings of gender identity pose for the child difficult questions about its relationships with mother and father; a boy is like his father but unlike his mother, and vice versa. A boy seeks a relationship with his father which is imitative and eases identification. But mysteriously there are limits to the modelling upon father: he finds that mother discourages him from relating to *her* as his father does. Something new is apparently called for in this relationship which up to then had been the mainstay of his life. How is he to give love to his mother and receive love in return? (Girls obviously have a less traumatic adjustment to make, because the fundamental link with mother is less disrupted.)

Since Freud, we have all been aware of so many things which can go wrong at this stage in a child's developing relationships (the 'oedipal' phase). The deep-seated and long-lasting effects of errors in negotiating these hurdles probably spring from the fact that nascent sexuality coincides with painful experiences of shame and guilt. Sexuality, shame and guilt easily become inseparable.

3. Righteous love and failure   From roughly seven to twelve years of age, a child's life is devoted to making sense of people and things in the immediate environment. At school there is rapid learning and energetic work. Concepts of number and language emerge, tied to concrete experience. Ideas are validated if they bring results. Building complicated structures and making things work occupy the child's attention. Achievements and rewards for achievement (stars, badges, points) matter greatly. They confirm a child's separate identity, slowly emerging from the safety of a family and home. Some discover, however, that they can achieve little; they have few gifts. They fall short and see themselves as failures. Life is perceived as unjust.

Similar issues colour relationships. Stories carry the child's glimpses of meaning so long as the stories are about 'real' people, the heroes of history who fought for right and justice. Everything is interpreted literally. The child's uncertain identity finds comfort in formal, structured and disciplined peer group organizations. Wearing uniform is the child's pride and joy. The rules of the group guarantee fairness and reciprocity in the relationships. In less structured contexts, anxieties are more common. In the home brothers and sisters become intensely jealous and angry if they feel that parental attitudes are anything less than scrupulously fair. Informal friendships are no sooner made than ended (sometimes with great anguish), as the child tests out whether self-interest can be fairly tempered by the interests of the other. Some children find towards the end of this phase of their life a deep loneliness. Few so-called friends can be trusted not to let them down when it suits them. Even authority figures (parents, teachers, leaders – and God) fail to run the world equitably.

4. Identity and nobodiness   Adolescence is a time of appalling upheaval. It is probably worse for girls than for boys. The onset of menstruation causes physical distress and emotional turmoil in an unending monthly cycle. The sexual self-consciousness which accompanies puberty disrupts with particular violence the daughter-mother bond, as the adolescent girl detaches herself with a mixture of love and hate from a mother whom she has trusted and identified with more or less without a pause since birth.

An adolescent is independent enough to create his or her own world instead of the jaded and compromised values and attitudes of the older generation. Youth is a phase of unsullied idealism. Though every young person quickly discovers life is not that simple. Independence means not only a distancing from childhood and parents, but also from peers. Individuality becomes the principle item on each young person's agenda. He or she discovers, 'I am unique'. A self-image comes into clear focus, if a little anxiously. (Many hours are spent in front of the mirror, choosing clothes, etc.)

'If, however, I dare to look at others (I sometimes feel gauche and shy), I notice from the look in their eyes and their tone of voice' – how subtle now are the signals of interpersonal relationship! – 'that their image of me is different from my image of myself. So what am I really like?' Young people have an 'identity crisis', to use Erik Erikson's suggestive phrase. This feels threatening and confusing. 'I feel isolated. I am not strong enough (yet) to go it alone. In the first instance I must cling to those most like me.' So young people nervously explore the first intimations of intimacy; they form into small groups of kindred spirits. There they forge intense, long-lasting friendships, marked by warmth, loyalty and trust. Between different close-knit groups of like-minded young people there are emotionally charged, sometimes vicious, conflicts.

What now of parents and other authority figures? Adolescents are ambivalent.[2] On the one hand they want to reject them. So they form a counter-culture, focused around youthful idols (pop stars, footballers) and expressed in fashions which are designed to offend or irritate the older generation. On the other hand young people want to respect their elders if the latter consistently adhere to their own values and authority structures because they are believed to be life-enhancing.

One of the primary aims of pastoral care of young people is to hold together these ambivalent feelings, in the hope that some measure of integration can be achieved. By this means a teenager is able to forge an independent identity, which in turn leads on to adulthood as an era to be welcomed.

Aiming for integration is more easily stated than achieved. The latent pressures within adolescence tempt young people to resolve their ambivalence about authority figures by embracing exclusively one extreme attitude or the other: either rejection or warm avowal of parental world views. Which option is preferred is influenced by fairly ruthless probing of the integrity of adult convictions.

Consistency among adults, for example, is a rare virtue. Given enough youthful provocation, many adults become aggressive and oppressive. They reveal deep-seated fears and insecurities. Young people readily discern this. They walk away from society's prevailing norms and expose its contradictions. Some set up hippy communes and the like. In other young people, collapse of confidence in society's constituted authorities means a failure to resolve their own crisis of identity. They feel nobodies. They enter adulthood in deep depression; or they find the black emptiness where their heart should be so painful that they falsely project an image of being a 'somebody' – effervescent, important and influential, determined to leave a mark on human history if only by bizarre, eye-catching actions of bravado.[3]

For those young people who opt for safe approval of inherited authorities (rather than rejection, or more creatively, integration), certain kinds of religious faith become attractive. They focus their needs and aspirations in a God who is symbolized as an intimate friend. The divine companion is sensed as some sort of presence, alongside or behind the young person. God assures the young person that he or she is valuable and lovable. God invites the adolescent into a private experience of confidentiality, openness, sharing and understanding. God protects and encourages the youth in difficult circumstances (there is much prayer to God before examinations, job interviews and so forth). God affirms traditional values, respect for authority, obedience of Christian leaders and conventional life-styles.

This sort of religious understanding concentrates on those

facets of the personality which constitute the heart: feeling, emotions, unequivocal commitments to precise (Christian) values and firm control of desires. The intellect is relatively uninvolved. The explanation of this may be along the following lines. It is only in adolescence that we become competent and confident at abstract thinking. Our educational system rightly seizes on this with intensive intellectual development and rigorous testing before the school-leaving age. Except in untypical situations (e.g. a Christian boarding school), the young person experiences intellectual growth as something contained within the boundaries of school. A school has to have a fairly tight discipline, to capitalize upon the teenager's need for intellectual mastery in a small number of subjects. In contrast, emotional and spiritual confusions (the identity crisis) have to be dealt with largely outside school, and are focused on the home and in peer groups. School and society (especially home) become divorced. Critical intellectual enquiry and religious faith are found in distinct compartments of life. A relatively conservative, uncritical theological tradition in the community of faith reinforces this division, but ironically increases the attractiveness of faith as a (one-sided) way of resolving adolescent ambivalence about authority.

Adolescence, then, is a period when huge distinctions emerge between and within us: disenchanted drop-outs, sometimes wallowing in satanic violence (the Hells Angels syndrome) over and against too-good-to-be-true, born again young people; analytical and abstract thought mastering the sciences, humanities and life-skills over and against a religion which is theologically uncritical. These are experiences of alienation.

An Interlude

Up to this point a fairly close relationship has been assumed between biological age and the patterns of emotional and spiritual development in children and young people. In adulthood, however, the way we structure our quest for meaning and purpose in life seems much less tightly connected to emotional needs and desires. The way in which we emerge from adolescence has a profound effect on how we tackle questions of meaning and the sorts of resources to which we turn to make sense of ourselves and of life. I illustrate this first by referring back to those who enter young adulthood having dodged the dilemmas of youth by adopting one or other extreme position on authority issues. Because something as fundamental as personal identity is at stake, young adults invest a great deal of energy in the option they choose. The polarization bites deep. It can become an underlying motif in life which effectively locks spiritual perception into one or other simplistic framework for the remainder of life, or for many subsequent decades. Many Christians, for example, find it necessary to live conventionally within the context of a conservative, uncritical and fairly directive religion throughout their adult lives; they isolate faith from the ambiguities, confusions, evil and brokenness of secular experience. Church and world, faith and life, are contradictory opposites.

Alternatively, adults inheriting adolescent dilemmas as rigid polarities may swing violently from one to the other. Someone who has been living in a thoroughly secularized counter-culture over several years is dramatically converted to faith, usually of a reactionary, almost fundamentalist kind. Or a devout Christian, a pillar of church and society, will overnight walk away from the Christian tradition, never to touch it again.

Within a fixed framework which copes with life's deepest puzzles only through alienation, the emotional conflicts, needs and social roles of men and women continue to change according to predictable general patterns, as it were independently of the unresolved issue of faith. I can here hint at these patterns only in the briefest terms.[4]

(a) Family versus career (20s–40s) Throughout this period there is a tension between the need to create an intimate family group (marriage, rearing young children, building a home) and the need to strike out alone, making a success of a

career. Put crudely, in the twenties one theme tends to predominate over the other, but in the thirties the importance of the themes is reversed. So those who marry young and quickly have children find in their thirties that marriage is under stress (the 'seven year itch'): mothers resent lost career opportunities and fathers resent the constraints on time and freedom imposed by the children; they want to break the bonds of marriage and family. Conversely those who remained single in their twenties often want to put down roots in their thirties; and drop-outs want to conform to conventional society. (It is important to note that it is only by about the age of thirty that adults feel liberated emotionally from their parents.)

(b) *Male versus female (40s–60s)* In these decades parents are dealing with the special pressures of adolescent children and their own ageing parents. These challenges coincide with the emotional needs of men and women diverging quite considerably, principally in the forties. Women typically want to take up new careers, and discover leadership and administrative skills not realized before. Men, in contrast, who have characteristically had long experience of competitive work situations, who feel on a sort of plateau because of failed ambitions and wasted potential at work, often take more seriously the nurturing dimensions of their personalities (see p. 105). In the frequent absence of a wife, now pursuing her own future, and in a world whose image is deeply influenced by his own teenage daughters, a man finds especially attractive a quasi-parental/experienced-lover role in relation to young women.

In the later fifties men's and women's interests converge once again. A new form of intimacy becomes possible, and hard-won wisdom as parents is focused on hoped-for grandchildren. New life-styles are created to cope with reduced physical powers and realistic pictures of their place in history and society.

(c) Pleasure versus death (over 60s)

> The sixth age shifts
> Into the lean and slippered pantaloon,
> With spectacles on nose and pouch on side;
> His youthful hose, well saved, a world too wide
> For his shrunk shank, and his big manly voice,
> Turning again toward childish treble, pipes
> And whistles in his sound. Last scene of all,
> That ends this strange eventful history,
> Is second childishness and mere oblivion,
> Sans teeth, sans eyes, sans taste, sans everything.[5]

Now detached from immediate responsibilities for social institutions, the elderly work emotionally on an agenda containing some difficult items. They must reconstruct their self-image to incorporate their experience of failing powers and faculties, and of doing foolish things; they attempt to come to terms with a despair about life's failures, unresolved conflicts, evils, unquenchable pains and lost opportunities, whose only conclusion must be death and nothingness. But in contrast they are able to rest in the pleasure of artistic creativity (pp. 48–50), the satisfaction which comes from true self-knowledge, and the calmness of a wisdom chiselled out of many rough experiences of caring and being cared for. In old age, especially great old age, it is less easy to conceal the true aims and values which have been operative surreptitiously throughout adult life.

Before introducing the fifth phase I remind you how we have arrived at this point. Throughout childhood human beings display predictable patterns in the development of relationships, emotional concerns and values which in later life will influence the shape that faith takes. In adolescence there is a predictable framework within which issues of personal faith and identity are explored. (By the end of the teenage years most young people have long since severed any connection with a Christian community. What we are discussing here, however, is not just Christian faith, but the ways in which any images are constructed in the adolescent mind which can be trusted as resources for coping with life.) In adulthood there is no longer a straightforward connection between age and the way we construct images of ultimate meaning and self-understanding. Many adults stay with those unifying frameworks for experience which first become habitual in adolescence. Emotional needs and social roles continue to change, but the question of faith in God, if it is addressed at all, remains locked in the relatively confined world of youth. God and religion are beneficent friends who underpin my identity and uncritically reinforce the aims and values of those close to me whom I respect. God has been domesticated.

> We come unto our fathers' God;
> their Rock is our salvation.[6]

It would be inappropriate to ridicule a faith of this kind in adults. It is legitimate, however, to respect such a faith and at the same time to question its adequacy. Is not an *adult* faith structured as in phase 4 above the root of religious tribalism and inter-communal religious conflict? Can such a faith integrate critical enquiry into itself? Can faith of this kind incorporate the evidence which accumulates overwhelmingly as we grow older: of life's ambiguities, of good and ill and infinite shades of grey co-existing, of success and failure, achievement and tragedy?

5. *Questions and commitments*　This is a phase which opens up the struggle to make sense of life to new and deeper challenges. Changes of a negative and of a positive kind must be explored in the inner life.

The *negative* element is the introduction, probably for the first time, of critical questioning into the tradition of faith. I refer to this as something negative in order to try and communicate its tone. It feels as if secure ideas about God are being painfully undermined, as if symbols which served the imagination well have been splintered, and secure authorities (the Bible, dogma and doctrines, and Christian leaders) are being ruthlessly toppled. Once a world of meaning generated by history, myth and symbol is exposed to critical investigation, it loses its capacity intuitively to sustain, nurture and encourage. Life seems bleak and colourless; prayer and worship seem unutterably boring and futile; and the emotional warmth of religious faith vanishes.

Those who find intellectual pursuits easy and enjoyable and who remain in contact with the Christian community now become absorbed in critical and abstract theology – to such an extent that they hide from themselves the haunting question mark which critical theology has planted deep in their souls. Intellectualism becomes more or less the be-all-and-end-all of discipleship. Emotional needs, desires, and feeling are dealt with separately. It is as if the compartmentalizing of life in the adolescent period (religious faith located in the heart; the intellect pretty well uninvolved) has been reversed. 'Academic' theology is dominant; spirituality is marginal, or pursued outside the cluster of Christian symbols and meanings. For example, it is not at all uncommon to observe coupled together in this phase a lively intellectual enquiry into Christian tradition, a spasmodic and superficial involvement in the life of the church, and a fascination with groups and techniques which claim to expand consciousness or promise heightened psychological states (transcendental meditation, yoga, drugs).

And what of those who are not natural intellectuals? Those who find intellectual activity difficult or dull (the vast majority) now bitterly criticize the theologians for callously destroying faith. There seems little left for them to cling on to.

In either case Christian discipleship virtually disappears, unless by good fortune the individual is held by sympathethic pastoral care. Pastoral care involves these skills: eliciting a rugged sort of loyalty to the framework of Christian discipline (e.g. occasional attendance at worship) even though it has gone 'dead'; evoking a reliable commitment to compassionate service of the needy, almost out of a sense of duty; and facilitating serious critical investigation of an appropriate kind centred on the Bible and the tradition. It is normally helpful to incorporate those involved in a group whose members are at roughly the same stage in their growth in faith.

Pastoral care must also support the *positive* aspect of this current phase of spiritual development. This is the exploration of what I call an 'initial vocation'. I use the word 'vocation' to suggest something more than earning a living. (In an era of high unemployment a paid job can by no means be taken for granted.) 'Vocation' includes the sense of an individual freely choosing to do something because it promises to develop distinctive gifts, interests and concerns within himself or herself. A vocation is a task which holds out some hope of contributing to further self-understanding and personal fulfilment. (I assume that the word 'vocation' can apply to a career, a course of study or a voluntary activity – and that there is no preference in the order in which I mention those possibilities.)

I also use the word 'initial' in describing vocation. 'Initial' may be contrasted with 'final'. This implies that in later life changes may take place not only in emotional needs (pp. 160–1) but also in the developing structures of faith (pp. 165–6). These may require a review of or drastic change from the initial vocation. 'Initial' may also be compared with 'complete'. A vocation discovered in the phase of faith development we are currently discussing is necessarily incomplete. It springs from inner promptings which are only partially understood and a self-awareness which cannot properly integrate ultimate concerns. Faith in this phase, we recall, is marked by themes such as these: the absence of any sense of God; aridity and doubt; broken symbols; habits and duties pursued with little commitment of the heart; and questions so puzzling that their outcome must be uncertain. In contrast to the feel of faith, vocation is about pleasure and satisfaction. A vocation is a sense of direction in which energies and potentialities are funnelled along creative channels.

Entry into the complicated developments described in this section can in principle take place at any stage in adult life. In practice there are certain favoured periods. They are the periods of transition between the predictable emotional patterns of adult life described above on pages 159–61, that is to say, roughly at ages 18–21, 29–31, 38–42 and the mid-50s. These are short periods of great turmoil and adjustment, where something like grieving processes accompany considerable losses, self-questioning and reconstruction. The first period mentioned is particularly significant for young people in their late teens who leave home in search of work or higher education. Chaplains to students are familiar with their needs and difficulties; and with the complicated dynamics created in student communities when the profiles I have summarized in phases 4 and 5 coexist.

While transitional stages in adult life may trigger entry into what I have described as *Questions and commitments*, there is no clear boundary to mark its conclusion. The issues outlined here may persist for long periods, up to, say, fifteen or twenty years, stretching to the limit (and usually well beyond it) any residual loyalty to a religious institution which may have been engendered during adolescence. For the same reason, late converts to faith who are still operating within what are basically adolescent faith-structures often fall away from institutional Christian allegiance as they struggle to move beyond the uncritical theological images and rigid church structures in which their religious experience was born. Pastors are called upon to encourage the spirituality of waiting. Not anxious waiting, like air raid wardens in the Second World War awaiting enemy bombers and V-rockets; but waiting in openness, for a gift – a gift which will come when it will come. This is waiting in hope (Ps. 123.2; Rom. 8.25).[7]

6. Integration and openness   This is mature adult faith which is a rare treat, and is unlikely to be apparent until the second half of life. It is, however, the sort of faith I have had in mind to explore throughout this book. Its contours will therefore be familiar. It transcends the limits of intellectualism. It is intrigued by the seemingly endless levels of understanding of human experience in its totality; it accepts the imprecision and limitations of our grasp of reality, but is open to new insights through conversation, story-telling, art and creative action. It integrates maleness and femaleness, conscious and unconscious, activity and passivity, individuality and corporateness and, as we shall see, stretches beyond all 'natural' bonds to embrace humanity. Love and service are given specific shape in a mature vocation. Personal growth continues as the Spirit inspires men and women towards wholeness, holiness and kingdom-life.

Pastoral care: specific and confused

How do we use the patterns sketched in this chapter in pastoral care? *First*, they help pastors to understand how faith is structured at different ages, and give fairly specific guidance for parents and others who work with children and young people. I assume that sensitive pastoral care of pre-adults involves the desire to enter into the world of feeling, emotions and concerns of the child, to address felt needs. The pastor needs to be fairly clear about appropriate and inappropriate expectations. The pastor wants to be relevant to the fears and aspirations of a child, and is helped by a knowledge of the child's age.

Two cautionary themes seem important in practice. On the one hand, while the patterns summarized above describe the *structures* within which children and young people attempt to make sense of life, they do not always prescribe the *content* by which issues are confronted and worked through. This becomes more evident as the child grows older. Thus, in the earliest years (phases 1 and 2), 'content' is not really an appropriate word; what matters are the relationships in which the child is nurtured by women (particularly) and by men. These relationships are, of course, impregnated with values. Adult attitudes to tender loving, to good and bad, to sexuality, to the degree to which the strictures of conscience are to be treated lightly or seriously affect profoundly the developing child's view of people and life. During junior and teenage years (phases 3 and 4), however, content becomes of increasing significance. For example, the pastor will want to tell junior age children stories of historical figures whose lives revealed heroic loyalty to Christian values; but must stimulate a conversation by which the child connects these stories with the range of complexity in relationships experienced at school and home, and among peers.

On the other hand, figure 4 reminds us that the phases of faith development are cumulative. A junior age child whose early years were marred by inadequate parenting will bring the destructive effects of mistrust, insecurity, and (by Christian standards) ill-formed conscience into the struggles appropriate to a child of 7–10 years. Already, therefore, the pastor is confronted with *more* than the agenda suggested by the child's age. He or she is also providing a context of reliable kindness, standards of behaviour and attitudes to people and property which may contradict what has been habitual at home. Without compromising the values and insights of his or her own faith, the pastor must take an appropriate responsibility for exploring with the child the tensions and confusions this may cause in the child. Immediately it becomes apparent that pastoral care of children and young people is impossible without that care extending to their homes, families and schools.

Second, pastoral care of parents bringing up children is assisted by the patterns of development in this chapter. Parents are frequently under inordinate stress. Their deep entanglement with each other and with their children leaves them little freedom to see their confusions, pains and pleasures in perspective, with a measure of detachment. Even at the physical level, parents can sometimes be blind to an emerging handicap or disability in their child. How much more difficult it is to perceive accurately what is happening in relationships! Not only do parents (understandably) fail to notice their children moving into new areas of emotional and spiritual conflict as they grow older; but they, as adults, are discovering so much about themselves and the unresolved issues from their own childhood from the intense involvement with their children, that they cannot disentangle their own needs from those of their offspring.

If that were not enough, further complications arise. Children in a family are at different phases; and husband and wife react differently to different phases in children's development. Mother and father treat their sons and daughters differently. Tensions therefore arise and invite married couples to reassess their own relationship (often in consider-able anguish). A pastor from outside the immediate family circle *may* be able to offer structured understandings of what is likely to be going on, drawing upon the patterns sketched in this chapter.

Third, we must confront the issue of how exceedingly complex it is to exercise pastoral care towards adults. For the overwhelming majority of adults (and this is significantly different from children and young people) there are discon-nections between needs in career development and the emotional and sexual life on the one hand and the struggle for faith and meaning on the other. The pastor usually finds his or her time and energy devoted to the former, with little or no reference to the latter. The ideal of wholeness becomes inaudible and invisible. The pastor feels like a second-rate psychotherapist. Moral and spiritual issues are marginalized. How rare it is to talk about God during pastoral conversation with adults![8]

Where there is a willingness to engage with issues of meaning, purpose, values and faith, adults may be in one of three phases (4, 5 or 6). Each phase needs its own sensitive engagement with the Christian tradition, its own spirituality and its own exploration of the inner life and of prayer. Once again, further complication is introduced from the residue of the earlier, pre-adult phases of life and the way they were negotiated. Usually the best the pastor can hope for is to provide structures of understanding of human development within which men and women can grow in self-awareness.

Fourth, therefore, the patterns listed above may be able to facilitate self-awareness – in the pastor as well as anyone else! Each phase comprises a dramatic tussle between positive and negative factors: trust against mistrust, power against fragility. . . . None of us ever works through these phases with one side in the tussle victorious over the other. We emerge with a negotiated compromise between them: trust in a range of circumstances, but mistrust and fear in other situations, and so forth. A wholesome and happy life is marked by the *predominance* of trust, the willingness to 'have a go' at new things, a capacity to make friends and a secure identity. As we grow older it is further enhanced by the freedom to enquire critically without inhibitions and to become committed, by openness to multiple insights into 'truth' and a growth to mature wisdom. But life never fully excludes mistrust, collapse under guilt and shame, a sense of failing to meet expectations, and a depressed feeling of being a worthless nobody.

What if the balance is the other way round? Or what if one particular stage was negotiated much less successfully than the others? (I write in the most general terms.) There is little value in resenting the harm our parents or others in positions of authority did us, or fatalistically wringing our hands with the words, 'That's the way I am; I can't help it.' Christian hope is the conviction that in discipleship the future is open to change; the past influences us but does not determine tomorrow's possibilities. We can know ourselves better, and begin to identify the feelings and fears which rob life of its joy and which block the inspiration of God's Spirit towards wholeness. We are then free to put ourselves in relationships where we can receive pastoral care which is specific to our perceived needs (Chapter 11). This can happen informally as well as formally. Children and young people can exercise a ministry of pastoral care to adults without being aware that they are doing so. As children and young people grapple with their own, largely age-specific issues in emotional and spiritual development, they open up for adults subjects and experiences which have been distorted, repressed or set solid since they themselves were at a similar phase of life. In one way or another the past is being redeemed.

11 Friendship

I must introduce the next three chapters with a disclaimer similar to those which preface the previous two blocks of material, on the structures of the inner life of the individual (Chapters 7–8) and the transitions in emotional and spiritual concerns during the course of a life-time (Chapters 9–10). The three chapters attempt to explore the networks of relationships, groups, institutions, communities and societies in which our lives are lived. No scheme can begin adequately to represent them; they are infinitely varied. In spite of its limitations, I shall in fact use a three-tier scheme, in order to get some leverage on what might otherwise be an overwhelmingly complex tangle. In this chapter the emphasis will be on one-to-one relationships; Chapter 12 will concentrate on small groups, and Chapter 13 on large groups.

I shall work on a deliberately restricted brief throughout these chapters. I want to discuss what we can see and experience in these different sorts of social structure; what pictures the Christian tradition offers us for imagining new possibilities for living within these structures; and what pastoral actions can assist the movement from current experience to envisaged alternatives.

Friendship

I have touched on the subject of friendship more than once already (pp. 44–6, 136–7). It cannot be overvalued as the normal context of pastoral care. It is strange therefore that the theme of friendship has been given so little attention in Christian reflection. How different was the ancient world of the Greeks and Romans! 'Friendship goes dancing round the world proclaiming to us all to awake to the praises of a happy life' (Epicurus). I suppose that one of the reasons for Christian disinterest in friendship was the claim that *divine* love had been embodied in Jesus, and could become the hall-mark of Christian discipleship. We should therefore dispense with the lesser good of friendship fully to incorporate divine love into our lives. In the light of Jesus' teaching, life and death, Christian reflection on divine love (e.g. I Cor. 13) portrayed a love which is universal in scope, unreserved in its self-giving, totally devoid of self-regard, yet focused with perfect precision on the concrete needs of each human being. Such love makes a neighbour even of an enemy (Matt. 5.38–45; Luke 6.28, 10.25–37).

None of us can escape the sense of absolute claim which divine love makes on our lives. Radical forms of Christian discipleship have always tried to imitate the portrait of Jesus in the Christian imagination and embody divine love. No one intrigues me more than Francis of Assisi.[1] What life could be more austere, challenging and attractive? But I am not a Franciscan. The reason is that a singleminded attempt to become a vehicle of divine love seems always to have been pursued at the expense of human love and emotion.

> Come down, O Love divine,
> Seek thou this soul of mine,
> And visit it with thine own ardour glowing.
>
> O let it [= the holy flame of divine love] freely burn,
> Till earthly passions turn
> To dust and ashes, in its heat consuming.[2]

There is a fundamental conflict here with the thrust of pastoral care and prayer as I have tried to describe them: they honour the fullness of our human faculties, gifts and loves; they seek ways in which human energies, meanings and purposes may be transfused with divine love, not consumed by it. This was Charles Wesley's sure instinct. 'Love divine,' he wrote, *'all loves excelling'*, that is to say, God's love transcends all our natural affections. But divine love filling the heart does not supplant or destroy friendships or any other facet of human existence; it suffuses them. 'Let all my powers thine entrance feel.'[3] God's love inspires friendship to fulfil its potential. Friendship is a relationship bounded by limits; these we shall examine in the next few paragraphs. So friendship can never embody divine love, which is infinite and manifests an 'undistinguishing regard' to all. But friendship can become a symbol of divine love.

We choose our friends. We make friends of those with whom we have a lot in common: shared interests and needs, and similar values in life. A friendship emerges when two people feel good about each other and in each other's company. They discover with each other an instinctive empathy; they feel 'on the same wavelength'.

A friendship is necessarily an exclusive relationship to some degree. I prefer to spend time with my friends rather than with colleagues, acquaintances, distant relatives, and so on. With friends I relax and gladly open myself to a depth and quality of relationship which is not typical of most other encounters. Here is a potential hazard in friendship: it can become a clique which is rigidly exclusive. Friends can be 'as thick as thieves'. It is the divine love which keeps friendship open to others to an appropriate degree; it questions any desire to cold-shoulder a neighbour in the name of friendship.

Friends choose each other. Friendship is a relationship of mutuality, of giving and receiving. Pleasure and enjoyment mark the reciprocity between friends. Sometimes the mutual enrichment flows out of the discovery by two people that they are kindred spirits: each affirms the other's attitudes, interests and character. In other friendships the mutual pleasure springs from complementary personalities: each supplies what the other lacks, so that two rather different people are attracted to each other and together make a 'whole' and balanced response to life. Friendship, however, is not ultimately dependent on two people experiencing mutuality every time they meet. A situation may arise where one friend is severely afflicted, a victim of an accident, bereavement, disappointment or attack. He or she is depressed and broken, with nothing to give. The other friend then gives unreservedly, with no thought of receiving, offering constant and costly support. Here, once again, friendship comes to its finest flower under the influence of the divine love.

Friendship is a relationship of warmth and openness which depends on arbitrary circumstances. Why did these two people happen to meet in this particular time and place? What mysterious string of events led to this fortuitous encounter?[4] We also know that as circumstances change, friendships wane or come to an end. There is no simple correlation between proximity and friendship: sometimes, contrary to our expectations, a friendship flourishes when two people see less of each other than at a former time in their lives. But normally we know that a significant change of context (e.g. moving from one neighbourhood or job to another) dislocates friendships. We never find it easy to leave friends. It is the divine love which aches within us with a longing for permanence in friendship ('I promise I'll write'; 'Do call in whenever you're passing; you'll always be welcome').

Friendship is an embodied relationship; it generates naturally a relaxed expression of affection and mutual enjoyment in physical contact. Our upbringing and social norms provide some guidelines for expressing physical intimacy in friendship. The conventions are much more diffuse in male/female friendships than in single sex friendships. This leads to uncertainty and anxiety in male/female friendships, and introduces threat where warmth and happiness ought to be enjoyed. The grounding of friendship in the divine love contributes wisdom and courage to these situations. Friendship between men and women flourishes when the partners to a friendship set their own boundaries for physical intimacy which are appropriate to the truth of their overall contexts. When one or both are married, for example, the manner in which friendship is embodied takes full account of these wider networks of obligation and joyfulness.

Traditionally pastors may have encouraged friends to sort out such complex webs of mutual enrichment with excessive caution ('Outside marriage don't cultivate close friendships with anyone of the opposite sex'). That attitude expresses our fears that in situations of close friendship we shall not be able to contain strong desires within any agreed boundaries, however rational and wise they may be. In contrast, God's love encourages adventures in friendship in which the relationship flourishes because *some* boundaries to affection and intimacy have been mutually agreed. The Spirit strengthens our capacity to observe these boundaries until they are freely and truthfully renegotiated.[5] This is what the biblical tradition refers to as a covenantal relationship. The mutual obligations agreed between David and Jonathan provide the classic example (I Sam. 18.3, 20.5–17). A covenant defines for a relationship the space where there 'Is wisdom, safety and delight' (to cite Richard Baxter's words). Covenant is a richer notion than contract: covenants 'have a gratuitous growing edge to them that nourishes rather than limits relationships'.[6]

Friendship and marriage

Companionate marriage in contemporary Western society is a relationship of friendship, with distinctive features. I recognize that in modern society there are echoes of different understandings of marriage; in some areas and social classes these historical alternatives remain dominant. But companionate marriage is of increasing significance. Its profile is described by four inter-related themes.

First, a marriage is a relationship of mutual love and friendship which each partner enters voluntarily and knowingly. In marriage two free adults respect and affirm each other's independence and unique individuality. Mutual enjoyment, reciprocity and mutual enrichment have to be experienced and tested as a pre-condition for marriage. *Second*, marriage incorporates an intention by both partners that their relationship shall be permanent. We have already noticed the difficulty of intending permanence in a friendship as circumstances change. Two elements in Christian marriage strengthen this intention, whose deepest source is the love of God. On the one hand is the making of vows 'before God and this company': 'When we make a vow we determine in our better moments what will strengthen our wills in our worst moments' (C. S. Rodd). On the other hand is the faithfulness of God into which we abandon, in faith, our noblest ideals and highest aspirations. Even so, such is the gap between intention and achievement in all human action that it becomes inevitable that many marriages based on friendship will fail, and all will have periods of severe strain. (I realize that many other factors affect the permanence and stability of marriage in today's society; I am concentrating here on the dynamics of the fundamental relationship at the heart of modern marriage.)

Third, in a marriage the partners in principle set no limits in advance to what may be shared between them. Sexual intimacy and intercourse represent and deepen this intention, and constantly startle us with the rapturous pleasure of uninhibited union. Outside sex, and in spite of its rich encouragement of total sharing, we find unlimited openness a frightening and impossible ideal. Our sharing is conditional. There is so much of ourselves of which we know little or nothing. Those deep forces, desires and concerns of the heart of which we are aware we guard jealously because we are anxious about what might happen if we were to let go, and what advantage even our marriage partner might take of us, to our hurt, if we made ourselves so vulnerable. There is, anyway, so much pain and suffering, guilt and shame, locked inside us that we resist all attempts to re-live it. These fears, which are conscious and unconscious, hold married partners at a distance from each other and generate conspiracies of silence, hurts, conflicts and jealousies. Is the intention of unlimited sharing therefore a fantasy; or simply a coded message for sexual explorations free of all imaginable constraints? It is certainly the case that many marriages negotiate a compromise where there are 'no go' areas and unmentionable subjects. They may be stable and good enough marriages.

In the Christian view, however, the possibilities of marriage are always open in the direction of greater sharing. This understanding is built on the idea of a marriage which is 'in God'. A marriage in God is one in which the partners are serious in their independent struggles to make sense of their lives in conversation with the Christian tradition; and to offer to each other pastoral care as spiritual counsel (see Chapter 8, especially pp. 115–18). The crucial factors for marriage in this mutually assisted journey towards God are the following: a willingness to face each other's pain and suffering, and to deepen those realities to the point where they can be uninhibitedly shared (usually accompanied by much crying); and a capacity for mutual forgiveness, not once but time without number (Matt. 18.22). When the God in one partner recognizes the God in the other partner, a depth of sharing becomes possible which transcends all normal expectations. It is perhaps worth emphasizing here that openness and sharing within a marriage in God need each partner to enjoy solitariness and activities outside the marriage relationship as well as for both to share intimate togetherness.

But let there be spaces in your togetherness.
And let the winds of heaven dance between you.

Sing and dance together and be joyous, but let each one of
   you be alone,
Even as the strings of a lute are alone though they quiver
   with the same music.[7]

A *fourth* distinctive feature which may apply to many marriages is this: the partners freely agree to cooperate in seeking the procreation and upbringing of children. This is not always appropriate, for example, when two elderly people marry each other. Similarly, if two young people marry and together choose not to become parents, this in no way invalidates marriage for what it truly is: a friendship of a particular kind where husband and wife commit themselves in the love of God to a life-long union in body, mind and spirit, within which relationship and by the help of God their love for each other may grow and deepen and find fulfilment in the wholeness of their life together, in mutual companionship, helpfulness and care.[8] On the other hand, marriage is the appropriate primary context for the nurture of children and young people (Chapter 10).

Pastoral care and friendship

I wish to draw out from the previous sections of this chapter the following themes:

> Marriage illuminates most fully what friendship is, though there are some features of marriage which do not apply to other friendships.

> Friendship and marriage are the *normal* contexts of pastoral care; through them the love of God can flow to make all things new and whole. This explains how every Christian person is caught up in the ministry of pastoral care: we all have friends. It is only ironic that within the Christian tradition we do not always give the highest priority in the use of time and imagination to cultivating and nurturing our natural friendships and our marriages. Conversely, those who trust and love God find within themselves the incentive and power to make friends. 'He wants [= lacks] not friends that hath thy love' (Richard Baxter). This is the root of the church's self-understanding as a community of friends and a communion of saints.

> All other one-to-one contexts of pastoral care are secondary to friendship and marriage. These secondary contexts must be shaped by our insights into friendship if they are to function well. With this in mind we turn now to consider briefly two sorts of one-to-one pastoral relationship which are not included within friendship and marriage.

(a) Neighbourly helping Imagine a situation like the following. David and Barry have little knowledge of each other; they are neither colleagues nor friends. One day Barry's teenage daughter Carol announced that she was pregnant,

refused to name the child's father and declared that she wished to become an unmarried mother. Barry was beside himself with anger and anxiety. This trauma brought David and Barry together. Seven years previously David had been confronted with a similar crisis in his own family. David offered support and understanding to Barry which were born out of a single shared experience. In a loose sense, David had more expertise in dealing with Barry's need than most people. What made possible a genuinely supportive empathy was David's friendliness in his approach to Barry when he was in the depths of shock and confusion. David's help was marked by an accurate memory of his own feelings years before; and by those rich spiritual qualities which result when a painful crisis has been worked through to greater self-knowledge and to a life lived more trustingly, that is, with less defensiveness and denial of pain and more openness to God in the anguish of human life (Chapter 9). Barry was glad to talk things through with David from time to time over the next few months. They went out of their way to meet in the pub most weeks. After that they hardly ever saw each other.

Another example of neighbourly helping is when two people meet to support each other as they simultaneously work through a common pressure, fear or need. Like Linda and Joan, who formed a bond because both had to cope with bringing up pre-school children by themselves for many months: Linda's husband was working abroad for six months, and Joan's husband was a scholar seconded to an overseas university for a year. Outside their shared experience as lonely and uncertain mothers, Linda and Joan had little in common, and friendship as such did not flourish. Five years later they would have been hard pressed to remember each other's names and addresses; but over a short period and in mutual response to a specified shared need, their care of each other was invaluable.

(b) Serving the stranger in need   It would be impossible here not to refer to the parable of the Good Samaritan (Luke 10.25–37). The story expresses perfectly what God's love may

stimulate beyond the confines of friendship, marriage and neighbourly helping. God sometimes calls for a costly care to be focused on an individual whose need confronts us unexpectedly and interrupts our plans. Pastoral care then starts as an act of obedience rather than a warm response evoked by friendliness. The Samaritan offered practical aid at the point of immediate distress; beyond that initial succour, without any thought of recompense or reward, he provided appropriate resources for the deeper and longer term needs of the victim (see pp. 118–32, and Chapter 9). Pastoral care in this context may be called forth by anyone we rub shoulders with in the course of life, but has a special reference to those who are in greatest need. 'Go always, not only to those who want you but to those who want you most'[9] (Ps. 146; Isa. 61.1–4; Luke 4.18– 19; Matt. 25.31–46; James 1.27). Absurdly, God's love inspires a preferential care for an alien who is also an enemy, and cuts through prejudice and fear so as to create a neighbour out of such a needy human being. Here is the infinite value of the Francis's of Christian history: they keep alive in our imagination this dimension of pastoral care and discipleship which demands everything of us. It may be rare and untypical, but its claim cannot be ignored if we would be faithful to Jesus.

Caring for a stranger in need in the sense sketched in Luke 10 is a risky form of discipleship. It is disinterested service offered by the strong to the weak. It is therefore exposed to the hazard of domination of the weak, or of authoritarian attitudes on the part of the strong. In the Christian tradition two themes have persistently challenged this profound danger. The first is a demand from God for radical humility on the part of anyone who would pretend to care for his or her neighbour. The person who practises pastoral care of the needy stranger must be as a servant or menial slave, kneeling deferentially, gently and diffidently alongside the injured and needy (Mark 10.41–5; Luke 18.9–14, 22.24–7; and supremely John 13.1–17.) Such spiritual maturity is a rare flower, not because God's Spirit in us is impotent or reluctant, but because our inner insecurity, brokenness, anxiety and selfishness are so slow to mend into wholeness and holiness. We want heroically to serve the world without the cost of inner change towards humility.

In the second place the Christian tradition assists us effectively to care for a stranger in need whom we stumble across by drawing on our experience of friendship. In John 15.13–17, Jesus is the strong one, the disciples are the weak. Jesus could have modelled their relationship on a master and his slaves. Instead he chose to infuse their unequal relationship with the essence of friendship. Friendship involves self-disclosure. 'I have called you friends, because I have disclosed to you everything that I heard from my Father.' The only safe way of being in a position of strength over and against the weak is to open one's heart to the weak, to be vulnerable, to share oneself, one's insights, knowledge, experience, strengths and weaknesses, and one's values, convictions and meanings. By this means we break through the normal self-protectiveness and fear which encourage us to keep the weak at a distance in case they grab what is ours for themselves and rob us of our superior position. In pastoral care, no attitudes on the part of the strong can change the facts of disproportionate need which fix the urgent claim of the other; but by offering himself or herself as a friend, the carer can prevent any help offered leading to the recipient becoming unhealthily dependent on the pastor, as a slave is beholden to a master.

It stands to reason that the relationship between a pastor and a stranger in dire distress cannot be a friendship in the full and normal sense. What the pastor is initiating is an asymmetric or skewed friendship. This is not just a condescending kindness towards the needy. It is an authentic imaginative leap into the feelings of the needy, as it were from a position alongside rather than above (Ezek. 3.15; Rom. 12.15). It is not, however, an attempt at total identification. What is opened up is the freedom for the pastor to receive as well as to give within the helping relationship.

Within this context of Christian caring for a neighbour, it is important to reflect further on the connection between pastoral care and the helping professions in modern society (see before pp. 5, 82–3):

(*i*) Professional helping roles do not provide the norm of one-to-one pastoral care relationships. Counselling and psychotherapy in particular may have become a seductive mode for middle-class Christians and particularly for many ordained ministers, whose status and role in society are imprecise; but that must not negate Christian experience and wisdom, which finds the norm in friendship and marriage.

(*ii*) The helping professions are not explicitly based within the Christian tradition of values, meaning and purpose for human being or Christian understandings of God. In a secular society it is inappropriate that they should be. It would be wrong to assume, however, that the helping professions contradict the values of Christian pastoral care. Some probably do, but the historic and widely established caring professions do not. God's love is not confined to individuals and groups who explicitly proclaim Christ.

Certainly pastoral care has much to learn from the experience of the helping professions, in terms of both theory and practice. For example: basic attitudes to people, definition of needs, strategies of care, contexts and limits set to caring relationships, codes of practice, confidentiality, and training, support and monitoring for helpers. C. Sandford and W. Beardsley set out much valuable material in *Making Relationships Work* (1986).

(*iii*) An appropriate relationship between pastoral care and the helping professions can be summarized under two headings: critical dialogue; and critical collaboration (accompanied by mutual trust and respect).

One example of critical dialogue between pastoral care and the helping professions concerns the nature of the helper's relationship with an individual in need. Often the professions use language which underlines a proper measure of detachment: a counsellor has a client or patient. I have stressed that pastoral care flourishes in friendship, even if occasionally a friendship has to be lop-sided. This debate actually takes place within the professions themselves. R. F. Hobson, for example, in *Forms of Feeling* (1985), argues the case for infusing professional relationships with friendship.

Now some remarks on 'critical collaboration'. I am not of the opinion that every time pastoral care focuses on a specific need, the pastor should refer the person concerned to a specialized counselling agency. Not every marriage in difficulty requires the skills of the Marriage Guidance Council. There is a mass of informal accumulated wisdom in the Christian community about stress and breakdown in marriage. It is not inappropriate normally to draw on this, to complement the overstretched resources of counselling agencies. Moreover, Christian pastoral care can sometimes operate in social classes for which counselling seems an alien, middle-class luxury.

Sometimes it is wise, indeed necessary, to encourage an individual with a severe emotional problem to seek specialized professional help. When this happens, it is crucial to confirm that pastoral care will continue alongside professional help. No situation can arise in which professional attention to one issue (e.g. drug addiction) cuts a person off from the overarching love of God, which seeks the freedom and wholeness of the total personality in its matrix of wider relationships and obligations. This is what continuing pastoral care represents and attempts to enact.

Making a judgment about whether or not a person in need should be encouraged to seek professional help is an exceedingly difficult thing to do. Pastors veer between two extremes: not believing enough in the validity and effectiveness of Christian pastoral care: and overestimating their capacity to cope in a creative way when involved beyond their depth with, for example, psychological illness. Better judgments would be assured if pastoral care were seen essentially as a collaborative ministry in the church. Within the Christian community, experienced pastors and helping professionals who are Christians can advise and support those who care informally and those with limited experience. This consultative and supervisory aspect of pastoral care needs urgent attention and improvement.

One particular difficulty in making a judgment about referrals to a professional is the (largely unexamined) assumptions we all carry of what is normal and what is destructively abnormal in psychological and spiritual terms. If we measure others against an image of an 'ideal' human being, we shall quickly fall into the fantasy that everyone we meet has a need which we can identify and help with. By and large it is better not to structure our pastoral care in terms of an assessment of others' needs and difficulties (Matt. 7.1–5), except in certain limited situations. Examples of such exceptional situations are these: when the other person initiates a conversation about their own perceived needs or fears; when the other person is obviously prevented from achieving what seems a reasonable ambition (e.g. an engaged woman who has a marked distaste for physical intimacy with her fiancé); or when the other person clearly disrupts or destroys what he or she claims to cherish. Normally a pastor accepts people as they are, however unlike himself or herself, and seeks to fulfil the aims of pastoral care (Chapter 6) positively: he or she builds on the other person's strengths, concerns, interests, struggles and self-disclosure. Pitying the handicapped for their handicaps is usually patronizing and degrading; it is a failure to see the person whole and to discern gifts, insights and spiritual achievements which may transcend those which are typical in the non-handicapped.[10]

Referrals can work both ways. Helping professionals – if they would consider referring a client/patient in any circumstances to a Christian pastor, which is rare – instinctively contact the member of the Christian community most like themselves, namely the ordained minister. There is no need for the minister to consider a referral as his or her exclusive task. Pastoral care is the cooperative work of all Christians, individually and corporately. It is important also to be alert to the terms on which professional helpers sometimes make their referrals: they may conceive of ordained ministers as 'religious specialists', concerned only with a narrow segment of human experience (e.g. guilt or exorcism of evil spirits). In fact pastoral care imaginatively and lovingly invites men and women to an experience of faith as a renewal in God of the totality of their existence and its meaning.

(*iv*) Helping professionals can profit from pastoral care as much as everyone else. Many helping professions provide resources and disciplines for the support, assessment and development of their members within the profession. Pastoral care complements this with its distinctive aims and agenda within a network of friends and family; and grounds all life in the love of God. The following quotation refers explicitly to a lawyer; it can, I believe, apply to all helping professionals. 'In this profession, as in any other, a man needs a line of retreat from the demands which are made on him. If he doesn't find it at home, then he may attempt either an impossible dedication or a dangerous identification with his client.'[11] I hope that I and all my fellow ordained ministers will take that to heart. It is a false guilt which in the name of human need inhibits a pastor enjoying time spent in the company of friends and spouse.

The dynamics of pastoral relationships

It would be ludicrous to suppose that in a few brief paragraphs the dynamics of interpersonal relationship can be summarized adequately. I wish only to touch on a few prominent features which may be experienced in all contexts of one-to-one pastoral care: marriage, friendship, neighbourly helping on the basis of an identifiable shared experience, and obedient, skilled service of a stranger in distress. There is a common thread in the matters I shall broach, which can be put in this way. Interpersonal relationships take seriously the immediate agenda which they throw up; they flourish when the partners to the relationship recognize that more items may be striving to get on the agenda than is at first apparent. Some books make this distinction in terms of a 'presenting' issue and the 'real' issue. This seems to me an unhelpful way of putting things because it implies that the 'presenting' issue is not real, and may be readily dismissed as trivial or distracting. The immediate and obvious is real, does matter and should be treated seriously. This does not negate the insight that relationships are hardly ever simple; there always seem to be layer upon layer of concerns, discoveries and problems which emerge in time. They also are important.

Noticing All relationships begin and develop by noticing shapes, movements and gestures made by another body. Visual impressions provoke inside us interest or boredom, sexual arousal, distaste, fear, acceptance or annoyance. The face and eyes in particular seem to be laden with signals about the other person. But as my eyes turn towards the face of another, I know that his or her eyes are turning towards my face and are noticing all sorts of things about me from my physical appearance. The result is considerable caution about the degree of initial eye-to-eye contact or face-to-face encounter. A fixed stare is inappropriate; it is a sign of emotional disturbance or deprivation. Instead we look and look away, or drop our eyes, in case we see too much too soon (or are seen into too deeply too soon). We devise adult ways of behaving like shy children, who are infinitely curious but need to structure their discovery into manageable doses by peeping – from behind a chair or mother's skirt, or through the cracks of the fingers placed across the eyes. In one way or another we acknowledge that each meeting with another individual is a voyage of gradual discovery, not a blindingly clear revelation. This remains true, however familiar we are with each other. We make an initial observation, or we notice a striking feature; after that we must amplify in stages our awareness of that individual as a person. We journey inwards (Chapter 8), but in the clear knowledge that the other person is simultaneously journeying into us (though maybe at a different rate and via a different route).

As the relationship develops, inner lives become open to each other to some degree or other. It is in the nature of all personal relationships that to some extent the physical boundaries around each individual become, as it were, pervious. Some of the emotions and desires being triggered off by the personal encounter seem to escape from one body and enter the other. So, as I attend to the emotions and desires aroused in me, what am I noticing? A strange mixture: my own desires and emotions stimulated by the other person and by what is being said or done; and the strong emotional responses and desires stirred up inside the other person and transmitted to me. Emotions and desires, from whichever centre of personal being, are expressive of yet more complex entities: the unconscious mind. It is therefore no easy matter to disentangle emotions and desires, and reflect on their meaning and significance. Yet their power is unmistakeable and unavoidable. It is worth the effort of trying to make allowance, so far as possible, for one's own emotions and desires. This is done by growing reflectively in self-knowledge.

'I remember occasions from the past a bit like this one; I have a rough knowledge of how I tend to react in such circumstances. My first guess is that any unexpected emotions or desires, or emotions and desires of surprising strength, are what have been transposed into me by the other person. I can therefore grasp in a very rough and ready way something of the inner response the other person is making to me and to our relationship, here and now, by paying attention to what is going on inside *me*. I can sense the other person's intense anger, jealousy, disinterest, sexual craving or whatever.'

It is important to stress how approximate and vague such guesses are. But at least they can become an indicator of what might be going on, and can be explored in open conversation.

In a similar way, with practice, developing self-awareness and a constantly critical approach to such tentative insights, a pastor can become sensitive also to the whole realm of feeling in another person, which is empathy (Chapter 3). And by prayerful attention human beings can begin to notice in one another what is in the other's heart, the ultimate meaning, values and purposes at the root of that person's life.

Receiving and rejecting   I mentioned in the previous section that the unconscious mind always plays its part in human interactions. There are two particular ways in which we normally describe some of the larger consquences of that phenomenon. They are projection and transference.

A projection happens when something in a person's unconscious is (unconsciously) taken out of the hidden recesses of the mind and is focused on the other person in a relationship. This 'something' has been locked away in the unconscious because it is unacceptable to the conscious mind: it may be morally revolting, or emotionally destructive, or a memory of a past experience repressed because its threat to a person's self-image is 'mind-blowing'. It is an alien part of the personality. If it is projected on to another person it appears to belong to that other person, who now seems to be a terrifying ogre. Such projections happen easily when an authentic feature of the other person resembles an aspect of what has been repressed. A woman who in childhood was 'frightened to death' by a violent father or abused sexually by her father may project a repressed anguish about her parent on to any male who is given a legitimate position of authority in her life. She reacts to male authorities as if they were her father of old, not recognizing that her feelings bear no relation to the facts of how authority is now being exercised over her.

Projections also happen easily when the other person in the relationship has a relatively weak personality, ready to be 'filled out' by images drenched in strong emotions. A man who unconsciously has a fairly masculine self-image (all Yang and no Yin – see p. 105) readily imagines that he is falling in love with every woman he meets who has a fairly bland personality. One way of describing this phenomenon is to say that the feminine/Yin facet of his own personality has been thoroughly denied and pushed into the unconscious; it is projected on the woman, who becomes in his eyes an ideal of womanhood – sexually attractive, tender, submissive, a perfect complement to himself.

When projections happen they evoke strong emotional reactions in both partners to the relationship, however much the facts of the case belie the emotional tone. The only hope of conscious and rational progress is for the person projecting something unconscious on to the other person to become aware that the projection in reality belongs inside himself or herself. He or she must 'own' what is alien as part of himself or herself. A pastor receiving projections may be able to notice what is happening and assist the other person to begin a process of self-awareness.

A transference is to do with unfulfilled needs. During childhood and adolescence, for example, a person needs good parenting, but never enjoys the attention of a perfect parent. We all grow up into adulthood carrying inside us feelings of resentment about the gap between an ideal parent and our real parents. We transfer to people we meet who vaguely match a parental role our unfulfilled need of a perfect father or mother. In relation to them we behave in many respects, especially emotionally, as children, rather than as fellow adults. We want them to take responsibility for our lives, to guide and protect us, to reassure and comfort us, to feed us and make us well. Some social roles are particularly susceptible to transferences of this kind. Female nurses, for example, are regularly idolized as angels of light, perfect mothers beyond all criticism, by hospital patients. Male ordained ministers similarly become in the imaginations of many people ideal fathers.

It is a seductive temptation to collude with such transferences. It bolsters morale, makes one feel needed and important, and very powerful. It seems to underpin the notion that a helper should help and *can* help the weak and needy of this world. Colluding with transferences, however, is to lock oneself and the other person in a world of illusion. No adult relationship can thrive on illusion and fantasy. Noticing what is going on, helping another person to see what is going on, and acknowledging that those who receive transferences are themselves tempted to transfer on to the other person in the relationship their own unfulfilled needs (counter-transferences), are the first stages in facing reality. Reality includes relating to another person with accurate judgments about one's own strengths and weaknesses and the other person's beauties and blots, successes and failures.

Conflict Reality also includes struggling in a relationship towards common understandings and common action (Chapters 1–2). This involves working with differences. Different values, ideals and intentions in a relationship produce conflict. So, of course, do the irrational factors which intervene in relationships and which the previous paragraphs have highlighted. A pastor, however, is bound to be particularly involved in conflicts which spring from collisions of moral values. This is one of the many situations where the intimate connection between pastoral care and ethics becomes evident. Most of us most of the time espouse particular causes or courses of action on the basis of a mixture of motives. Obedience to God and the pursuit of goodness and justice are intermingled with self-interest, the maintenance of the interests of our social class and the bolstering of personal prestige and power. There is no such thing as purity of heart; though striving for that ideal by reflection, repentance and faith is one of the marks of the disciples of Jesus.

Pastoral care attempts to create a context within which critical moral reflection and repentance can fruitfully take place. The marks of this context are forgiveness and acceptance. These are not actions which condone sin. They are creative initiatives which re-establish broken relationships, break the spiral of mounting conflict and mutual hurt, and provide new conditions within which moral issues can be discussed. Acceptance and forgiveness precede confession. Nothing has more movingly mediated to me this theme of pastoral care than these famous words of Paul Tillich:

> Grace strikes us when we are in great pain and restlessness. It strikes us when we walk through the dark valley of a meaningless and empty life. It strikes us when we feel that our separation is deeper than usual, because we have violated another life, a life which we loved, or from which we were estranged. It strikes us when our disgust for our own being, our indifference, our weakness, our hostility, and our lack of direction and composure have become intolerable to us. It strikes us when, year after year, the

longed-for perfection of life does not appear, when the old compulsions reign within us as they have for decades, when despair destroys all joy and courage. Sometimes at that moment a wave of light breaks into our darkness, and it is as though a voice were saying: 'You are accepted. *You are accepted*, accepted by that which is greater than you, and the name of which you do not know. Do not ask for the name now; perhaps you will find it later. Do not try to do anything now; perhaps later you will do much. Do not seek for anything; do not perform anything; do not intend anything. *Simply accept the fact that you are accepted!'*[12]

Because all our behaviour is affected by emotional needs, unconscious longings and mixed motives, the situations in which the pastor is called on to change the context towards acceptance and forgiveness are exceedingly fraught. The pastor does not operate in a detached way. He or she has to act while immersed in tumultuous conflicts which are more likely to bring out the basest rather than the noblest facets of his or her character. Here is one example, which I shall leave open-ended. I do this to encourage the reader to enter imaginatively into the situation (of Harry) and to try to envisage the cost of pastoral care.

Harry Smith is head of a large comprehensive secondary school. He is much respected as a leader and teacher, and as a human being of integrity and fairness. This respect has been won not only in school, among staff and pupils, but also in the wider community. Over a period of time Mr Smith found the high principles on which he runs the school being constantly besmirched: the boys' lavatories were being vandalized in a most objectionable way. Slogans and pictures of a perverted and pornographic nature were being daubed over the walls. The culprit could not be caught. Dire punishments were threatened before the whole school. But they had no deterring effect. At last, however, the case was solved. The culprit was caught in the act, and hauled before the headmaster. It was Harry Smith's own son, Robert. 'You have undermined my authority and demeaned my good name.' To make matters worse, Robert remained defiant and impenitent. What should be done? Harry Smith had no doubt where his duty lay. Setting aside his fatherly emotions, he administered to Robert the promised punishment: a severe caning and suspension from the school.

At home that night, what was Harry to do? He wanted to be his son's father, to be reconciled, to arrest the inevitable drift into violence and resentment. But how had he and Robert got into this state of affairs? What did it all mean? What could now ever put things right?

12 Fellowship

'No man is an island entire unto himself' (John Donne). I hope
the reader has recognized this theme beating rhythmically
throughout the pages of this book. To find ourselves and to
know God, we need communication and relationships with
others. It would not be too much of an exaggeration to claim
that during the twentieth century pastoral care has concentrated its concern for human growth through relationships
almost exclusively on one-to-one relationships (Chapter 11).
This has been encouraged by the rampant individualism of
Western European society and by the extraordinary influence
of psycho-analysis and counselling on Christian pastoral
practice. In some quarters, indeed, the phrase 'pastoral care' is
irredeemably locked into one-to-one relationships; other categories have to be invented to highlight more corporate
dimensions of Christian witness and service. This seems to me
to be an unhelpful move because in our experience there are
no rigid distinctions between one-to-one relationships and
our life in small groups, institutions and large communities.
The different levels of belonging and personal significance
that we find in relationships of increasing size and complexity
glide into one another. So I would prefer to break the mould
which imprisons our understanding of pastoral care in one-to-
one relationships. Pastoral care and pastoral theology have as
much to do with the dynamics of groups, sociology, politics,
social policy and social ethics as with the interactions of two
people meeting face to face.

In fact I want to take this theme one stage further. The
corporate groupings to which we belong are the *primary*

influences in our personal formation. We carry around inside us wherever we go images of our family structures and traditions, our social class and culture. They influence one-to-one relationships far more profoundly than interpersonal encounters affect our life in groups. In every one-to-one relationship, therefore, there is a hidden meeting between two sets of family traditions, social custom and class culture.

The family of our upbringing is the small group which influences us most throughout our lives. A family is a complex system of roles, rules, traditions and inter-relationships. The ways in which authority was exercised in our family of origin, the roles given to father and mother, the relationship between individual freedom and family loyalty, the weight given to ritual and unexamined habit, the significance attributed to moral and social values, the isolation or the openness of the nuclear family in respect of its neighbours and the 'extended' family: these stay with us. They may be modified and questioned by experience in later life, but they are not erased.

Like every other living system, when looked at as a whole a family functions to minimize change and to maintain equilibrium. So when one of the family members is changing role (e.g. an only child becomes one of two children when a brother or sister is born), other parts of the system unconsciously compensate so that the family as a whole retains its stability. When a family is under stress it regularly designates one of its members to be the representative sick person or the scapegoat. By this means, physical and emotional disturbances are sloughed off on to one (usually fairly willing) family member; other members can carry on their family life, so it appears, much as they have always done, and can heap blame, difficulties, frustrations and anger on to the 'black sheep'. Scapegoating is an unconscious device to avoid perceiving the family for what it truly is: a family is an interconnected system of individuals who in different ways *share* responsibilities for a common life. Only when that insight is grasped are members of a family, individually and together, able to work at what is always threatening and distasteful:

change, conflict and the pervasive sense of evil and of things never quite working out as we might hope.

When we meet an individual outside his or her family setting we have little idea of how that person performs roles and sees himself or herself within the family. The family scapegoat is often a paragon of virtue at school or work. It is only when the family assembles that apparently hidden factors reveal themselves. This experience provides the fundamental criticism of one-to-one pastoral care and counselling on marriage and family matters when it is performed outside the family system.

I am not, however, going to draw the conclusion that pastoral care should always be located in the home. Much of it can usefully be centred there, and visiting people in their family settings is a theme to be re-emphasized in the church's ministry. Some secular professionals (e.g. family therapists) are also discovering the importance of the home location. But however influential families are in our struggle for personal self-knowledge and meaning in life, they are but one of a number of formative groups to which we belong. Each of us is conscious of having an identity which is larger than that which our family (even at its best) makes possible. In non-family groups, each of us is literally a different person from the person we are at home. Different groups (work, tennis club, church, etc.) illuminate and set free our different 'selves'. The real 'me' seems to be a community of selves, and self-discovery and the richness of my life are enhanced by finding a sense of significance and belonging in several quite different groups. I need to be part of a network of inter-locked small group systems if I am to be whole and free. If the family makes disproportionate or exclusive claims as *the* experience of small-scale community, it feels claustrophobic and imprisoning.

Small groups (by which I mean groups of not more than twelve members) have time and again demonstrated their ability to renew not only individual well-being but also larger societies.[1] This may seem a rather puzzling statement in the light of the preceding paragraphs about families, which have noted some of the limitations of small groups. Before this chapter is finished, more of the complexities and difficulties of small groups will have been touched on! Yet experience shows that small groups can be creative. This is the heart of the matter as far as pastoral care in relation to groups is concerned. Pastoral care does not naively assume that groups are an inherently good thing, but works towards an awareness of how groups behave and how we feel and act in groups. Out of this come realistic expectations, a knowledge of the limits of what groups can achieve, but also a sensitivity to flashes of kingdom-life which emerge as corporate tasks are completed. Faith holds to this hope in spite of sin and evil working to distort and undermine everything (Matt. 18.19–20).

The purposes of groups

Helping a group to define its purpose and aims is a major facet of pastoral care in relation to groups. A group with an uncertain or confused purpose finds it very difficult to define sensible jobs to do or programmes to follow, and causes endless frustration and acrimony among its members. It is then likely to disintegrate, leaving behind bitter memories. Even groups like families, whose structures and functions are deeply entrenched in a culture, are helped by understanding their purposes. A family, for example, exists to give form and stability to the processes of procreation and primary nurture of the next generation; to incorporate all its members critically and creatively into the wider society in which it is set; and to maximize the growth towards autonomy and fulfilment of each of its members. Families remain true to themselves if this last mentioned purpose is tackled in such a way that both individual and corporate responsibilities remain on the agenda (i.e. people grow up in families neither selfishly individualistic nor forever sacrificing private needs and gifts to the demands of the family).

Most small groups are, compared with families, short-term and fairly *ad hoc* constellations of individuals. Conscious definition of purposes needs to be more explicit. Experience suggests it is helpful either for a group to form around a clear purpose announced in advance, or for a group to meet on an open basis and to negotiate together a purpose for themselves. Groups which fail to attend to their purpose in meeting are prey to the strong personality who imposes his or her will or needs upon the remaining group members.

There is a wide range of purposes appropriate to small groups, from which each group needs to choose and define its own goal. Groups may be formed to achieve specific practical tasks (e.g. organize a fete, write a policy report or raise money for a project); they may have an educational purpose; they may exist to facilitate an interest or hobby; or their purpose may come under the general heading of 'nurture' (e.g. therapy groups, mutual support groups or groups designed to initiate conversation between antagonistic or mutually suspicious factions).

I am taking it for granted that pastoral care in relation to small groups is not confined to church-based groups. The vision of God's kingdom includes the renewal of all that exists in human society and, indeed, the whole created order. This, however, should not blind us to the truth that church-based groups will sometimes take on a specific form and purpose which reflect Christian understandings. Church-based groups may be formed with the sole purpose of worship or prayer; and educational groups may take the form of Bible-study groups. Particular attention needs to be given to Christian nurture groups, or discipleship groups, whose purpose may be defined by the understandings of pastoral care and pastoral theology expounded in the chapters of this book. They will be groups whose programmes will provide opportunities for their members to explore the meaning of their lives in a wide spectrum of activities (discussion of concerns, challenges and values; creative self-expression; appreciation of art; exploring history and science; digging into the Christian tradition; prayer and silence). Members' care for one another in a nurture group and their action in church and community will be shaped by psychological and sociological understandings as well as Christian insights (Chapters 7–14).

The structure of a group is best determined by the purpose for which the group exists. The group structure comprises items such as the following: size, frequency of meeting, layout of the group, style of leadership and the life-span of the group (i.e. the period of time over which the group will exist). Accumulated experience and rules of thumb govern the structures which most efficiently serve particular purposes. For example:

(*a*) A group of two or three talking intensively for five minutes is an effective way of releasing all sorts of interests, insights, fears and agenda items connected with a precisely defined theme, which can then be taken up and worked on by a larger group. (This is often called a 'buzz' group.)

(*b*) A group of four (but never five!) can efficiently create a report for a larger committee or consultative body, provided one of the four is appointed convenor and the four have equal status within the larger community. (This would not work, for instance, if the four were two staff and two students from an educational institution.)

(*c*) A group of eight to ten meeting fortnightly for two hours over three years, in a relaxed context and more or less circular configuration, is ideal for a Christian nurture group; leadership may reside in one person, or may be shared between two, or may circulate in an agreed way.

Leadership

The degree to which small groups flourish or flounder is related to the quality of leadership. A great deal of the work of pastoral care of small groups is therefore rightly devoted to leadership training. The best way of managing leadership training of this sort is within a small group comprising group leaders whose purpose in meeting together is to reflect on their experience as group leaders and to become more aware within the group of how groups function and how people feel and act in small groups.

We shall now hint at some of the themes which need to be examined expansively within a group like the one described above, in the light of the members' experience and feelings.

(a) Purpose and structures   The preceding section has emphasized how important it is for a leader to be aware of a group's purpose, or to help a group to define a purpose; and to create structures most appropriate to its explicit purpose. In fact, all the members of a group need to be clear about the group's purpose and to own for themselves the group's aims and objectives. The primary task of a leader is to encourage the formation of a common mind about and a common responsibility for the group's intentions. From this flows a common loyalty to meeting times and places, and to the tasks which the group must undertake.

(b) Trust, initiative and freedom   No group can function without a measure of trust between the members, and between members and the leader. This is as basic to group life as it is to individual growth and development (Chapters 9–10). A leader must recognize that individuals bring to any group from their personal history widely differing degrees of openness and caution, of security and fear. The group is a new creation at its formation, and in a sense the leader must be to the members as a mother to her new-born child. Time has to be devoted to the cultivation of trust, openness and mutual acceptance between members. The personal qualities of a leader are particularly exposed in this process: is he or she made anxious or afraid by what the group members might think or say? is he or she afraid to reveal his or her own thoughts and feelings, preferring to hide behind a role? is he or she the sort of person who has fixed ideas formed outside the meetings of the group about the group's agenda, timetable and objectives, or does the leader have the confidence that the group members acting together can contribute to and take responsibility for such things?

A wise leader knows that the question of mutual trust between members is bound to be implicitly present in the early meetings of a group whatever may be the explicit agenda. This may make progress slow in pursuit of the group's aim. It is usually worthwhile breaking away from the formal purpose of the group, certainly in the early stages and from time to time in its maturer life, specifically to give more attention to the dilemmas of trust and mistrust, and to build up trust. This can be achieved in a number of straightforward ways: a group shares in a meal together; the leader introduces a space in the group's work to allow members to ventilate their fears and mistrust about where the group is going to and in particular about the leader and his or her motives; the leader makes an opportunity from time to time for members to itemize the gifts, needs, visions and experience which they could contribute to the work of the group and which seem to be overlooked or neglected. In these sorts of ways group members grow in confidence that they can take initiatives within the group and that their distinctive personalities and contributions are being respected and incorporated within the group. Communication flows from trust. The greater the level of trust within a group, the more ready the members will be to give and assimilate information, insights and feelings relevant to the group's purpose, and to work together towards a common aim.

Whenever a group has paused from its formal purpose to build up trust or reflect on levels of mistrust, it is important that the leader delineate clearly when the group is returning to its formal work and that he or she remind the group (in no more than a sentence!) what the task and purpose are.

No small group exists in isolation. It has connections with other, comparable groups or with larger groups and communities. Sometimes the relationship between a small group and a larger community is formal and precise (e.g. a sub-committee which must report back to a larger committee). In all circumstances a leader is responsible for keeping open lines of communication and building trust between the small group and the wider network in which it is set.

(c) Authority   The leader and the group need to be clear about who has given authority to the group to pursue its purpose and, in particular, who has authorized the leader to lead.

Uncertainty in these areas creates deep anxiety. Within a small group, anxiety prevents the group making progress; within the wider network of groups and society, anxiety about the authority of a particular small group and its leader (e.g. a private clique within a congregation) creates fear, suspicion, prejudice and hostility.

The way in which a leader exercises legitimate authority is related to the personal needs, experience and integrity of the leader. Not everyone is emotionally, spiritually and intellectually gifted to lead well. Good leadership is a distinct vocation. Behind these statements lie assumptions about the sorts of groups and the styles of leadership which best enable human beings to grow into freedom and maturity. These hidden values are derived from the Christian tradition. The Bible, for example, is full of material germane to these issues. There is space here to mention only two samples.

First is the notion of fellowship (e.g. Acts 2.42; II Cor. 13.14; Phil. 1.5, 2.1–3; Philemon 6). A fellowship is a whole which is larger than the sum of the constituent individuals. It is more than a conglomeration. It is a living organism (a 'body' in Paul's language in I Cor. 12). Individuals flourish and grow *within* a fellowship as the relationships which connect each individual to every other and to the fellowship as a whole are infused with divine love (I Cor. 13). Love enables participation. Each and every member contributes to the fellowship according to his or her gifts, experience and maturity; and receives from all the other members and from the organism itself (Acts 2.44–8). Fellowship is therefore authentic interdependence. It is characterized by openness, sharing, grateful receiving, cooperation, mutual companionship and reciprocal empowering. Individual and corporate actions are judged by their intention of nurturing the common good of the fellowship. (Biblical examples: the collection of money in the Pauline churches for the poverty-stricken Jerusalem church was to foster fellowship, Rom. 15.26, II Cor. 8.4, 9.13; and the holy communion is a ritual act to celebrate and to deepen the unity of the fellowship, I Cor. 10.16–17). Fellowship is a gift of the Spirit and a foretaste of kingdom-life (Rom. 14.17).

Second, some reflections on leadership and authority.

Issues of *authority and leadership* were inevitably part of the church's experience from the beginning (I Thess. 5.12–13). Leadership is among the relatively small handful of ecclesial ministries given great prominence in the New Testament (Acts 1.15–26; Rom. 10.14–17, 12.6–8, 15.16; I Cor. 12.28–30; Eph. 2.20, 4.11–13; Heb. 13.7, 17). 'There can be no church community without a leader or team of leaders.'

Leadership is given by the spirit. Thus
(*a*) In the Christian view, attention is focused on the personal and spiritual qualities of those with a vocation to lead. Autocracy, authoritarianism, self-seeking and manipulation of other people are unacceptable. Servanthood, modelled on the ministry of Jesus, is basic (Mark 10.42–45; John 13.1–17). Leadership is a *ministry*. In Paul's experience (II Cor. 4.1–12) leadership involved the capacity to enter deeply into another human being's weakness, hurt and confusion, and to speak creatively out of the leader's own vulnerability so that the other person found new life and courage.

(*b*) Leadership cannot be confined to those formally authorized as leaders. Leadership can arise spontaneously or from an unexpected quarter when a situation demands that an initiative be taken (I Cor. 6.5, 12.28, 16.15). Those formally authorized as leaders exercise their oversight by encouraging church members to contribute their gifts and, where appropriate, to take initiatives, and to enable and sustain the gifts of their partners in ministry. They also carry responsibility for the church remaining true to its nature and mission (II Cor. 11.28; Phil. 1.9–11).[2]

In the light of these biblical perspectives, pastoral care in relation to small groups has a special interest in the ways in which authority is exercised. This is a concern which applies to all groups, not just church-based ones. Figure 5 represents three distinct options.

Figure 5

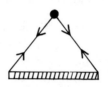

Authoritarian   Representative   Permissive

● Leader

ⅡⅡⅡⅡⅡ Membership

⟶ Direction of ideas,
initiative and decision-making

Authoritarian leadership discourages human growth and fulfilment because it undercuts the values enshrined in themes like fellowship and kingdom; it displaces justice and freedom with oppression and slavery (at the emotional level).[3] Permissive leadership frustrates human growth and fulfilment because it foregoes order in favour of chaos; it makes the group prey to paranoiac forms of informal, unauthorized leadership, unwitting ideological oppression, and hidden agendas projected on to the group by disaffected and inadequate members.

Small groups flourish under representative leadership. A representative leader encourages group members to share in the leadership function, without losing sight of his or her ultimate accountability and responsibility. An interchange between leader and members is encouraged by the leader minimizing his or her 'emotional distance' from the members. Within the representative model, leaders with different personalities can flourish and be true to themselves. Leaders with fairly forceful and extrovert personalities, who like initiating projects, will veer *towards* the authoritarian model, without necessarily becoming the domineering persons who inhibit members' contributions and impose solutions on the group. They are best described as directive leaders. At the other end of the spectrum, leaders who are more introverted, who enjoy seeing quiet and retiring people enabled to blossom and who like operating within agreed procedures and constitutions, will veer *towards* the permissive model; without necessarily becoming merely a figurehead or spokesperson who is unable to contribute to the group's life. They can be described as democratic leaders.

Under stress, directive leaders may become authoritarian, and democratic leaders may opt out of their responsibilities into the permissive mode. Good leadership within the representative model emerges when leaders become self-aware about their leadership style, and explicitly eschew authoritarian and permissive styles.

Within the representative model, different emphases may be appropriate at different phases of a long-term group or for different sorts of group. A directive style may assist the establishment of a new group whose purpose is to grasp and give concrete form to an adventurous vision. (Sometimes a directive leader inspired to act tirelessly to such an end is called 'charismatic' by sociologists.) A democratic style will be much more fruitful as the group settles down to routine tasks or the evolution of long-term structures for a well-established project whose value is widely accepted in the larger society.

(d) Management   Enabling a group to effect change towards agreed targets consistent with an explicit purpose is an art of its own. Too rapid or drastic change provokes anxiety and resistance. Too slow change reduces morale, loosens loyalty and increases restlessness. All change provokes conflict and defensiveness. Every group generates, usually unconsciously, emotional energies which are dedicated to preventing change and therefore undermine the work the group has

consciously set its hand to. The unconscious dimension of a group is as real for the dynamics of a group as the personal unconscious is for the emotional and irrational life of an individual. W. R. Bion first described the three basic forms of unconscious group behaviour, in a book which unfortunately is not always easy to read.[4] His thesis is that a group always has unconscious as well as conscious features which contradict each other; and the prominent form of unconscious assumptions in a group (one of three possibles) can vary from one phase to another of the group's life. Here is a simple, brief description of the three forms through which a group unconscious seeks to frustrate a group's work.

(i) *Dependence* The group behaves emotionally as a class of little children in the presence of a teacher. The eyes of each 'child' are on the teacher, wanting to win the teacher's approval and permission to speak. There is little energy or interest devoted to the 'children' relating to one another. The teacher is perceived as having infinite knowledge and wisdom, an unchallengeable authority and resources to cope with every need and emergency. The children therefore relax into a secure dependence on this god-like provider. The children feel comfortable. They feel that in due time and with the utmost fairness each will be given teacher's undivided attention; then each can make his or her points, raise questions and express needs. He or she will be heard and nourished, because the teacher will respond in language which is ideally suited to his or her child-like level of understanding.

I have described 'dependence' in terms of primary school experience; but it is important to realize that this is only a metaphor. Dependence is a set of unconscious emotional roles adopted by *adults* in a group. Leader and group members, usually without realizing what is happening, collude with a fantasy of this kind. All sorts of unconscious games are played to maintain the fantasy. For example, members will set up what to an outside observer must seem ridiculously simple problems for the leader to solve; in reality any group member is perfectly capable of solving the problem unaided, but within the group it feels as if only the leader can rescue the group from a hideously confusing crisis. The leader in turn feels needed, admired, paternal and strong as he or she, effortlessly and with great panache, produces the solution which sets the mind of the group at rest. The leader is a genius, or a magician, or God himself! The leader is not like any other group member. The leader and the group must symbolize this vast difference of knowledge, experience and power. The ways in which this happens in a dependent group are infinitely various: the leader can be separated from the group in a special chair, or behind a table, for example; or the leader may dress to look different from the group members.

I hope my descriptions will suggest the sorts of group which are particularly prone to unconscious dependence on a heroic leader. They are adult education groups and religious groups (especially those led by someone who in the religious consciousness is 'set apart', namely an ordained minister). But dependence can become a feature of any group's life. Dependence stops the group working effectively because it shuts the group off from its tasks and its involvement with the messy and complex environment in which in reality it is set. Dependence soaks up group energy into a quest for security, knowledge poured out 'from on high', and relief from feelings of guilt and inadequacy. Dependence holds adults in childish emotional states.

The strong and competent leader is often the one who notices what is happening in a dependent group and wishes to explode the fantasy. Ironically, an initiative by the leader usually reinforces the emotional *status quo*. A leader who privately chooses not to 'play the role' of omnipotence and omnicompetence is perceived by the group as a *mysterious* god, who cannot be approached directly; or the leader is felt to be unwell, perhaps even a little unbalanced (the eccentric parson or the dotty professor?). In the former case, the group maintains its dependent mode, in spite of the leader's intentions, by unconsciously electing one of its members to mediate between themselves and their puzzling deity who is shrouded in mystery; the mediator alone now puts group members' questions and needs to the leader, and alone relays replies or interprets the leader's enigmatic mind. In the latter case, the group familiarly chooses one of its members (often the one who is most obviously inadequate, ill or weak) to be a new leader who is deemed to be worthy of deference, support, flattery and obedience. Presumably the unconscious hope is that relieving the 'true' guru of leadership will hasten his or her recovery and underline in his or her mind what is already well-established among group members, namely the indispensability of the true leader for the group's well-being.

(ii) *Fight/flight* The group behaves emotionally like a be-leaguered fighting unit facing an enemy with far greater forces and firepower which is more or less surrounding them. The leader perceives himself or herself as the commanding officer facing impossible odds. Morale and discipline must be maintained among the troops, or else the group will disintegrate in terror. So pictures are painted of the group's cause being unquestionably righteous, while everyone and everything outside the group are identified as an evil threat and abused with slogans. The leader calls the troops to self-sacrificial loyalty: injuries and death (i.e. people leaving the group) are the inevitable and noble cost of fighting for what is right; and there must be no free thinking or disaffection among the troops to distract from singleminded obedience to the commander's orders. The leader alone holds the group's life and future in his or her hands. The leader will decide when to stand and fight, and when to flee for safety to a new stronghold or a more easily defended position.

Once again, an emotional fantasy of this kind deflects a group from working effectively at its tasks. Instead of being devoted to the rational pursuit of sophisticated goals, energy is used up ventilating group members' anger, aggression and jealousy, which are projected on to the wicked world outside the group. A simplistic black-and-white picture of 'us' (the good) and 'them' (the bad) does not relate to the complex ambiguities of individual members' lives or the mish-mash of commitment and reticence, good and evil, freedom and imprisonment, which is within the group and in its environment. Working towards goals is not in reality fighting a war (except in the very rare circumstances of a genuinely military action by professional soldiers or trained guerrillas).

Fight/flight assumptions figure largely in the unconscious life of groups with insecure leaders, or with leaders who have little standing in the wider society or network of small groups in which a particular group is set.

(iii) Expectancy The group behaves emotionally (and unconsciously) like a class of older secondary school children awaiting a teacher who has not arrived on time. They feel like sheep without a shepherd or like people drifting on the open sea in a small boat awaiting rescue. (In reality the group has a leader, but he or she is perceived to be inadequate or weak or failing to get on with the job of leading.) So the 'adolescents' use the waiting time not to work together as a group at the subject they all know is on the timetable. They are paralyzed until the teacher arrives. Instead they chat among themselves. Boys and girls flirt with each other. Sub-groups form in different parts of the room; there the teenagers natter about extra-curricular activities like pop, fashion, gossip and romantic liaisons. These fascinate them and bind them closely together in warm peer-group friendships. From time to time, one of the members looks at the clock, or at the door, to discern signs of the teacher's appearing. Occasionally someone raises the question, perhaps with a note of anxiety, of whether the teacher will *ever* come. Ought they to take some initiative to find out if something's wrong, or if there has been a change in the arrangements for the scheduled class? 'Will you come with me to the staff room?'

Groups operating unconsciously on the expectancy model look to their salvation in the future, when a heroic leader will appear to set them on a new and clear course. They await the coming of a Messiah. Those who 'merely' wait find the sub-groups into which the group has disintegrated congenial, friendly and undemanding. Those who actively *prepare* for the Messiah's coming are like parents planning the arrival of a new-born baby: there are strong sexual overtones to their collaboration, and not a little anxiety and pain. But they are convinced the future will bring a joy which will more than compensate for current anguish. All in all, the group stops working at its formal tasks; it leaves work until the new, messianic era has dawned.

Expectancy is prevalent unconscious group behaviour when the group is short of good leadership resources and when a group knows that its accredited leader is leaving, to be replaced by someone new and unknown.

Dependence, fight/flight, expectancy: three modes of unconscious emotional energy, any one of which will be operating at a particular phase in a group's life to inhibit change and obstruct the attainment of rationally defined and corporately agreed tasks, goals and purposes. One of the perennially puzzling features of group life is how difficult it is to become aware of these hidden, emotional dynamics. That is in the nature of the unconscious. Nothing is achieved (and groups get nowhere), however, if its reality is denied; or if groups avoid the difficulties of interpretation by uncritical collusion with the subterranean pull towards fantasy and escapism.

Interpretation cannot be left to the leader, however skilled and well-trained. (Dependence again!) The best hope is for the leader to operate on the representative model and invite and respect contributions from group members to be placed alongside his or her own. The aim is for the group together to discover a common understanding of what is going on in its emotional life, and to use that insight creatively in its continuing work.

Here is an example of a group doing this. I will leave the reader to sort out the issues of authority and unconscious behaviour which this illustration provides.

Ralph was leading an adult evening class. The ten people present were sitting at desks set out in an oblong shape, as they had done on the previous six evenings together. It was a narrow room. Ralph always sat in the same place at one end, from where he operated the overhead projector. The evening followed the usual pattern: an introduction of about twenty-five minutes from Ralph, then open discussion. Ralph is not the sort of teacher who gives deliberately balanced presentations, looking at things from all angles. He argues a case, sometimes provocatively, and encourages the class members to react.

It was about twenty minutes into the discussion. Actually it wasn't a discussion at all. Peter and Hazel, who were on opposite 'long' sides of the rectangle, were the only two who had spoken. They were deeply opposed to each other's point of view. Their argument became increasingly heated. The funny thing was that they didn't look at or speak to each other. Each spoke to Ralph. Furthermore, Ralph felt he had to make a comment back each time Peter or Hazel spoke to him. Ralph was much more sympathetic to Peter's position than to Hazel's. He wanted to win the argument. He seemed always to be able to dig up from nowhere further evidence to strengthen Peter's insights; and he had no difficulties criticizing Hazel's ideas.

And what was going on among the other group members? Jack yawned. All except Peter and Hazel noticed, and in a sense Jack was expressing the boredom that several felt. Ken could have contributed a lot from his experience, but he had opted out, feeling he couldn't be bothered to break into the speech-making. Jane was becoming increasingly agitated. There was a lot she wanted to say on the subject, but she was frustrated and angry at the three-way monopoly.

Eventually Jane could contain herself no longer. It was an emotional explosion and barely coherent. Ralph looked at her, confused, feeling assaulted and hurt. He was moved to reply to Jane. He spoke at length, with a lot of feeling in his voice, of the importance of the debate between Peter and Hazel. He reviewed the evening's progress, obviously trying to justify his handling of their work so far.

Ralph's speech was followed by an uneasy silence. Then Heather spoke, in a calm and assured voice. 'I need to get my own thoughts straight on this subject. It would help me if we had a short break, to stretch our legs. Then I was thinking, if we start again in ten minutes' time, we could each write down the most important two things as we see them on the subject you've introduced. After that we could split up into two smaller groups for a quarter of an hour to discuss what we've written down. Then we could come together again and share what the two groups have been talking about. It's just a suggestion.'

Suddenly the atmosphere felt more relaxed. Ralph spoke next, now more in control of himself. 'Thank you, Heather. That's a very valuable suggestion. I guess we've lost sight this evening of what sort of group we are. You're quite right: we've all got experience and points of view which are relevant to our subject. I'd be happy to support your suggestion, but let's see what everyone thinks about it.' . . .

Good management enables a group to do three things:

To keep at the forefront of its mind its purpose and the particular tasks it must achieve in pursuing its goals.

To become aware of unconscious emotional drives operating in the group to frustrate its task.

To resolve the tensions and work through the conflicts which arise between conscious aspirations and emotional needs.

Experience indicates the sort of group in which the third of these tasks is best achieved. It is a group which allows to all its members free self-expression; which accepts all the members as individuals regardless of their personal opinions and attitudes; which respects variety of conviction and does not coerce conformity or force minorities into a corner where they feel victimized, oppressed or prejudicially treated. (This is a restatement of the representative model for the exercise of authority in a group.)

Given time, it is possible for group members to understand and adjust to one another's varied contributions and insights without everyone feeling they have to conform to a single point of view. This process can be described as 'incorporation'. This is a name which reminds us that group discussion can be fruitful in much the same way as conversation in one-to-one relationships (Chapter 1). Incorporation is an achievement of corporate creative imagination. It is the fusion into a novel artefact of all sorts of bits and pieces which before the creative act were unconnected or only loosely connected. Incorporation is community art which evokes in the group the pleasure, meaning and memorability we experience individually when we invent and create (Chapter 3). The conclusion I draw is that work in groups towards specified goals is a thoroughly human activity, expanding in a collective context our capacity for thinking, feeling, imagination and action.

13 Relatedness

This chapter is about life in the public sphere, that is, in groups, institutions and communities with more than, say, twenty-five members. The distinction between small groups (fewer than thirteen) and large groups is important. It seems to be based on a straightforward experience: there is a limit to the number of people in the same room who can retain reasonably comfortable eye-contact as they speak to one another. When numbers get above twenty-five, the limit has clearly been passed; when the number is twelve or less, we are still unquestionably within the limit. There is an indeterminate series of group sizes in between (13–24). My general experience of in-between size groups is that they seem unable to sort out whether they are operating as a small group or a large group, and soak up endless hours and much energy unconsciously dealing with that issue instead of working effectively towards their chosen goals.

The individual and the large group

Large groups feel very different to their members from small groups. They are more impersonal, and the larger the group the greater is the experience of faceless, bureaucratic management, indirect forms of communication (memos, rotas, directives) and de-personalized information (e.g. impossibly long computer reference numbers instead of names). Large groups are more formal and structured than small groups in the way they conduct their affairs. It is therefore impossible in a large group for all the members to enjoy (or reasonably to expect) warm, intimate relationships with one another. In large groups we often feel lonely, lost or uncertain about who we are or what we are supposed to be doing. It seems as if whatever an individual does will have little or no effect in the large group, and perhaps will not even be noticed. The individual's insights and concerns are marginalized, or over-whelmed by the group's unstoppable, ponderous movement towards its destiny.

The large group is perceived as a whirligig. At its centre are a few anonymous and powerful individuals who control the levers, in their own interests and to the oppression of the majority. The oppressed feel that they are being thrown off the edge of the merry-go-round to land, damaged, as an isolated unit on a concrete surround. Large groups therefore make us feel as if each of us is on his or her own; they also seem to act to diminish rather than enhance individual well-being.

There is one long-established school of thought[1] which reacts to this experience as follows. 'Don't let large groups get you down! All they are doing is showing you what you really are: an autonomous individual. We were created to live without "society", that is, as an association of free individuals. That doesn't seem possible in practice, so we have invented large groups to hold in check those forces which always work to rob us of our human destiny. Groups and society have no more to do than this: to protect us against enemies, disease, theft, violence and the like. For the rest, we ought to be on our own as much as possible, looking after our personal interests and seeking to reach our full potential. Club together, by all means, from time to time, to offer resources or buy into resources for personal development. But drop out as quickly as you buy in, if the group doesn't help you to get what you want.' Contracts and market forces are perceived to be the pivotal notions by which groups and societies are held at a distance, their power held in check.

This is an ideological perspective on large groups. Its power lies in its utterly realistic estimate of human beings in large groups as being irredeemably selfish. But it has to compete with alternative and contradictory ideologies, for example

Marxism. For Marxism, 'society' is *necessary* if human beings are to flourish; but not society as we know it, which is flawed and frustrates the meeting of human needs. So Marxism envisages a future era in history when society will reach an ideal form. It will be classless and free of the organs of state power (armed forces, police, bureaucracy); within it each individual will find fulfilment in interdependence, giving and receiving to one another according to need and ability. Marxism also suggests what must be done to move towards that ideal – class analysis, proletarian revolution and rule by the working class.

No ideology seems comprehensive or convincing enough to engage the multi-levelled complexity of our experience in large groups. A Christian theological point of view, concerned with reality and truth, is bound to live in critical conversation with all ideologies. But Christians are divided about how to pursue such a conversation. Some argue it is best fostered from a base of commitment *within* an ideological framework; others argue that it *must* be from such a base, preferably the one which is least congenial to those who hold power. Others seek a detached, neutral (fanciful?) platform untainted with any ideological commitments from which to criticize creatively those who wield power and exercise authority.

One example: in Marxist analysis, alienation is a form of impoverishment experienced by individuals in large groups. Roles are imposed on us which fragment our personal lives. Work is set against home, intellectual and technical skills against emotions, feeling and spiritual concerns; practice against theory; competition against cooperation. We feel more like cogs in a machine, mere things, than persons. None can doubt this general insight. Is it the case, however, that roles are always and comprehensively imposed? Surely they can to some extent be freely chosen. Within limits I can pay attention to what I have experienced about myself (my gifts, skills, needs, potentialities) and elect a vocation. From a Christian perspective a vocation is the coherent application of personal powers on behalf of others. Inspired by that goal, I can put myself in the way of training resources in order to develop to the full my vocational opportunities and aptitudes, the better to serve others. Of course, large groups being what they are, coupled with our experience of evil and brokenness being all-pervasive, a freely chosen vocation is not always realized. Employment opportunities may not exist for my chosen vocation; or I am too old to gain access to training; or I fail to reach a level of competence required by a profession. But at least the question is open as to whether roles are always impersonally imposed or whether we are free to move towards a goal where 'Work is love made visible'.[2] This possibility is greatly enhanced if we can challenge, and perhaps overcome, the alienating distinction between high status paid employment and low status unpaid voluntary work (mother, PTA committee member, pastoral visitor, etc.).

As soon as we feel from within ourselves that our contribution to society, in paid or voluntary work, has some value, we need a way of understanding how we relate to all the many others who play a part. Our expectations must be realistic to the context of a large group. We relate in terms of the role we perform, which can only engage a *part* of our total personhood. We become colleagues. Colleagues work well together when there are between them respect, trust, friendliness and common understandings about their roles. But it is confusing and disruptive in a large group to demand or expect colleagueship to become friendship. Colleagueship is relatedness; friendship is relationship. They are different, but relatedness is at least a positive concept which overcomes the sense of loneliness which large groups so easily impose on individuals.

We must note the pressure we all feel in large groups to turn relatedness into relationship. We feel we ought to build friendships with colleagues. This is a snare and a delusion. Possibly the pressure springs from the mysterious power which all large groups exert on us to give to the group an inordinate pride and loyalty. Large groups claim from us a commitment which is beyond reason, for which we seem willing to sacrifice our deepest personal loves and concerns. (Examples: going to war for my country, right or wrong; fanatical support for a football club; uncritical pride in a school or university.) We can justify such allegiance only if we can convince ourselves that the large group provides a web of deeply meaningful relationships, worth dying for. Hence the irrational longing to make the large group a network of friends.

The dynamics of large groups

There is more to large groups than their effects on individuals. They are essentially corporate structures, to be understood, moulded and used in their own terms of reference. This is the task of sociology. It is a huge undertaking which gives detailed attention to many disparate forms of social organization (e.g. urban and rural society; class structures; family and kinship patterns; educational, welfare, industrial and religious institutions; work and unemployment; the place of minorities; and political groupings). We cannot begin to delve into the details here. From a theological point of view, it is important to reflect on the creative and destructive possibilities inherent in social structures. Our vision of the kingdom of God, inspired by the Christian tradition, guides our critical reflection; though experience in large groups, and structures of understanding drawn from the social sciences, can be expected to challenge and inform elements in the tradition. In other words a genuinely interdisciplinary conversation needs to be established between sociology and the Christian tradition, whose outcome in principle is creative for both in shared understandings. My limited tasks in the remainder of this chapter are: to sketch some general features of all large groups; and to reflect on what social structures best correlate with the demand of the kingdom for change towards justice, peace, freedom and human well-being.

Large groups, like small ones, have an unconscious emotional resistance to change. In large groups the basic models of unconscious group emotion apply, but often in more complex configurations and mixtures than is the case in small groups. However difficult it may be for any individual or small group to discern clearly what is happening in the larger society, that *something* is going on becomes apparent when irrational energy is unleashed to disable or destroy all who threaten the *status quo*. Those in power, pledged to act on the noblest principles, act corruptly to eliminate opposition. Acts 6.8–8.1 illustrates how something like a demonic power commonly overwhelms those in authority in large groups: Stephen holds his own in a disputation, pleads his case eloquently in terms of Israel's tradition, but is murdered on the evidence of false witnesses and an emotional response to criticism. The persecuted prophet becomes a martyr (a witness to divine love) precisely by meeting with love the irrational evil and conservatism in large groups. 'It is when we stand in the righteous all-seeing light of love that we can dare to look at, admit, and *consciously* suffer under this something in us which wills disaster, misfortune, defeat to everything outside the sphere of our narrowest self-interest.'[3]

In the tension between demands for change and resistance to change, large groups respond in characteristic ways. First comes the polarization of opinions and convictions. The middle ground – the place of conversation and the quest for shared understandings, cooperation and mutually agreed compromise – is lost. The large group then splinters into smaller groupings. The sub-groups take up extreme stances, and prepare for battle. Usually the polarized attitudes and the stances of the warring parties encapsulate oversimple pictures of the issues confronting the large group. Complex reality is reduced to ideology and fantasy pictures which reinforce the cohesion and identity of the sub-groups and the loyalty of their members. Each sub-group projects on to its opponents or on to the all-encompassing environment of the large group the negative feelings and the evil forces that are in reality as much part of its own inner life as of everything else. 'Them' and 'us' conflicts become heroic struggles between evil and good, or between death and life.

Illustrations of the previous paragraph abound in everyday experience: employers versus trade unions; political right versus political left within a party or between parties; Protestant versus Catholic in Northern Ireland; suburban versus rural versus new town versus inner city in the struggle for social services and resources. The last of these illustrations is particularly instructive. We cope with belonging to a nation state by investing a great deal in the idyllic pictures we create of the neighbourhood in which we have our homes, or in which we aspire to live. Every local community is in reality a large group which is an extremely complex sub-system of the larger network of the nation. But we think and feel about the community around our homes in simplified terms. Although our pictures are a fantasy, they have practical effects.

An English village, for example, is perceived to be a fully integrated group of friendly families displaying a profound, kindly, but unobtrusive knowledge of one another. The whole village operates on a common value system rooted in the soil, in natural rhythms and in history (represented by the ancient village church on the edge of the village green). Here are social stability, a rounded life and harmony. But this flies in the face of many harsh realities in modern villages: conflicts between newcomers and long-established residents, and between the *nouveau riches* and the council house poor; and the clash of interests between those who use the village only for leisure and residence and those who need the village also to provide shops, employment and public transport. The idyllic picture, however, reinforces social divisions in English society, and certainly exerts pressure against ethnic minorities settling in the countryside.

An even more pervasive fantasy is one which perceives any small locality as a coherent community, a neighbourhood. In a neighbourhood individuals of all ages and families of all types can inter-relate and find a wholesome life, incorporating friction, passion, birth and death. Planners of housing estates operate on this picture, which is endlessly underlined by television soap opera (EastEnders, Coronation Street, Brookside, Albion Market). The practical effect of this is to make people blind to the political decisions and social structures which operate at regional and national levels. In reality these profoundly affect people's lives in their local communities.

It is the lot of some groups in society to work at the interface between the small-scale locality and the larger social and political structures. Social and community workers often find themselves in this uncomfortable position, facing in two directions at the same time. Those who exercise power at regional and national levels have a vested interest in encouraging community workers to concentrate on the needs of individuals, families and parishes. Ironically, any serious reflection on needs in a neighbourhood must make community workers attentive to centres of power outside the locality. They will see the importance of cooperation between independent, adjacent neighbourhoods, to exert joint pressure on external authorities.[4]

Community and social work is caught up in political controversy. These conflicts remind us of the simple fact that large groups always control power. Greater size equals greater power. Power often means wealth, but can also include a wide range of resources like information, means of communication, the right to make decisions and access to physical force. All experience underlines the truth that power corrupts and absolute power corrupts absolutely. There are totalitarian tendencies in every large group.

Management of large groups

Good leadership of large groups (which can be everything from a large committee to a national government) takes seriously the negative factors outlined above. It tries to deal with them realistically and creatively so that the large group can perform its tasks and enhance the quality of life. There is no need here to repeat the material in Chapter 12 about ways of exercising authority. The representative model still holds pride of place. In large groups, however, authority is often vested not in an individual but in a team, who operate as a small group within the system, dedicated to management of the large group.

The obvious themes in good management of large groups are these:

(*a*) Identifying the primary purpose of the group. In any large community the overall purpose is bound to be fairly abstract in character. It is therefore crucial that managers define also the concrete aims whose fulfilment will contribute to the attainment of the group's purpose. Even the aims are often distant goals which can be reached only through a series of intermediate objectives. Leadership skill is therefore about planning tactics and strategies of a flexible kind which enable various intermediate stages to interconnect and serve the overriding purpose. None of this is effective unless all the members of the large group are enabled to discuss, agree and own the group's aims, strategies and purpose. (I return to this in paragraph (*f*) below.)

(*b*) Structuring and ritualizing the polarization of attitudes and the conflicts inherent in any large group. Giving formal expression to these divisions (e.g. a formal debate instead of a free-ranging discussion) enables the group to use conflict creatively and to reach decisions which incorporate differences. Without structure and ritual, conflicts lead to groups splintering or violence erupting.

(*c*) Appointing representative small groups to do most of its work, for example, a large group appointing committees. Large groups function well as consultative bodies and at agreeing policy outlines; they are inefficient at executive action, research and analysis. Small groups can do these tasks well (Chapter 12). It is crucial that there is clear authorization from the large group to the small regarding its terms of reference; a genuinely representative membership in the small group; and mutual trust between the large and small groups.

(*d*) Devising checks and balances in the large group regarding the exercise of power (elections, length of service, rules about expenditure of money, requirements of consultation before decisions are taken by leaders, team leadership in preference to individual leadership, etc.) This involves writing constitutions which win the assent of the whole group, and institutionalizing procedures. From time to time checks and balances need review and revision. Large groups are so notoriously slow to acknowledge the need for any constitutional change that it is wise, wherever possible, to incorporate periodic reviews in the initial constitution.

(*e*) Affirming the value of criticism, in other words permitting sub-groups to form of their own volition to pursue their vested interests within the overarching structures of the large group. This is usually the element of management which the large group finds most threatening to its authority. The fewer the checks and balances on those who hold power in large groups, the less easy it is for critical small associations to flourish; the tendency is always towards autocratic suppression of 'opposition' and 'subversion' (as sub-groups are perceived). Totalitarian leaders prefer to oversee monolithic institutions which favour the virtues of 'male stereotype' behaviour (efficiency, discipline, tidiness, rationality, regulations covering all contingencies). This, however, is not necessarily the most desirable ethos for any large group or community. Looser, untidier, more short-term and experimental structures can characterize institutions ('female sterotype' groups); within them the members feel more free to initiate change.

When sub-groups are *not* seen as inherently dangerous, arrangements have to be made for their concerns and insights to inform the large groups.[5] This requires structures for mutual conversation; in particular, the large group needs to affirm the status of the sub-group leaders, without being paternalistic.

(*f*) Underscoring the human character of every institution, organization and large group. This means that in the midst of all the procedures, structures and planning, people matter. Furthermore, people acting cooperatively at every level of belonging in the large group need easy access to resources to fulfil their roles in the system. Large groups therefore need always to pay attention to how people participate. From the point of view of the leadership, this is best enhanced if they see themselves as working *with* people (visiting and consulting, enabling and empowering them), rather than *for* people.

The large group then becomes a genuinely collaborative venture in which, without confusion of roles and responsibilities, men and women relate to one another in interdependence and mutual respect (i.e. as colleagues). Relatedness is experienced.[6]

The institutional church

The Christian denominations are large institutions; many congregations are large groups. They reflect the variety of types of large group which the previous paragraphs have touched on. Some denominations are highly centralized, tightly structured 'male' institutions (e.g. Methodism); others are more loose-knit, decentralized and 'female' national churches (e.g. the Baptist Union).

Some congregations see themselves as having been appointed by the local community as a 'representative work group'. Characteristically a Church of England parish church is a representative focus of the religious needs and ritual processes latent in the parish. Its visible presence in a community, its accessibility to all parishioners for 'rites of passage'; its reliable liturgy, its holding in trust the religious symbols of the parish's history (war memorials, graveyard) provide transcendent roots for the community, a clear identity and continuity. Few worshippers there may be, but they work on behalf of everyone at the interplay between a community's instinctive religious needs and the Christian tradition.

Other congregations see themselves as voluntarily formed sub-groups which operate as grit on a sore palate, the moral and spiritual conscience of the local community.[7] Such are many free churches, witnessing to the light of Christian faith and love over and against the world's darkness and wickedness.[8] As with all non-appointed groups, their problem with respect to the large group is one of status, a problem whose solution is in the hands of the local community (and its authorized religious 'representative work group').

Ordained ministers have traditionally played a pivotal role in the management of churches. They have been the authorized leaders *par excellence*. Their 'universal' authorization[9] and their local appointment have ensured that they operate in that uncomfortable interface between the personal/family/neighbourhood and the regional/national/world-wide. They have classically represented the 'cement' which holds the whole church together in unity and love.

Much confusion has crept into the self-image of ordained ministers in recent decades as churches have rediscovered the ecclesial ministries of all God's people. Ordained and lay are having to learn new styles of collaborative leadership. By making their voice heard, the laity contribute insights and world-views from many professions, social classes and human needs to the churches' understandings of ministry and mission. Ordained ministers no longer have an exclusive claim to formulate the church's aims and purpose.

Church management is a highly skilled task within the ministry of pastoral care. Church councils, synods, assemblies and conferences endeavour to build authentically human institutions – just, peaceful, participatory, open to change according to the purpose and aims of the church. They draw upon professional management skills and learn from their chequered histories.

There is, however, a persistent uneasy feeling about the church being institutional in form. Sociologically and historically it is inevitable. The consequences are that the church becomes a bastion of conservatism, drawing the loyalties and energies of the Christian community unduly towards itself, and constantly encouraging theological reflection to centre on the church's identity and needs. Critical conversation with the biblical tradition affirms the church as an integral part of God's purposes in history (Eph. 1.4). But the Bible constantly raises questions against the church's rigidity and its self-concern. Witnessing to Christ and the coming kingdom always take precedence over the church; institutional features of the church (buildings, a settled leadership pattern, etc.) are relativized by a picture of God's pilgrim people travelling light through the desert (Exod. 12–40; Acts 7; Hebrews). The church's inner life and security are made subservient to its calling to participate faithfully in God's mission to the whole created order (Matt. 28.18–20; I Peter 2.9). What all this means in practice is that church management must be exercised in critical dialogue with the ministry of the word and sacraments.

Historically, the ordained minister has focused in himself – classically a male! – both the conserving ministry of church management and the prophetic, unsettling ministries of word and sacraments. The general result has been clear: word and sacraments have been blunted in the interests of good order, stability and resistance to change. The true interests of the ecclesiastical institution and of its creative management require a diversity and separation of roles in the church. Team leadership (incorporating lay and ordained) can achieve this better than leadership focused in an individual (the ordained minister). And within the community of the ordained there needs to be a fairly drastic shift in consciousness. Left behind must be the picture of each individual ordained person being capable of doing almost everything well (preaching, presiding at the sacraments, reflecting theologically, performing the whole range of pastoral care ministries including church management). Embraced must be a picture of each ordained person being gifted to do well *one* or a few of the focal ministries on which the church depends, in critical association with others (lay and ordained) performing complementary ministries.

Pastoral care in secular large groups

The idea dies hard that the norm of discipleship consists of activities to support and nourish the ecclesiastical institution and large congregations. The church as a large group is infinitely seductive, institutionalizing and clericalizing church members as well as ordained ministers. In contrast, throughout this book I have tried to locate pastoral care, theology and spirituality primarily in the human concerns, struggles, actions and crises of everyday life. This is not to denigrate the church, but to shift the balance from an 'ecclesiastical paradigm' to a 'secular paradigm'.

The same shift of perspective is needed in the ministry of pastoral care of large groups. There is a proper pastoral task of church management, which needs to be done well (see the previous sections). Most energy and attention, however, needs to be devoted by appropriately gifted Christian people (and not exclusively lay members) to pastoral care of large groups, communities and institutions which have no ecclesiastical foundation. The gospel is about God's kingdom – embryonicly present in Jesus and still to come. The present-and-coming kingdom transforms all creation; it is not reserved for religion or the righteous (Mark 2.17).

I mention now four ways of pursuing a ministry to the structures of large non-church groups. These are distinguished by the role and status that individual Christians have in their particular large group. There are tensions and conflicts between these four approaches which need to be faced realistically by those involved.

(a) For *those with formal leadership functions* in a large group (e.g. teachers in a school, managers in a business, leaders of a trade union or professional body). They are called upon to manage well, within the terms of reference summarized on pages 219–22. They will normally operate alongside men and women who exercise leadership on different assumptions. The obligation on Christian leaders is not to create conflict and friction, but to increase cooperation and shared responsibility. They allow their own values to speak for themselves, quietly to infiltrate structures devoted to self-seeking, oppression, self-aggrandizment and corruption.

There are two particular pastoral and theological tasks which will always figure largely in good management. The first is critical reflection on the purpose of the group or institution. Is the purpose laudable when judged against Christian images of God's kingdom? Does it enhance the possibilities of justice, freedom, peace and participation, not only within the group but in wider society? Does the group's purpose pander without restriction to human selfishness or narrow ideological convictions, without reference to altruism and the common good?

Second is the need to remain self-critical about the fantasy pictures and dominant ideologies which large groups construct for themselves, or which become fixed in polarized confrontations within large groups. Common examples: we are the 'righteous' over and against all others, who are evil; we are the 'best,' while comparable groups are all perceived to be indifferent, less capable, more reactionary . . .; this locality is perfect, a true 'village'. Reality in all its complexity is always preferable to simplistic fantasy (especially when the latter can generate practical effects which undermine the struggle to renew the whole of humanity and the natural order).

Neither of these tasks is easy. Progress is not possible without public compromise of high principles and deeply held beliefs. Accommodation to the prevailing powers of a wicked world hides, and maybe threatens, inner integrity. Controversy is inevitable. A historical example of such a ministry was that of Matteo Ricci (1552–1610), a Jesuit who went as a missionary to China in 1582. He indigenized himself in Chinese culture, gained a position of influence, performed the kowtow and refused to condemn ancestor worship. Yet his Christian influence was substantial. Leaven in the dough, maybe; but hardly a light set on a lampstand.

(b) For *those who create and lead new groups and institutions.* Existing large groups are profoundly reactionary, or seem perversely to entrench death-dealing values in preference to life-enhancing possibilities. Some with leadership skills have therefore felt a compulsion to create new, alternative institutions. The hope is that the new community will enshrine human values in fresh structures, and be a witness against the older (and usually larger) institution. Hence the long and honourable history of Christians pioneering new institutions of pastoral care in many sectors of life, to question and transform existing indifference or evil. Examples abound in housing, education, industry, care for the elderly and for children in need.

One striking illustration from the recent past was the creation of a hospice by Cicely Saunders, to give practical expression to new and Christian ways of ministering to the dying. The hospice movement stands over and against the style of geriatric medicine and care which had become traditional in the hospital system. The alternative has demonstrated its creative possibilities, and is now transforming assumptions, aims and methods of care within the NHS.[10]

(c) For *those who take up a specialist role on the edge* of large groups. This is a difficult option because it requires that a special role of a sophisticated kind be created within the normal structures of an institution. It is more like a consultancy than anything else. Some chaplains have tried to create it, especially in polytechnics and colleges of further education.[11] To work, the role has to be authorized by church authorities, but not in a way which makes the pastor obviously beholden to a congregation or the church institution; he or she must be given as much freedom as possible. The role has also to be authorized by the secular institution, but must be distinct from the normal patterns of staff/student or officer/member; the pastor must 'belong' to the institution, but on its edge. The role works best if it is not confused with other perfectly proper pastoral options within the institution (e.g. caring for individuals, working with explicitly Christian small groups or leading worship – traditional chaplaincy functions). Possible tasks are the following:

Bringing a critical perspective to the management of the institution, by having the space and time to attend to what is actually happening and the way all the members react.

Keeping in the consciousness of the large group the complex interconnections between the institution and the environment in which it is set, and to assist the development of these links.[12]

Convening small groups in which polarized opinions, vested interests, warring sub-groups, and complacent and critical points of view can interact in a common concern for the institution's welfare and for human values.

Witnessing to the mysterious depths beneath all human existence, which are more readily squeezed out of consciousness in bureaucratic institutions than anywhere else. One famous metaphor for this task is a clown in a circus.[13]

Everyone else in the circus appears to display extraordinary skill and competence in a highly specialized field: trapeze artist, conjurer, animal trainer or stunt artist. They evoke from the audience awe, respect, amazement and pleasure. But what of the clown? He appears to have no skill, to be clumsy and foolish. (In reality clowning is a very skilful business, requiring as much practice and dedication as any other circus profession; but it does not seem like that.) Yet he evokes responses which no one else in the circus can touch, responses which relate easily to the common experience of the audience: pathos, failure, humour, being tripped up and looking silly, and of being incompetent and weak in a world of specialists. The clown may seem merely to fill the gaps in the circus programme; but he better than any other can point us to suffering and pain, and to God.

(d) For *those who find themselves on the edge* of the large group, but *with no role or power*. Christian instinct, the biblical tradition and the emergence of liberation theologies in the so-called Third World all point to this as the normal and major way in which pastoral care is to be exercised in large groups. We often picture liberation theology as something which has in it the seeds which will eventually topple governments and transform the culture of continents and of the world church. Whether that is so or not, it is the case that the fundamental methods and aims of liberation theology apply just as naturally among the dispossessed in large groups and institutions of a far smaller size than nation states as among the poor and destitute in Latin America and Asia, or among oppressed blacks or women throughout Western culture. Liberation theology is about structural and political change towards kingdom-life for the marginal, weak and powerless in *every* large group, institution and community.

Liberation theology, like the gospel itself (Mark 1.14–15) begins with a call to repentance, or conversion. It is a claim addressed to the rich and powerful to be converted *to* the poor. 'Poor' is, of course, a relative term: it is a piece of shorthand for those in any particular large group who are on the edge, who are consulted least and most often dealt with paternalistically, dismissively or oppressively, and who have no voice among those who manage and wield power in the institution. Christian pastoral action springs from solidarity with the poor, a commitment to be alongside the oppressed. This requires a specific break from any attempt to remould the large group towards kingdom-life by taking up positions of leadership or any specialist role (paragraphs (*a*) and (*c*) above).

The gospel follows the imperative of repentance with a call to radical discipleship (Mark 1.16–20). Earlier chapters have hinted at some of what this involves: a journey inwards towards self-awareness and God, whom we contemplate in silence and faith; and actions of love flowing from a changed heart. The practice of discipleship precedes reflection, knowledge of the tradition or intellectual constructs about God. In particular, alongside the poor, actions of love involve struggling with the oppressed for justice, dignity and freedom.

Critical reflection on what is done must indeed follow action. This is how action remains essentially human (pp. 23–7). But to be genuinely critical, a new framework of thought and feeling must be established among the poor which challenges the ideology of the powerful who manage the large group. This new framework is shaped by alternative understandings of power and alternative social structures. The alternative understandings of power derive from Marxist analysis of history, economic forces, class structures and property. The alternative social structures are small groups, in which leadership is distributed as democratically as possible (p. 203). The members of the cell, aided by Marxist thought, see their predicament in a fresh way, and are inspired to persist in the struggle for the transformation of the large group. The small group also attempts to manage creatively the polarized emotional attitudes prevalent among the poor: either apathy (the 'happy slave', acquiescent, deferential and fatalistic) or intense anger. The cell can challenge the former (creating a 'new consciousness') and constructively channel the latter.

To be genuinely theological, action needs also to be reflected on critically in the light of the Christian tradition. But even the Bible is not a 'neutral' text which sounds the same to the powerful and to the poor. What is read in the Bible is to a large extent coloured by the dominant ideology, interests and concerns of those who read. So in liberation theology, in open discussion among small groups of the poor, the Bible reveals fresh insights. The point, however, is not that there are various ways of reading the Bible. Rather, the insights about the God of the Bible which can be discovered only among the poor as they struggle to overcome and understand their oppression are more authentic than any other insights. The Bible is revealed in its true light among the poor, as a collection of books whose prevailing concerns precisely mirror the struggles of the marginal people in every large group and community. To the eyes of the poor the true God reveals himself. God has a 'preferential option' for the poor. He rescued the oppressed Hebrew slaves from Egypt; he restored to Palestine the humiliated and broken exiles in Babylon; he announced his gracious salvation for all creation in the crucified peasant from Nazareth; he made his gospel known to the weak and lowly, the scum of humanity (I Cor. 1.25–31). God is not the God of the rich and powerful; on the contrary, as the Magnificat declares, 'he has brought down monarchs from their thrones, but the humble ones have been lifted high. The hungry he has satisfied with good things, the rich sent empty away' (Luke 1.52–3).

To marginal people in large groups pastoral care gives a prophetic voice, and an ultimate meaning to their actions to change history and society. We have reminded ourselves earlier of the common fate awaiting prophets: they are silenced by the powerful. But even a cross can be embraced as a symbol of hope for God's coming kingdom.

IV The Pastor

14 Pastoral Education

It is all too easy when writing about pastoral care to give the impression that a pastor is someone who knows what he or she is doing, has gifts of discernment refined by training and experience, and can make a difference to human situations. The pastor, for example, can encourage growth, respond to needs, facilitate movement in groups. . . . In practice it is not often like that. The reality of personal and social life is so unutterably complex that the pastor easily flounders, becomes confused, or loses a sense of direction. What makes pastoral situations even more difficult is the simple fact that the pastor becomes part of the very situations he or she is trying to understand and serve. Pastoral care cannot be carried out in a neutral or detached way; of necessity it requires personal involvement, interaction, receiving and giving. Individuals and societies have first to be experienced before any understanding can arise. I shall try to highlight this in a story about a sick visit.

Peter visits Joe

The characters in this story are the following. Joe Clark is seventy-two years old. He is a regular worshipper at his church, a devout person and a member of a Bible fellowship which meets weekly. He has recently suffered a severe heart attack. After a period in hospital he has returned to his home, a bungalow in Willow Terrace. There he lives with his wife Anne, who is in her late sixties. Anne has been suffering for about fifteen years with severe arthritis in her hands and knees; she is virtually housebound and nearly immobile. Anne has never been a churchgoer. She has a reputation for being crotchety and blunt. Normally Joe does everything for Anne, as well as run their home.

Joe and Anne have three children. One of them is Helen, aged forty-four, who is a primary school teacher. She is married to Paul. They have two children. Margaret is at university; Kate, sixteen years old, is unemployed, but is contemplating a YTS offer to learn about hairdressing. Helen lives nearly ten miles from Willow Terrace. Normally she visits her parents each Tuesday tea-time during term-time, and also on Sundays during school holidays. She accompanies her father to church at festivals and for other special services.

Peter Briggs, an accountant by profession, is the leader of Joe's Bible fellowship. He is also a teacher in the junior church. Peter is in his late forties and married to Julia; they have no children.

Peter decided to visit Joe on a Thursday evening. He arrived at Willow Terrace at about 6.45 p.m., and knocked at the front door. It was Helen who answered the knock.

'Hullo! I'm Peter Briggs, from St Luke's.' By this time Peter had got over his initial surprise at the door being opened so promptly. Even as he had walked up the garden path he had been wondering how he would get inside without causing too much trouble: would Anne understand if he went to the back door and simply walked in? He had also had time to recognize the person in the doorway. He had seen her in church once or twice. He remembered her because she had striking auburn hair, such a contrast from Joe's frizzled, non-descript mane. 'You must be Helen. I think we may have met at church. Actually I've called to see Joe.'

'Come in, won't you?'

Peter was shown into the lounge. The television was on, very loud.

'Turn the telly off, darling, please.' Helen had followed Peter into the lounge, and had moved straight towards Kate who was sitting, almost stupefied, on the settee watching the screen directly opposite.

'Please don't feel you have to turn it off because I've come.'

Helen looked round towards Peter, with almost a look of relief and pleasure on her face. 'Well, can we at least have the volume down a little?'

Kate moved reluctantly to the volume control, turned it down, but didn't return to the settee. She pulled an armchair close to the television and enveloped herself around it. She sat round-shouldered on the edge of the chair with her back towards Helen and Peter.

Peter smiled a little nervously at Helen. She was an attractive woman, round, mature features, prominent lips without lipstick, and a pale complexion. She exuded a sense of calm and control. 'Her father's daughter,' thought Peter.

'How is your father today?'

'He's getting on slowly. The doctor came this morning and gave him some new pills. He wants dad to get up and potter about. He tried it for a bit after lunch, I think, but soon got tired. So he's back in bed. You won't stay too long, will you?'

Helen showed Peter into the bedroom. Close to the door and immediately in front of him was Anne, sitting in an easy chair with a blanket over her knees and a shawl round her shoulders. 'Hullo, Anne! It's good to see you!'

'Why, it's Peter Briggs from the church! They've sent you, have they, instead of that Mr Giles?' (The Revd John Giles was the minister.)

Peter laughed nervously and walked beside Anne to the side of the bed where Joe was. He leaned slightly over Joe, held out his right hand and felt Joe's warm, sincere and generous clasp.

Anne: 'You're not to get Joe excited. He's got to take it easy.'

Joe (looking away from Peter towards Anne, but still holding Peter's hand): 'I don't think Peter will do me any harm. Anyway, the doctor said I should be more active.' Looking back to Peter: 'He wants me to run around like a spring chicken!'

'That doctor's no good. He treats us all like guinea pigs, stuffing us with the latest pills and new-fangled ideas. They only produce side-effects no one has thought of. The last state's worse than the first, if you ask me.'

'Mum, that's not fair!' Helen was still standing in the doorway. 'The doctor's been very caring to dad. I'm sure what he says is for the best.'

'Trust you to take your father's side,' muttered Anne, her eyes cast down towards her gnarled hands.

Peter felt caught in the cross-fire of a family feud. He was uncomfortable. Fortunately from Peter's point of view, Helen ('Has she sensed my embarrassment?') changed the subject. She offered to make a cup of tea for everyone, and shut the bedroom door behind her as she left for the kitchen.

'She's a good girl,' said Joe. 'She's stepped in here with no complaints. She looks after us both now.' He looked up into Peter's eyes. 'She comes every day after school. I can't think how we'd manage without her.'

The thought of Helen's love seemed to give Joe a feeling of pride and peace. A sort of calm rested on the bedroom. Peter at last felt free enough to take stock of where he was. He looked round the bedroom, where he had never been before. It was small and cluttered. It had not been decorated for many years. The overwhelming impression was that yellowy-brown colour so typical of the 1950s, but now a generation old. On top of a chest of drawers Peter's eye caught a photograph of Joe as a young man, in soldier's uniform. He had never before thought of Joe as young, and Joe had never mentioned military service. What had Joe done in the war? How much did Peter really know about him?

'Do sit down, Peter.' It was Joe who interrupted Peter's meditation. The only vacant chair in the bedroom had clothes draped across it, so, hesitantly, Peter sat on the edge of the bed. 'How's Julia?'

'She's fine. She sends you her love, of course. And how are *you* feeling, Joe?'

Anne: 'That's a damn silly question. How would you feel if you'd been at death's door?'

Peter was irked by Anne's intervention and attitude. He had come to see Joe!

'I'm very fortunate, Peter,' said Joe. 'I. . . .' Before he could say any more, the door opened and Helen brought in the tea. As she distributed the cups and saucers, Helen said, to no one in particular but presumably (so he thought) for Peter's benefit, 'It's been a nice day, today. Mind you, we could do with a bit of sunshine. Schools are so claustrophobic when children can't get outside. It's been driving me mad lately – that, and worrying about dad here.'

'Not to mention your dear old mum!'

'Don't be silly, mum. Of course we care about you. But dad's the one we've got to concentrate on at the moment. Anyway, you'll have to excuse me. I've got to be off now. I've promised to take Kate to a friend's party tonight. She'll give me no peace if we're late.'

Helen quickly summarized instructions about the food she had planned for her parents, kissed them farewell and politely took her leave of Peter. When she had gone, Peter, who in the previous few minutes had increasingly felt like an intruder into a private and intimate family ritual, now felt like a spare part. What was going on all around him? He was useless. He had ignored Kate. Indeed, it was only just as Helen was leaving that he realized that the teenager he had vaguely encountered in the lounge was Helen's daughter, Joe's grandchild. He had certainly noticed Helen (and enjoyed the noticing), but hadn't got to know her in any sense. Now Helen and Kate were off. Here in the bedroom, he couldn't see how to break into the conflict between Joe and Anne and the doctor. He knew what he *wanted* to say: he must affirm the doctor's advice. But how, without making Anne angry? He *wanted* to talk to Joe about so many things that they valued and shared – last week's Bible fellowship and last Sunday's morning service. He wanted to talk to Joe about the future, how he could adjust to new circumstances. Was there any help members of the congregation could give: devising new diets, perhaps; or organizing a rota of people to help look after Anne? He wanted to *pray* with Joe. But none of this was going to be possible, it seemed, with Anne in the room and so dominant. What a saint Joe must be! he thought. Where did he learn such patience? What did he do with his anger and frustration? In contrast, Peter felt depressed.

As soon as Helen left, Anne said: 'That Kate's no good. You notice she didn't come in to say goodbye.' (Peter had in fact overlooked this. Now it was brought to his attention it did seem odd – or intriguing.) 'I blame her for Joe's illness, you know. Joe's been worried silly over her. She's in with the wrong company. Idle good-for-nothings, they are. Helen's found out she's been taking drugs. Paul ought to take her in hand, but he won't – or can't.'

Here was a totally new agenda, for which Peter was unprepared. Should he follow it up? He must, if it was really worrying Joe. But now it would all be so indirect, almost like gossip. If only he had known about this before Helen and Kate had left! He was angry with himself for not paying more attention to Helen and Kate. The anger prompted in him a stronger resolve to take the initiative.

'I'm sorry Kate has been such a worry to you, Joe. And it must be difficult for Helen on top of everything else.'

'Don't pity her.' It was Anne speaking again. 'She's only getting what comes to every mother who thinks she can run a home and hold down a job at the same time.'

Peter kept his eyes on Joe. Inwardly he was seething, but tried to hide that emotion. He spoke deliberately a little more softly and slowly: 'I was really wondering how *you* feel about Kate and Helen, Joe.' As he said it, he was conscious of putting Anne down. Was that the right thing to do? he asked himself.

Learning from experience

Here we can leave the story of Peter's visit to Joe, even though the encounter in the bedroom is far from over. It is a fictitious story. But it represents, I believe, what is commonly experienced in a visit to someone at home – not in the details but in the complexity of what was going on and the bewilderment, uncertainty and strong feelings aroused in Peter. How was he to make sense of this experience? 'How can I understand unless someone will give me the clue?' (Acts 8.31).

There is unlikely to be a single clue which unlocks the maze of interactions in a seemingly straightforward visit; but at least the poignant question on the lips of the Ethiopian eunuch just cited from the story in Acts 8 correctly suggests that Peter will not easily comprehend his experience *in situ*. He needs to come away from Willow Terrace and reflect on it; and he needs someone else's help, insights and encouragement. From this starting point I wish now to set out in a systematic way how we learn from our pastoral experience. In the course of this I shall try to start drawing together some of the threads from earlier chapters in this book.

I begin with the basic premise that *all* learning takes place from experience. Learning is prompted particularly by experiences which are puzzling, challenging or unexpectedly inspiring and revelatory.

To make sense of experience we need a language. I do not mean by 'language' a dialect or, say, the English language, or French. I mean a set of devices for understanding experience, and therefore for use in communicating our experience to others. The early chapters of this book looked at some of the language we all use to make sense of experience: art and culture, stories, rituals, the ways people act and react, legends, myths, history and science. In addition I have tried to show that pastoral experience can also be understood by special reference to the human and social sciences and to the Christian theological tradition (which is rooted in the Bible). Put all together, this makes a veritable 'rag bag' of bits and pieces, which must be most uncongenial to those who want life to be ordered and tidy like a Bach cantata or a mathematical theorem.

In spite of its messiness, we can make some general comments on this 'language'. All the language we use is by nature symbol and metaphor (Chapter 5). In other words, the language we have enables us to probe what we do not understand (the puzzling, challenging and startlingly revelatory) in terms of what we know and understand already. But metaphors and symbols do not simply accumulate and add up understanding, like a pile of neatly stacked bricks. Each metaphor we use highlights some aspects of the mysterious and unknown but overlooks other aspects.

In the titles of Chapters 7–13 I have made extensive use of the metaphor of a journey. This suggests pastoral care is about movement towards a goal, a sense of direction, a familiar route with predictable landmarks. Furthermore, *love* is often thought of as a journey ('I feel our relationship is *getting somewhere*'; 'Since we talked honestly to each other, I feel we've *turned the corner*'). And the Christian life is regularly portrayed as a community pilgrimage, a journey of love towards a perfect love.

> Didst thou not make us one,
> That we might one remain,
> Together travel on,
> And share our joy and pain,
> Till all thy utmost goodness prove,
> And rise renewed in perfect love?
>
> Then let us ever bear
> The blessed end in view,
> And join, with mutual care,
> To fight our passage through;
> And kindly help each other on,
> Till all receive the starry crown.[1]

But the 'journey' metaphor disguises the fixity and dependability of love, which nothing can shake ('an ever-fixed mark . . . Love's not Time's fool', p. 45).

So we need many metaphors, of different sorts, set side by side. We need constantly shifting constellations of metaphors drawn from all the sources we have available, for new mixtures bring new insights (just as they equally assuredly leave us with new questions). Sometimes we cannot make sense of our experience unless a new metaphor is invented. So the quest for understanding is a rolling process, never complete. We need constantly to refresh our resources (from the prevailing culture, from history, scientific developments and the Christian tradition). Most of all, we need the rich diversity of metaphors and partial understandings that others can offer us, to broaden our own insights and discoveries.

In all this dipping, searching and juggling, this trial and error, what are we seeking to do? We are trying to get a good all-round fit between our language (mixtures of metaphors) and our experience. I. T. Ramsey once used the helpful analogy of shopping for a pair of shoes.[2] I take size eight; but it's no good simply buying a pair of eights from the shelves and taking them home. I have to try them on before I purchase, because each pair of eights has a unique set of variables besides the length – width, shape of the toes and heel, slip-on or lace-up, leather or plastic. I decide what's comfortable by what fits well over the whole foot. Even then, there's no such thing as a perfect fit: left and right shoes may not be exact mirror images; and my feet are unlikely to be identical in all dimensions. But I buy when the fit is good enough – sometimes hoping that with use, the sensation of a bit of pinching here or there will wear off.

To learn from experience, then, we must honour the breadth and depth of our experience. Reflection (searching for understanding) is never an exclusively cerebral activity. It incorporates the irrational elements of our experience (e.g. instincts, emotions and intuitions) and spiritual awareness as well as the rational (intellect, feeling and volition). Reflection must also look for understandings that fit well enough not the situation by itself (apart from the pastor) and not the pastor in isolation, but the total experience of a-particular-individual-interacting-with-a-unique-situation.

Shoes are for wearing on journeys! That's the final test of whether we have bought a good pair of shoes. Our 'rounded' understanding of experience is like that. It drives us back to action and activity. The metaphors of meaning are metaphors to live by, not to gloat over in detached intellectual glee. Unlike mathematics and some of the natural sciences (physics and chemistry), there is no such thing as an isolated theoretical branch of pastoral care or pastoral theology. *Pastoral education is never far away from the practice of pastoral care.* Pastoral education is a search for a language which affects perceptions, attitudes, values and actions. Peter indeed needed to draw back from his confusing experience in the Clark's home, to seek with others clues for understanding that complicated system. But only to return to his pastoral task more self-aware, better equipped to notice what was happening, more realistic about his aims and more flexible and sensitive in his responses. There is a constant interplay, or oscillation, between experience and reflection, between action and learning. However vast and wide may be someone's experience in pastoral care, no situation can ever be reached where experience and learning stop illuminating each other.

Structures for pastoral education

The normal and classic structure for pastoral education is a small group. In earlier chapters I have referred to an appropriate group under names like nurture group, discipleship group (p. 196) or, in the context of liberation theology, a cell (p. 229).[3] In other words, for most purposes, pastoral education does not need separate structures. Pastoral education is typically another way of describing the purpose of the most basic structure for growth in Christian discipleship.

It might be useful here to expound one or two guidelines for a pastoral education/nurture group. (I will take for granted that such groups will assimilate the material in Chapter 12.) Its purpose: to search for life's meaning as deeply and with as much integrity as possible; and to assist one another in confronting and overcoming all that frustrates growth into what the members together discern as a fully human life.

It is crucial that a nurture group builds its life around the concerns and interests of its members. Work and play, family and society, moral and political questions, indeed every conceivable issue of human existence is potential material for exploration and reflection.

Exactly *how* members bring their concerns and interests is a very difficult matter. Take Peter's bewilderment, for example. Imagine he belonged to a nurture group (in the story he didn't: he belonged to a Bible fellowship, which is different). Would it be appropriate for him to recount in detail what happened, what he thought (about Anne) or what he learned (about Kate, say) during his visit to Willow Terrace? I think not. Visiting a home places a pastor under obligations to respect confidentiality and resist gossiping. Is Peter, then, reduced to silence? A way forward might involve tackling things tangentially or indirectly. 'I can't tell you the details; but something's really upset me this week. I want to share with you my concern about young people and drugs/caring for elderly and frail parents/why I feel so ill at ease when people argue with each other in my presence/what I'm supposed to be doing as a pastoral visitor.' Or Peter might do what I've done: construct a story for the group to look at together, a story with no references to known individuals or circumstances but reflecting typical experiences and feelings.

A nurture group should resist the intrusion of outside visitors – whether so-called 'experts', people it is thought will stimulate, or the local ordained minister (assuming he or she is not a member). It is fundamental to Christian understanding that within the fellowship of believers men and women can counsel, guide, inspire and edify one another. Group members therefore need to trust their own judgments and their own capacity to contribute to the work of the group. Each member can legitimately presume upon the Spirit to mediate God's love, wisdom and care through other members' insights and through the group (Deut. 13.1–4; Jer. 31.33–4; Matt. 11.25, 21.6; Luke 10.36–7, 18.9–14; I Cor. 6.1–8, 12.12–27, 14.26). I take it for granted that mutual edification happens best in groups which represent the variety and richness of human experience, where the membership comprises male and female, several occupational groups, different social classes and a wide age span (Matt. 21.14–17; Gal. 3.28; Col. 3.11).

A group's agenda will need to be flexible and broad-ranging. Method and style of working together also need to be variable, to match the varied tasks the group may choose for itself. So, while discussion may be the staple diet, there will also be meetings devoted to many other activities (making things; visiting together a sporting, cultural or political 'event' in the community; listening to music, radio or television; looking at pictures; eating a meal together; undertaking a limited community project). I am not hinting that these or any other suggestions should be imposed on a group; only that the group should be open to many and adventurous possibilities. One of the tests of a group's maturity and freedom is its capacity to respond positively to an unusual suggestion for a group activity which springs from one member's desire to explore or share something meaningful.

Flexibility and breadth are not, however, to be equated with a completely open agenda. From its inception a nurture group needs to find its distinctive identity by adopting the following discipline:

(*a*) It must agree that over a suitable period of time (a year?) it needs to build into its agenda some engagement with topics from a specific set of broad categories. These categories are the ones we have referred to many times throughout these chapters: art and culture; social and political issues; inter-personal relationships; history and science; the theological tradition; prayer and worship. There is no prescription about the relative weight to be given to any of these categories; and there is no prescription about the sorts of detail or breadth with which they must be tackled. (Is 'prayer' one occasion in six months when a member shaken to the core with a family bereavement asks the group to sit in silence with her; or is it fifteen minutes' formal devotion at the beginning of each meeting?) Each group finds its own way of engaging in the human struggle for sense and meaning in life.

(*b*) It must appoint someone to keep a log of what the group actually does.

(c) It must agree every so often to review its evolving life against the discipline in paragraph (a). This must not lead to artificiality ('We haven't done anything serious about history for six months; who can mug up something about William the Conqueror before we next meet?'). Rather, the task of the group is to reflect together whether its common experience authentically suggests that a historical dimension relating to a particular issue could illuminate present perplexity or enrich present perspectives. Another advantage of the periodic review against a yardstick is that it enables a group to confront issues (sexuality? death? conflict? studying the Gospel of Mark?) which are easily avoided because they are painful, difficult or challenging.

(d) It must seek always to make connections between areas of experience we habitually segregate from one another. Learning from experience involves discovering *mixtures* of varied metaphors which together fit reasonably the complexity, subtlety and depth of our concerns. So a group needs always to make time to say: How does what we're now discussing/doing/feeling relate to what we were up to in previous meetings? (What's the connection between, say, prayer and music, or between sport and politics, or between daily work and the kingdom of God?) Insight comes when sparks leap across the gaps, connecting in creative ways things which have long been isolated from each other. Nurture is about overcoming alienation, developing towards personal and social wholeness, and deepening participation in the world's renewal.

Pastoral education for formally authorized pastoral care

Those who are formally appointed by the church to particular responsibilities within the ministry of pastoral care (e.g. lay chaplains to a wide range of secular institutions, ordained ministers, pastoral care assistants in congregational settings, or leaders of Christian voluntary organizations) require, I suggest, an education in pastoral care which is identical in intention and structure to what I have just described for all

Christians. Inevitably, formal authorization should be contingent upon a more formal embodiment of experimental learning in a nurture group. I mention four ways in which the basic model may be developed for more formal educational purposes.

(*i*) There needs to be a more systematic general introduction to some of the resources which are distinctive of pastoral care and pastoral theology. These are the human and social sciences, personal and social ethics and the theological tradition. Each of these, of course, contains vast accumulations of varied concepts, knowledge and methods. It would be bizarre to suggest anything more than an elementary grounding in a few characteristic features of each discipline; or a study in depth of just a small handful of typical topics from the various fields of learning. (If selections are being made, as they must, from the human and social sciences, it is not obvious to me that psycho-analytic concepts and sociology must always be preferred to, say, politics, economics or anthropology.) It would be equally unrealistic to suppose that a period of initial training, perhaps prior to authorization, should attempt to cover anything like a complete syllabus. Initial training must be integrated into a thorough programme of continuing pastoral education. Authorized ministries of pastoral care must include in their job description and discipline flexible requirements for participation in a structured programme of development.

Methods of learning will be drawn from those which have become characteristic of the different disciplines, for example, role play, group project work, discussion, case studies and placements from the human and social sciences; a disciplined participation in worship and ritual, a common life, witness and practical service in the community from the theological tradition. (In this last sentence there is an implied criticism of traditional university departments of theology, who perpetuate the captivity of 'theology' in philosophical and historical studies. I do not suggest for one moment that there should not be a relationship between the universities and pastoral education for certain highly responsible pastoral care ministries. But I think it is always important to underline the practical nature of theology by building firm links with other forms of practical education in the university, e.g. social work, medicine, education and business studies. Just as important is the creation of a link with non-university institutions of higher education which are founded on the integration of practice and theory, i.e. polytechnics, colleges of education and other professional training centres.)

(*ii*) The intermingling of metaphors (from the sciences, the Christian tradition and everything else culture and history can supply) as a *necessary* path to understanding needs to be given structured expression. I have tried to outline samples of what this might be like in Chapters 7–13. It is worth reflecting on how these structured statements of 'mixed metaphors' relate to the insights which spring to life out of the more haphazard conversation of a nurture group. The simplest analogy I know is drawn from chemistry. Imagine a large test tube full of a liquid. The liquid contains in solution all sorts of substances, many of them unidentified. You add a catalyst, and some complicated chemical substance is precipitated. A different catalyst may re-dissolve the first solid formed at the bottom of the test tube, but replace it with a different one. The advantage of having a solid precipitate is that the chemist can withdraw it from the test tube, analyze it, amend it and use it.

The formal educational process is comparable to the addition of a catalyst to the liquid (= the rich, puzzling, alluring, unanalyzed experience of life which is the common heritage of informal nurture groups and of groups training for authorized ministries). The hybrid structures of understanding (which are simultaneously structures to guide the practical tasks of pastoral care), for example, Chapters 7–8, 9–10, 11–13, are the solid precipitates. Looking at three such complicated molecular substances gives some hope of grasping what was in the original liquid. But it does so in a way which suggests that effective pastoral care is *coherent* activity which attempts to remain faithful to life's 'dome of many-coloured glass.'[4]

I want to stress here what I have *not* attempted to provide: a coherent philosophical framework for pastoral care (that would be falsely abstract); a so-called 'integrated theology' (another intellectualist dream); or a theory of pastoral care crying out to be applied. What I am seeking are constellations which have a reliable form of their own, and which are made up of many diverse ingredients drawn directly from life's experience.

Three corollaries can be drawn from this analogy. First, different catalysts will produce yet further sediments. I make no claim that the structures in Chapters 7–13 are definitive. They do arise from my own teaching and pastoral experience. But I hope others will be keen to describe different 'chemicals' which have precipitated from their educational work.

Second, I press the analogy by reference to molecular biology. Imagine one of my 'structures' is like DNA. Without destroying the basic shape (a double helix), it is possible to add or subtract enzymes along the chain. Such modifications change the properties of the molecule. This leads me to expect that any one of my 'models' can be tinkered with, adapted, certainly improved.

Third, the precipitated solids, when they have been looked at and used (the formal educational task), need to be put back in the test tube. Withdraw the catalyst, or add a 'neutralizing' catalyst, and we have again a tube of liquid. That is true to the experience of pastoral care. With all the formal training in the world, life is still incredibly problematic, hazardous, question-begging and downright stupefying. The process of experience and reflection has to start all over again from scratch. Pastoral care involves taking risks, that is, involvement in human discoveries and needs which may shatter all previous ways of feeling, relating, acting and believing. The solid is dissolved into liquid. 'A man becomes a theologian by living, dying and being damned; not by reading, thinking and speculating' (Martin Luther).

(*iii*) Structures of supervision need to be built not only into training situations but into the practice of formal pastoral care ministries (see pp. 181–4).

(*iv*) Attention needs to be given to the special features of situations to which pastors will be formally authorized. Those who will work in industry and commerce need to know what is distinctive of those institutions. (I use the word 'know' in the experience/reflection sense, i.e. by supervised experience in an industrial placement followed by careful reflection which draws on many facets of understanding.) If Peter were, say, a deacon with special responsibility for sick visiting, he would need to grapple at length with the Christian meaning of health, the relation between cure and care, and the connection between his work and the medical, nursing and welfare professions. At this point the list of special areas for pastoral care becomes infinite. Sensitive care from formally authorized pastors certainly requires detailed knowledge of the particular factors which shape the areas of their responsibility. So while it is true that there are structural similarities between bereavement and being made redundant (Chapter 9), they are far from identical. This element of pastoral education itself is not a 'one off'. Understanding the distinctive tints, odours, harmonies and textures of a particular sector of work needs to grow through reflection, not least because nothing remains static in the modern world. As always this reflection is best done in a supportive group, now comprising members with a similar or connected area of speciality.

Resistance to pastoral education

'Your pain is the breaking of the shell that encloses your understanding.'[5] Resistance to change is therefore something which must be confronted imaginatively in every educational process. In addition it will be apparent that certain attitudes and assumptions will be in direct conflict with the aims and methods of pastoral education which I have tried to describe. Familiar examples are these:

Those who deny that pastoral care and reflection is a vocation given to all Christian people, but reserve it to ordained ministers and 'theologians'.

Those whose perspective on life is uncompromisingly individualistic.

Those who find their personal security in abstract, propositional 'truth' or comprehensive theories, which are guaranteed by accredited authorities.

Those who feel a need for 'right answers' to pastoral puzzles; or a certificate which publicly demonstrates their pastoral competence; or an objective guarantee that they are doing God's will.

Those who exalt the Bible or the theological tradition above all other resources in the struggle to make sense of life and to act lovingly in the world.

Those who insist that theology is essentially an intellectual and systematic discipline.

Those who wish to practise pastoral care without any continuing accountability for developing self-awareness, learning or growth.

None should underestimate how tense are the relationships in the church between those who advocate pastoral education of an experiential kind and those who favour aims and agenda which spring from other, more traditional educational theories and understandings of theology. Part of the self-chosen vocation of pastors must be to enable this conflict to be tackled openly and creatively (Chapter 13). One of the many sets of insights we need to bring to the argument is the material in Chapter 10. This may suggest a way of breaking down the polarization of perceived needs in theological and pastoral education, and giving more careful attention to individuals' needs according to where they are in the normal processes of human development.

The following scheme needs enormous expansion and refinement, for which there is no space here. While all pastoral education needs the structures and aims outlined above for authorized ministries, the *stress* will be age-specific. For those in their twenties: an intellectual grappling with concepts in the human and social sciences and in theological studies (so long as there is simultaneously responsible pastoral work to do, which may remain to a considerable degree disconnected from the educational process). For those in their thirties: a supervised development of specialized pastoral skills, and research. For those forty and above: a comprehensive experiential pastoral education which moves as closely as any formal education can to the informal nurture group; particular attention always to be paid to each individual's perception of his or her own needs for growth and development.

On top of such a basic set of variations other themes need to be heard whenever possible. Interaction and encounter across age bands is always valuable, for example. So is every move to break down walls of silence and suspicion between initial training and continuing education, and between those who practise formal and informal ministries of pastoral care.

The structures within which these ideals can be secured have yet to be set up. A period of adventurous experimenting is called for.

15 Pastoral Identity

Why 'pastoral'?

Throughout this book I have used the word 'pastor' to describe the person who practises pastoral care. This has been a risky procedure. So much of the Christian tradition and ordinary parlance confines 'pastor' to an authorized church leader, normally an ordained minister. My emphasis, in contrast, has been to break out of a clerical monopoly and argue that pastoral care is a ministry in which all God's people participate. Its normal *modus operandi* is informal, in friend-ships and families, and where people work, live and relax: in brief, wherever Christian people have a concern for human possibilities being realized in a just and free society. All are pastors, though not all pastors have identical ministries. So I am attempting to broaden the scope of 'pastor'. Some may think it is in danger of becoming so wide in its use as to be virtually meaningless. This is a danger we can live with to challenge the dominance of ordained and professional models of pastoral care.

But why the word 'pastor' at all? Its origins lie in a cultural and historical setting which is utterly remote from contempor-ary life. A pastor was classically a shepherd. This metaphor has a rich and suggestive use in the Bible and in Christian tradition; but the criticisms we must make of it seem insuper-able. In the first place, images of shepherd and sheep ring no bells with the experience of the vast majority of men and women in an urban, industrial and technological society. Pastoral scenes belong for most of us in the realm of nostalgia, and idyllic fantasies about pre-modern times. An additional difficulty is that 'sheep' is just about the least successful metaphor we could devise for human beings; it does not fit well enough to be useful. Sheep are notoriously dumb and stupid; they congregate in flocks which seem unable to protect themselves or initiate a search for good pasture; sheep in a flock provide no insight into the struggle for individuality or personal vocation.

Sheep need a shepherd. That leads us to the most damaging criticism of the church's persistent clinging to this imagery. For shepherd/sheep relationships are essentially about dependence (Chapter 12). There may be many positive things we can cull from the tradition, to prevent us concluding too quickly that ecclesiastical 'shepherds' simply capitalize on the drift towards autocracy in every large group. (For example: the shepherd guards the flock against wild beasts and thieves at great personal cost; the shepherd remains loyal to his flock; the shepherd knows each sheep individually by name and cares for each sheep; the shepherd seeks out and saves the lost sheep; the shepherd does for the sheep what they cannot do for themselves – finds water and pasture.) This helps us envisage a shepherd as a paternalistic provider rather than a tyrannical despot. The fact remains, however, that shepherd and sheep are radically different. It has indubitably been in the interests of those who rule in the church to perpetuate this way of exercising authority. Now, however, we are rediscovering the ministry of all God's people: models of acquiescent dependence are exploded in favour of interdependence, common struggles towards agreed goals, mutual ministry, and the pooling of resources to encourage individual fulfilment.

If 'shepherd/sheep' metaphors necessarily underlie 'pastor' and 'pastoral', I agree with the critics who insist that they must now be dispensed with. Many are replacing 'pastoral' with 'practical'. I have no difficulties with that, except that it seems wooden and pedestrian instead of imaginative. But in fact I have not discarded 'pastor/pastoral'. Instead I want to revitalize this way of speaking by appealing to a different metaphor.

It is drawn from literature, in particular from the plays of Shakespeare.

'The best actors in the world, either for tragedy, comedy, history, pastoral . . .' (Polonius, in *Hamlet*, Act II, scene ii). Shakespeare puts into this speech the main categories of play current in the sixteenth-century theatre. The true artist in him immediately wants to burst through the straightjacket of any rigid system, so he makes Polonius continue in a mocking tone, 'pastoral-comical, historical-pastoral, tragical-historical, tragical-comical-historical-pastoral.' What, however, is the meaning of 'pastoral' in this context? It is a category of plays in the Shakespearean corpus which are nowadays called romances. It comprises four plays which are the final fruit of the Bard's genius, from the period 1608–1611: *Pericles Prince of Tyre*, *Cymbeline*, *The Winter's Tale* and *The Tempest*.

The simplest way of seeing the distinctive nature of the pastorals/romances is to compare them with the earlier comedies and tragedies. The comedies celebrate life's humour and brightness; they sparkle and entertain, and exude confidence in happiness. They do not overlook human wickedness (e.g. the vengeful Sherlock in *The Merchant of Venice*), but it is handled with lightness and wit. In complete contrast stand the tragedies. Here heroic individuals struggle against awesome, passionate energies released from deep inside their souls, and against the destructive forces of nature and fate. They battle to become human in the face of these uncontrollable onslaughts, but are broken in the process. Madness and death are the cost of learning tenderness, love and humility. Now the romances. They draw together the insights of the comedies and tragedies into a new synthesis. Here men and women, young and old, all find that life is wracked by sin and destructiveness. Inner passions bubbling up from within, and tempests raging in nature and in the unpredictable course of events are no less traumatic; but now they do not lead inexorably to disaster. There is no need to react to the feared death of a loved one with suicide (as was the case in *Romeo and Juliet*). Rather, there is in life's puzzling brokenness and suffering a challenge to personal growth in character. Moral and spiritual values can ultimately mould the impersonal forces of fate; hate and violence can be redeemed. Beyond seeming tragedy lies re-creation, resurrection and new life. All the romances have a happy ending – not a trite or forced conclusion, but an expression of a conviction about a transcendent joy underlying and eventually overcoming life's hurts and damage. This is 'pastoral' insight, so resonant with the Christian gospel and the tradition of Christian caring. A 'pastor' therefore is someone who sets about the truly dramatic task of mediating God's redemption to individuals and communities.

The pastor as community artist

Drawing on the metaphor of Shakespearean drama to illuminate the meaning of 'pastor/pastoral' is bound to excite all sorts of vibrations between the vocation to pastoral care and the calling of an artist. I wish now to elaborate a little the basic elements in the artist's quest for truth, to illustrate parallels with the spirituality of a pastor. Here are four themes in which poets and painters reveal what lies near the root of pastoral identity.

(i) *Interrogating the silence* Here is a poem by George Mackay Brown, entitled 'The Poet'. In it the poet makes a foray into a local fair to sing a few songs, show his lyrical skills and join in the fun and games. But, contrary to popular opinion, he must return to his proper task: questioning and probling the silent mystery at the heart of life, searching for the hidden meaning in life.

> Therefore he no more troubled the pool of silence
> But put on mask and cloak,
> Strung a guitar
> And moved among the folk.
> Dancing they cried,
> 'Ah, how our sober islands
> Are gay again since this blind lyrical tramp
> Invaded the Fair!'

Under the last dead lamp
When all the dancers and masks had gone inside
His cold stare
Returned to its true task, interrogation of silence.[1]

A similar emphasis is found in John Donne (1572–1631), the great Catholic/Anglican metaphysical poet who was Shakespeare's contemporary.

Churches are best for Prayer, that have least light:
To see God only, I go out of sight:
    And to 'scape stormy days I choose
      An Everlasting night.[2]

Solitude and silence reveal their grace at the end of the journey inwards (Chapter 8). They challenge self-images which regularly bedevil the pastor's identity: of frenetic activism, or of accumulating knowledge, information and ideas with which to win one's way in life. Artist and pastor both embrace the one thing needful which Mary saw and Martha missed because she 'was distracted by her many tasks' (Luke 10.38–42). 'Mary seated herself at the Lord's feet and stayed there listening to his words'; in her silent attention she confronted the unutterably mysterious, transcendent God whom none is like in heaven or on earth (Ps. 113.5). This God, in Mother Teresa's words, is 'the friend of silence'.

We need to find God, and he cannot be found in noise and restlessness. God is the friend of silence. See how nature – trees, flowers, grass – grows in silence. The more we receive in prayer the more we can give in the active life. We need silence to be able to touch souls. The essential thing is not what we say but what God says through us.[3]

(ii) Uncovering the glorious   The God whose glory is above the heavens is portrayed in the tradition as the creator of everything that exists. His creation is self-revealing: 'every labour of his hands Shows something worthy of a God' (Isaac Watts). The artist's vocation is to uncover what the Stoics called the 'divine spark' in everything and in everyone – in

people and nature, in human thought, construction and creativity. Glory is truth: more like a richly coloured seam in the rock beneath the river bed than a pretty young girl perched daintily on a punt in the summer sunshine. So the artist needs the courage of the potholer exploring dangerous subterranean caverns, the wit of the satirical comedian performing in front of the high and mighty, and the tenacity of an investigative journalist exposing corruption and deceit. It has been said of the artist Joseph Beuys that he is constantly 'digging away, not only industriously but fanatically, where maybe no one else has thought to dig before. His purpose is to get to the truth and to help society. He is not concerned with beauty, with painting beautiful pictures, or with playing games to do with art; he is only concerned with digging, a primary activity, because the truth, the reality, is more important.'[4]

Artists must therefore resist all pressures in human society to reduce deep engagement with the world and its life. Abstract thought and philosophy are by and large inimical to the artistic task. The nineteenth-century French painter Odilon Redon (1840–1916) wrote: 'Art owes nothing to philosophy'; and 'Metaphysical minds occupy themselves too much with abstractions to be able to share and taste to the full the pleasures of art.'[5]

This is akin to the calling of the prophet and the pastor. They want to scratch beneath the surface of things and reveal untold wonders hidden in the deeps: the truth of God, a vision of Christ and the power of the Spirit, which redeem human values, passions and concerns. Pastoral care is enriched by speaking and acting in ways which question and expose what is taken for granted. Wisdom and imagination combine to invent parables, create stories, devise dramatic 'events' and to bring humour and pathos into what is dull and heavy. Pastoral care is about discovering life's meaning – not as a philosophical principle or a theological dogma but as discipleship, a lived faith. The glory of God is revealed as actions of love.

(iii) Entering human pain One of the paintings which has scaled the Olympian heights in the twentieth century is Pablo

Picasso's *Guernica*. It was painted in 1937 in response to the horrendous bombing of the Basque capital city during the Spanish civil war; it breathes the air of a pained Spaniard (Picasso was born in Malaga in 1881). In a poem inspired by the painting, R. S. Thomas defines Picasso's genius in these words:

> The painter
> has been down at the root
> of the scream and surfaced
> again to prepare the affections
> for the atrocity of its flowers.[6]

To this voluntary identification with human suffering, the artist must add a pain which is inherent in all creativity. When a work of art is finished it is normally shared with the public. The artist has invested a great deal of himself or herself in an artefact: now it is exposed to the response of audiences and the scrutiny of critics. The pleasure which creativity generates in an artist is experienced as a precarious gift. The artist's self-confidence and self-esteem as much as the work of art become vulnerable to questioning. They are as likely to receive ignorant or vicious rejection as warm acclamation.

The connection of the artist's vocation with the cross at the heart of the Christian tradition is clear. Marc Chagall, the Russian-born Jewish painter, makes the link in these words: 'Christ is a poet, one of the greatest, through the incredible, irrational manner of taking pain on himself.' No pastoral care is worth the name which does not plumb the depths of human pain and suffering to a point where it can be shared and absorbed. And no pastor can exercise such a ministry to others unless he or she has discovered *inside* his or her own heart an experience of confusion, pain, hurt and aggression. This alone unites the pastor in solidarity with those who receive pastoral care.

(iv) Living from the inside The artist is someone who lives from the inside out. Creative action is the expression of imagination and vision formed within. This is not to say that

the artist cannot or chooses not to react to external stimuli; but reaction is infused with a consistent way of seeing or hearing which issues from a deep-seated point within the personality. The opposite of an artist is the person who 'lives for kicks', or responds to life's events without consistency like a de-masted yacht in a cyclone, or calculates advantages with Machiavellian cunning.

The memory is a crucial faculty for an artist. Depth and breadth of experience, glory and pain and mystery, are of little use if particular moments of insight cannot be recalled or if connections cannot be made between the present and the past (which includes the history and tradition of art). Art is not like science in making 'progress'. Art is the re-expression in ever new configurations, contexts and amendments of classic symbols drawn from resources stored deep inside a living personality.

Towards the end of his life C. P. Snow, scientist and man of letters, wrote from memory the first draft of a book which was never revised and was published in 1981 as *The Physicists*. It is the story of the development of the 'new physics' in the twentieth century. In the introduction W. Cooper writes: 'When an artist calls upon memory, what he writes has a life and a moving quality which scarcely ever infuses the product of the filing cabinet which we nowadays refer to as researched information.'[7]

In a comparable way, prayer and caring are nourished by memory and a vision of Christ in the heart inspired by the Spirit. These are inner resources (Phil. 4.11; I Tim. 6.6) which, in Christian experience, are constantly refreshed and renewed ('they are new every morning', Lam. 3.23; John 7.37–9). They stimulate the disciple to want to live consistently in love. They relieve the disciple of anxiety about external things; the mind can be set 'on God's kingdom and his justice before everything else' (Matt. 6.25–34; Phil. 4.19).

In drawing parallels between artist and pastor, it is as important to resist idyllic pictures of the former as of the latter. There is no such thing as a 'pure' artist. The vocation of artist is muddied by personal defects, imbalances and inconsistencies like everything else in creation. Interrogating silence, for instance, can sometimes tilt a person towards becoming an obsessive recluse, like Emily Dickinson (1830–1886), the distinguished American poet. The desire to uncover the hidden glory in nature can make an artist besotted with colour, as it made Vincent van Gogh (1853–1890), to such an extent that the rest of life is immature or out of control. None of these deviations from an ideal invalidates artistic achievement any more than pastoral care is invalidated by a pastor being less than Christlike.

There is, however, a word of caution that seems necessary here. It is part of our culture to *expect* the artist to be eccentric, to live on the edge of madness and to be uncontainable within groups, institutions and stable patterns of society. The 'heroic genius' view of the artist (usually poor, unrecognized, battling for truth in a cold garret) thrusts him or her into Bohemian extravagance. It is not so with pastoral identity.

It would be equally unhelpful to swing to the opposite ideological extreme, which identifies the meaningful only with what emerges from a Marxist collective (p. 213). Our human existence is a more subtle and complex interplay between the individual and the corporate. In her novel *Bliss*, Jill Tweedie has an amusing skit on extreme collective attitudes in the women's movement, in the course of which she writes: 'They refused to see an obvious truth, that every effort, every book or painting or poem or piece of music or newspaper article done by an individual was also, by definition, collective because no one lived in a vacuum. The unconscious itself was collective; hadn't Jung called it the *racial* unconscious?' (p. 298).

Tweedie's comment is an important corrective to individualism and collectivism. Even so, pastoral identity is best encapsulated, I believe, in the notion of community art, a cooperative exercise practised, for example, by musicians in a band or orchestra. In a fascinating section on metaphors for love, Lakoff and Johnson expound a novel notion, LOVE IS A COLLABORATIVE WORK OF ART.[8] They list the principal insights such a metaphor entails:

Love is work.
Love is active.
Love requires cooperation.
Love requires dedication.
Love requires compromise.
Love requires a discipline.
Love involves shared responsibility.
Love requires patience.
Love requires shared values and goals.
Love demands sacrifice.
Love regularly brings frustration.
Love requires instinctive communication.
Love is an aesthetic experience.
Love is primarily valued for its own sake.
Love involves creativity.
Love requires a shared aesthetic.
Love cannot be achieved by a formula.
Love is unique in each instance.
Love is an expression of who you are.
Love creates a reality.
Love reflects how you see the world.
Love requires the greatest honesty.
Love may be transient or permanent.
Love needs funding.
Love yields a shared aesthetic satisfaction from your joint
efforts.

This seems to me to throw much new light on the practice of pastoral care; in association with the earlier perspectives on the artist's vocation, it cements the metaphor of the pastor as a community artist. Much of the work of pastoral care is working with others, building relationships and reshaping community. This utilizes all the wisdom we can muster from culture, history and science; but it is worth little without imaginative flair. Pastoral care is a contribution to the reconstruction of human life founded upon shared creative insight into the presence and the call of God. Henri Nouwen movingly describes such a disclosure:

I vividly remember the day on which a man who had been a student in one of my courses came back to the school and entered my room with the disarming remark: 'I have no problems this time, no questions to ask you. I do not need counsel or advice, but I simply want to celebrate some time with you.' We sat on the ground facing each other and talked a little about what life had been for us in the last year, about our work, our common friends, and about the restlessness of our hearts. Then slowly as the minutes passed by we became silent. Not an embarrassing silence but a silence that could bring us closer together than the many small and big events of the last year. We would hear a few cars pass and the noise of someone who was emptying a trash can somewhere. But that did not hurt. The silence which grew between us was warm, gentle and vibrant. Once in a while we looked at each other with the beginning of a smile pushing away the last remnants of fear and suspicion. It seemed that while the silence grew deeper around us we became more and more aware of a presence embracing both of us. Then he said, 'It is good to be here' and I said, 'Yes, it is good to be together again,' and after that we were silent again for a long period. And as a deep peace filled the empty space between us he said hesitantly, 'When I look at you it is as if I am in the presence of Christ.' I did not feel startled, surprised or in need of protesting, but I could only say, 'It is the Christ in you, who recognizes the Christ in me.' 'Yes,' he said, 'He indeed is in our midst,' and then he spoke words which entered into my soul as the most healing words I had heard in many years, 'From now on, wherever you go, or wherever I go, all the ground between us will be holy ground.' And when he left I knew that he had revealed to me what community really means.[9]

The pastor as eucharistic companion

One test of a new metaphor is its effect on long-established metaphors: can it bring to fresh life old images which, though classic, have become tired or jaded? The image of a pastor as a community artist passes that test for me. It has revitalized the use of eucharistic symbolism to illuminate discipleship.

Formal exposition of the significance of the holy communion is familiar. The eucharist is essentially a corporate act and a collaborative ministry. It is the focal expression of all God's people working together to praise God. It is also a ritual which builds community. Those who share the eucharist, adults and young people and children, are bound together as companions (i.e. those who share bread together). Like every ritual, the eucharist also suggests something larger and deeper. It represents and begins to bring into being what God wants for the whole universe; it is a 'foretaste' of God's kingdom. But how does this way of speaking relate to our pastoral identity?

In the first place, the eucharist can be perceived as a structured way of becoming silent together in the face of the awesome mystery of life and of God – like the 'silence in heaven for what seemed half an hour', of which the Apocalypse speaks (Rev. 8.1). Here is time to attend to life's meaning, and, like Job, to interrogate God.

This is achieved in the eucharistic liturgy with which I am most familiar ('The Sunday Service' in *The Methodist Service Book*) by the instructions about periods of silence which punctuate the service. The effect is analogous to listening to music, and therefore to losing our obsession with the passage of time.

Music offers [an] avenue to simplicity, since it communicates both spontaneity and order at a level which words cannot reach. In responding to its mysterious powers of rhythm, sound and silence, we are released from the domination of clock time, with its measured reminders of passing minutes and hours, and are free to enter [a world] where all is immediacy and where anxiety has no sway over us. We no longer need to justify each moment by what has been achieved in it, but can appreciate time, not as demand, but as gift.[10]

Secondly, we take bread and wine – signs of nature and human work. As they crystallize in our imaginations, our own struggles to pray, to become disciples and to care for all men and women, they become transparent of divine grace. Immersed in Christian tradition, they are symbols of God's saving love in Christ, sacramental figures of Christ's body and blood and therefore full of wonder and glory – like everything else God has given us.

But before that is clear, the bread must be ripped apart, unveiling to us the world's pain and sin, revealing to us above all the pain of the Crucified. Here the true glory of God is fully disclosed (John 12.23–33, 13.31–8). While the bread is being broken and fragments are torn off for us and our neighbours, Christ hangs motionless on the cross.

> Hidden is love's agony,
> Love's endeavour, love's expense.[11]

Now in the eucharist we have reached such a depth of identification with God's pain and God's love that we can sense true community with one another. Loneliness and alienation have been overcome. 'By his wounds [we] have been healed!' (Isa. 53.5; I Peter 2.25). The unknown Stranger next to us is revealed as none other than the living Christ. The moment we have glimpsed that, we no longer need to cling close to one another, like anxious lovers fearing that their passion will wither once they are out of each other's sight and each other's arms. Wherever we go and whether or not we ever meet again, all the ground between us has become holy ground. So the eucharist ends with our rapid dispersal.

Pastoral identity has been reshaped and pastoral vocation renewed. Our calling is to transmit the silent music and the hushed poetry of God in and beneath practical deeds of love. There are no limits to where such a ministry may lead: God's peace is for those who are far off and for those who are near by (Eph. 2.17). So we travel inwards, forwards and outwards. We plumb unfathomable depths; embrace the future in hope, even its suffering and death; and transfigure every bond, system and structure with the values of the kingdom. The ministry of pastoral care is drawn along by the boundless grace of God.

O Love, how deep, how broad, how high!
It fills the heart with ecstasy.

Notes

1. *Basic Resources: Words*

1. D. G. Deeks, *Calling, God?*, Epworth Press 1976.
2. T. S. Eliot, 'Little Gidding', in *Collected Poems, 1909–1962*, Faber.

2. *Basic Resources: Deeds*

1. C. Christo, *Letters From A Prisoner Of Conscience*, Orbis 1978, p. 65.
2. In 1986 the Tate Gallery mounted an exhibition entitled *Forty Years of Modern Art 1945–1985*. In the foreword to a book accompanying the exhibition, R. Alley wrote: 'Free from the constraints of tradition which seemed to inhibit so many European artists, artists of the post-war American school have continued to show extraordinary freshness and boldness . . . In their search for new forms of art which would avoid the stale imitation of what had been done before, many artists of the post-war period have attempted to go back to the basics of art, the very beginnings, in order to make a fresh start.'
3. A Bold, 'Topless Poem', in *Penguin Modern Poets 15*, Penguin 1969, p. 27.
4. A. Pope, *Moral Essays*, Epis. i, 1. 109.
5. N. Lash, *Concilium*, 171, p. 76.
6. R. Harper, cited in C. Morris, *The Word and The Words*, Epworth Press 1975, p. 138–9.
7. L. Fischer, *The Life of Mahatma Ghandi*, Harper & Row 1950; M. Ghandi, *The Story of my Experiments in Truth*.
8. K. Lorenz, *On Aggression*, Methuen 1966.
9. J. -P. Sartre, *Words*, Penguin 1964, p. 76.
10. H. Fletcher, regarding Oliver Cromwell; see A. Fraser, *Cromwell Our Chief of Men*, Panther 1973, p. 702.
11. M. Proust, cited in H. A. Williams, *True Resurrection*, Mitchell Beazley 1972, p. 135.
12. H. Arts, *With Your Whole Soul*, Paulist Press 1983, Ch. 1; A. Hardy, *The Spiritual Nature of Man*, Clarendon 1979.

3. Basic Resources: Feeling

1. J. Bronowski, *The Visionary Eye*, The MIT Press 1978, p. 21.
2. K. J. Narr, cited in W. Pannenberg, *Anthropology in a Theological Perspective*, SCM Press 1985, p. 482, n. 234.
3. I. Murdoch, *Nuns and Soldiers*, Penguin 1980, p. 131.
4. Here is a beautiful modern poem which points in the same direction: 'To my Daughters', by M. Seymour-Smith in *Pen New Poetry 1*, Penguin 1986, p. 134.

My child (whichever) my love for you's more dear
As fatherhood becomes more clear
Not to be my own ghost spying
On your mind after my dying:
Sitting in the shaft of this same sun,
Going through my dusty stuff and saying
'This was his but does not matter any more.
Nor did it ever much. Moon in Cancer,
Always he felt compelled
Crab-like to collect
Detritus of a past which now's
No longer anyone's at all,
Unless the Moon's.'
But what is never past, my child (whichever)
Is my blessing on you
As adamantine now as when I saw you first.
Love like mine for you's almost
Too much to bear
And undoes history quite.
It never can be told except
Beyond death's care, as now;
But then it's heartfelt as the sun is warm.
Now, as you muse upon these relics,
Now, as I write you these words.

5. F. Sagan, *The Unmade Bed*, Penguin 1978, p. 50.

4. Broadening the Search

1. J. D. Watson, *The Double Helix*, Weidenfeld & Nicolson 1968; J. Goodfield, *An Imagined World*, Hutchinson 1981; C. P. Snow, *The Physicists*, Macmillan 1981.
2. Much of the controversy surrounding Darwin's work in the middle of the nineteenth century related to this point. Darwin himself was reluctant to spell out explicitly the implications of his work on evolution for our understanding of the emergence of human beings: he could foresee their controversial nature. Lyall and Wallace

prevaricated; they wanted to except *homo sapiens* from natural selection. The infamous debate between T. Huxley and the Bishop of Oxford was primarily on *scientific* grounds rather than, as the popular imagination has it, on evolution versus creationism.

3. J. Bronowski, *Science and Human Values*, Penguin 1961, ch. 2.
4. Herodotus, *History*, intro.
5. Thucydides, *Peloponnesian War*, i.22, ii.2; Luke 1.1–4.
6. A. Solzhenitsyn, *The Gulag Archipelago*, Collins 1974, p. 272.
7. The 'official' history is contained in three volumes, *The History of the Methodist Church*, eds G. Rupp *et al*, Epworth Press 1965.
8. A. Solzhenitsyn, op. cit., p. 175.
9. O. Goldsmith, *The Vicar of Wakefield*, 1766; A. J. Russell, *The Clerical Profession*, SPCK 1980.

5. Pastoral Theology

1. G. Eliot, *Middlemarch*, 1871–2, p. 240: 'Mortals are easily tempted to pinch the life out of their neighbour's buzzing glory, and think that such killing is no murder.'
2. H. -G. Gadamer, *Truth and Method*, 1975.
3. Even in the New Testament itself, in its latest and most philosophically minded documents, e.g. the Gospel of John, a movement towards incarnational ways of thinking can be detected. See J. D. G. Dunn, *Christology in the Making*, SCM Press 1980.
4. J. Cary, *Mister Johnson*, 1939, p. 212.
5. Much of the lively discussion among theologians in the modern era has revolved around this theme. Severe criticism of the traditional view was first given coherent expression by F. Schleiermacher (1768–1834). At the beginning of the twentieth century K. Barth (1886–1968) and others revived what they called neo-orthodoxy. In spite of the criticisms of Barth's position by theologians like D. Bonhoeffer (1906–1945) and P. Tillich (1886–1965), L. Newbigin, in *The Other Side of 1984*, WCC 1983, seems to want a neo-Barthianism. Pastoral theology has often attempted to operate within one or other of these theological frameworks, as *applied* theology. A famous example from the Methodist tradition was F. Greeves, *Theology and the Cure of Souls*, Epworth Press 1960. The pastoral theology advocated in the present volume differs markedly from this tradition.
6. Gregory the Great illustrates this. An outstanding pastor and writer, whose influence was enormous for centuries. His works are today unknown and unread. See T. Oden, *Care of Souls in the Classic Tradition*, Fortress Press 1984.

6. Pastoral Care: Purpose and Aims

1. *This is suggestively argued by W. A. Visser't Hooft in S J Th* 38(4), pp. 481–90.

2. 'Improvised comedy' flourished in Italy in the 17th and 18th centuries. A troupe of actors who knew each other well were given a story line by their director. Thereafter each actor had to improvise to create the theatrical experience. Something similar happens in a traditional jazz band.

3. E. Schweizer, *The Good News according to Saint Mark*. SPCK 1975, p. 386.

4. G. Baum, cited by D. Evans, *Faith, Authenticity and Morality*, 1980.

5. *Antony and Cleopatra*; the illustration is given in J. Bronowski, *The Visionary Eye*, pp. 77–8.

6. Since the Nazi holocaust, that truth is now built into the Jewish experience of God. See E. Wiesel, *Night*, 1969.

7. A Map of the Terrain

1. U. Eco, *The Name of the Rose*, Picador 1983, p. 57.

2. M. Luther, 'Your God is that around which you entwine your heart and on which you place your confidence' (*Little Catechism*).

3. In very rare instances this can be confused, e.g. a hermaphrodite.

4. S. Colegrave, *The Spirit of the Valley*. This was reviewed in *The Guardian* (30.5.79) by Mary Stott, who pointed out that this is a more helpful way of putting things than appealing to 'female' and 'male' qualities, because the latter reinforces female/male stereotypes.

5. A wise and theologically acute perspective on psychic phenomena is to be found in M. Perry, *Psychic Studies*, The Aquarian Press 1984, and in J. Heaney, *The Sacred and the Psychic*, Paulist Press 1984.

6. J. Tweedie, *Bliss*, Penguin 1984, p. 45.

8. Inspirited to Love

1. F. Sagan, *The Unmade Bed*, Penguin 1980, p. 47.

2. J. Goodfield, *An Imagined World*, p. 63: this refers to scientific discovery, but it captures well the feeling of a spiritual counsellor.

3. Put on the lips of Jung in M. West, *The World Is Made of Glass*, Hodder & Stoughton 1983, p. 26. The maenads were the ecstatic female followers of Dionysus (or Bacchus), the Greek god of wine.

4. G. Eliot, *Middlemarch*, p. 147.

5. *The Classics of Western Spirituality* is a series which reproduces the primary works of many of these. R. Williams, *The Wound of*

Knowledge, Darton, Longman & Todd 1979, surveys Christian spirituality up to St John of the Cross. A helpful introduction to St John of the Cross in particular is M. Tillyer, *Union With God*, Mowbray 1984.

6. In what follows there is some connection with what the psychologist A. Maslow called a 'hierarchy of needs'. A good account of Maslow's work can be found in F. Wright, *Pastoral Care for Lay People*, SCM Press 1982, ch. 2.

7. N. Ward, *Friday Afternoon*, Epworth Press 1976, p. 20.

8. M. West, op. cit., p. 82.

9. M. West, *Daughter of Silence*, Pan Books 1961, p. 133.

9. From Night to Morning

1. This figure is largely taken from J. van Dongen-Garrad, *Invisible Barriers*, SPCK 1983, p. 66.

2. It seems that the internal images we have of our friends and family are often vague, possibly because they are always being adapted to the developing experience of personal encounter in a living relationship. It can be distressing to discover how inadequate is our mental picture of a spouse or child if we are asked, in their absence, to fill our mind's eye with the details of their face. We find our mind is almost blank. In grieving, this anxiety about losing for ever a clear inner picture has to be overcome.

3. The Litany, *The Alternative Service Book*, Hodder & Stoughton 1980, p. 99.

4. *Hymns & Psalms*, Methodist Publishing House 1983, 726, v. 4.

10. From Birth To Decay

1. A mother's role in the earliest months does not necessarily have to be fulfilled by the child's biological mother. See J. Bowlby, *Child Care and the Growth of Love*, Pelican 1953.

2. Adolescent ambivalence is imaginatively presented in stories of, say, two sons in a family interpreting their lot in contradictory ways, e.g. Matt. 21.28–30; Luke 15.11–32.

3. J. Fowles, *The Aristos*, Jonathan Cape 1964/1980, ch. 3, expresses this with great clarity.

4. A fuller, popular, if controversial account is given in G. Sheehy, *Passages*.

5. W. Shakespeare, *As You Like It*, II, vii.

6. T. H. Gill, *Hymns & Psalms*, 453: the whole hymn well expresses the sentiment.

7. W. H. Vanstone, *The Stature of Waiting*, 1982.

8. In the case of the elderly, the need for physical oversight and for

security (pp. 120–1) becomes uppermost, because of the rapid deterioration of physical functioning. This needs specialized attention.

11. *Friendship*

1. R. J. Armstrong, I. C. Brady (eds), *Francis and Clare: the Complete Works*, SPCK 1982; L. Boff, *Saint Francis*, SCM Press 1985; M. de la Bedoyere, *Francis*, Collins 1976.
2. Bianco da Siena (d. 1434), *Hymns & Psalms*, 281, vv. 1–2.
3. *Hymns & Psalms*, 282, v. 5; more expansively in 791, v. 3:

Take my soul and body's powers;
Take my memory, mind and will,
All my goods, and all my hours,
All I know, and all I feel,
All I think, or speak, or do;
Take my heart, but make it new.

4. C. Wesley again:

Why hast thou cast our lot
In the same age and place,
And why together brought
To see each other's face,
To join with loving sympathy,
And mix our friendly souls in thee?   *Hymns & Psalms*, 374.

5. I have found the following references particularly helpful on this theme: J. V. Taylor, *The Go-Between God*, SCM Press 1972, ch. 3; M. Britton, *The Single Woman in the Family of God*, Epworth Press 1982; W. Kraft, *The Sexual Dimensions of the Celibate Life*, Gill & Macmillan 1979; J. B. Nelson, *Embodiment*, SPCK 1979.
6. A. V. Campbell, *Moderated Love*, SPCK 1984, pp. 102–4.
7. Kahlil Gibran, *The Prophet*, Heinemann 1923, pp. 16, 19.
8. The phrases in this definition are drawn from the preface of 'The Marriage Service' in *The Methodist Service Book*, Methodist Publishing House 1975.
9. J. Wesley, *The Twelve Rules of a Helper*, 1744, No. 11.
10. 'They have shown me what it is to live simply, to love tenderly, to speak in truth, to pardon, to receive openly, to be humble in weakness, to be confident in difficulties, and to accept handicaps and hardships with love. And, in a mysterious way, in their love they have revealed Jesus to me', B. Clarke, *Enough Room for Joy*, 1974.
11. M. West, *Daughter of Silence*, p. 118.
12. P. Tillich, *Shaking of the Foundations*, SCM Press 1949, p. 163.

12. Fellowship

1. H. Snyder, *The Radical Wesley*, IVP 1980, especially ch. 10.
2. 'The Ministry of the People of God', *Agenda of the Methodist Conference 1986*, p. 603. The quotation is from E. Schillebeeckx and is a paraphrase of Jerome.
3. The willing connivance of human groups with authoritarian styles of leadership must never be underestimated. Experiments inspired by S. Milgram suggest that about two-thirds of the population would be willing to inflict pain on innocent victims in obedience to authorities who present themselves as beyond question and who claim to be willing to take moral responsibility for what their 'subjects' do.
4. W. R. Bion, *Experiences in Groups*, Tavistock 1961.

13. Relatedness

1. It goes back to philosophers like T. Hobbes (1588–1679), J. Locke (1632–1704) and J. J. Rousseau (1712–1778). Its economic expression is capitalism.
2. K. Gibran, *The Prophet*, p. 33.
3. D. Hammarskjold, *Markings*.
4. A. V. Campbell, *Moderated Love*, ch. 4.
5. Granting freedom to small groups to inform the large group is not just a piece of wisdom learned from the experience of humane management. It is also a profoundly theological insight. Through the Bible runs the theme of election. This is the way God acts in the world to transform it. He chooses insignificant Israel to be his witness among the nations; within Israel he chooses the righteous sufferer and the poor to be the vehicle of his purposes; from among the marginal groups in Israel (John 1.46; Mark 6.2–3) God's purposes are revealed in Jesus, particularly when he is most thoroughly victimized on the cross (Isa. 52–53.12; Mark 15.39). (See also pp. 228–30.)
6. The principles in this paragraph have been very thoroughly enshrined in community work and community development programmes.
7. 'Solomon's Proverbs, I think, have omitted to say, that as the sore palate findeth grit, so an uneasy consciousness heareth innuendoes', G. Eliot, *Middlemarch*, p. 333.
8. Usually it is impossible to understand a congregation as simply either a representative work group (communal church) or a voluntary association. Because a congregation is itself often a large group, its identity and relation to its environment is a complicated mixture of interests, needs and experience.

9. Each denomination claims its ordinations are ordinations into the Church of God – one, holy, catholic and apostolic. Sociologically, authorization of ordained ministers cannot run more widely than the boundaries of the denomination in which the ordination takes place (or, in these ecumenical times, than the boundaries of mutually recognized denominations).

10. C. Saunders, D. H. Summers & N. Teller (eds), *Hospice: The Living Idea*, E. Arnold 1981.

11. E. Sherrington, *Christian Ministry and Further Education*, 1985; *Going Public*, 1985; W. Carr, *The Priestlike Task*, SPCK 1985. Terminology is difficult. By and large 'chaplain' is not a good name, for historical and sociological reasons. Historically, a chaplain was a minister in a chapel, a place of worship in an institution, or an alternative to the communal parish church. Sociologically, chaplains in many institutions, e.g. prisons, hospitals, factories, have focused their attention on caring for individuals rather than engaging structures.

12. One example of this for Western society as a whole is K. Lorenz, *Civilised Man's 8 Deadly Sins*, Methuen 1973.

13. H. Faber, *Pastoral Care in the Modern Hospital*, SCM Press 1971.

14. *Pastoral Education*

1. C. Wesley, *Hymns & Psalms*, 374, vv. 3–4.
2. I. T. Ramsey, *Models and Mystery*, OUP 1964.
3. The phrase 'Base Christian Community' (BCC) is also frequently used in literature on liberation theology. In Latin America BCCs are often not small groups at all, in the sense I have used that phrase, but much larger (e.g. up to 100 people).
4. Life, like a dome of many-coloured glass,
   Stains the white radiance of eternity (Shelley).
5. K. Gibran, *The Prophet*, p. 61.

15. *Pastoral Identity*

1. *Selected Poems*, Hogarth 1977, p. 37.
2. *A Hymn to Christ*.
3. Mother Teresa, *Something Beautiful for God*, Collins 1971.
4. A. Seymour, *J. Beuys' Drawings*, 1983.
5. M. Wilson, *Nature and Imagination*, Phaidon 1978, p. 48.
6. *Ingrowing Thoughts*, Poetry Wales Press 1985, p. 9.
7. C. P. Snow, *The Physicists*, 1981, p. 8.
8. G. Lakoff, M. Johnson, *Metaphors We Live By*, University of Chicago Press 1980, ch. 21.

9. H. J. M. Nouwen, *Reaching Out*, Collins 1976, p. 45.

10. A. V. Campbell, *Rediscovering Pastoral Care*, Darton, Longman & Todd 1981, pp. 60–1.

11. W. H. Vanstone, *Love's Endeavour, Love's Expense*, Darton, Longman & Todd 1977.

Suggestions for Further Reading

Introduction

A. V. Campbell, *Moderated Love*, SPCK 1984.
A. Bloom, *School For Prayer*, Darton, Longman & Todd 1970.
'The Ministry of the People of God', in *Agenda of the Methodist Conference 1986*, pp. 603–38.

1. Basic Resources: Words

H. Arts, *With Your Whole Soul*, Paulist Press 1983.
B. W. Anderson, *The Living Word of the Bible*, SCM Press 1979.
G. Lakoff & M. Johnson, *Metaphors We Live By*, University of Chicago Press 1980.

2. Basic Resources: Deeds

North-South: A Programme for Survival, Pan Books 1980 – the Brandt Report.
D. Capps, *Pastoral Care and Hermeneutics*, Fortress Press 1984.
E. N. Jackson, *Understanding Loneliness*, SCM Press 1980.

3. Basic Resources: Feelings

J. Fowles, *The Aristos*, Jonathan Cape, 1964/1980.
J. Bronowski, *The Visionary Eye*, The MIT Press 1978.
H. Kung, *Art and the Question of Meaning*, SCM Press 1981.

4. Broadening the Search

B. Jenner (ed.), *Future Conditional*, Home Mission Division of the Methodist Church 1983.
P. Medawar, *The Limits of Science*, OUP 1985.
H. McLeod, *Religion and the People of Western Europe, 1789–1970*, OUP 1981.

5. Pastoral Theology

M. D. Hooker, *The Message of Mark*, Epworth Press 1983.
R. Williams, *The Wound of Knowledge*, Darton, Longman & Todd 1979.
F. Young, *Face to Face*, Epworth Press 1985.

6. *Pastoral Care: Purpose and Aims*

A. V. Campbell, *Paid to Care?*, SPCK 1985.
A. Louth, *Discerning the Mystery*, Clarendon Press, Oxford 1983.
A. O. Dyson, *We Believe*, Mowbray 1977.

7. *A Map of the Terrain*

Ed. C. Jung, *Man and his Symbols*, Aldous 1964.
D. E. Saliers, *The Soul in Paraphrase*, The Seabury Press 1980.
J. Dominian, *The Capacity to Love*, Darton, Longman & Todd 1985.

8. *Inspirited to Love*

A. & B. Ulanov, *Primary Speech*, SCM Press 1985.
G. S. Wakefield (ed.), *A Dictionary of Christian Spirituality*, SCM Press 1983.
Understanding Christian Nurture, BCC 1981.

9. *From Night to Morning*

C. S. Lewis, *A Grief Observed*, Faber 1961.
E. Kubler-Ross, *On Death and Dying*, Tavistock 1970.
C. Murray Parkes, *Bereavement*, Penguin 1972.

10. *From Birth to Decay*

J. W. Fowler, *Stages of Faith*, Harper & Row 1981.
L. Kohlberg, *Essays on Moral Development*, Vol. 1, Harper & Row 1981.
M. Jacobs, *The Presenting Past*, Harper & Row 1985.

11. *Friendship*

G. C. Meilaender, *Friendship*, University of Notre Dame Press 1981.
C. Sandford & W. Beardsley, *Making Relationships Work*, Sheldon 1986.
R. F. Hobson, *Forms of Feeling: The Heart of Psychotherapy*, Tavistock 1985.

12. *Fellowship*

H. Anderson, *The Family and Pastoral Care*, Fortress Press 1984.
C. M. Olsen, *Cultivating Religious Growth Groups*, Westminster Press, Philadelphia 1984.
C. Holloway & S. Otto, *Getting Organised*, NCVO 1985.

13. *Relatedness*

E. Butterworth & D. Weir (eds.), *The New Sociology of Modern Britain*, Fontana 1984.
Going Public, National Standing Committee of Polytechnic Chaplains 1985.
G. Gutierrez, *We Drink From Our Own Wells*, SCM Press 1984.

14. *Pastoral Education*

P. Ballard (ed.), *The Foundations of Pastoral Studies & Practical Theology*, University College, Cardiff 1986.
J. Rogers, *Adults Learning*, Open University Press 1971.
J. M. Hull, *What Prevents Christian Adults from Learning*, SCM Press 1985.

15. *Pastoral Identity*

A. V. Campbell, *Rediscovering Pastoral Care*, Darton, Longman & Todd 1981.
F. Wright, *The Pastoral Nature of the Ministry*, SCM Press 1980.
H. J. M. Nouwen, *Reaching Out*, Collins 1976.